Challenges for midwives

volume two

Other titles in the midwifery series include:

Birthing Positions by Regina Coppen

Challenges for Midwives, volume one edited by Yana Richens

Demystifying Qualitative Research in Pregnancy and Childbirth edited by Tina Lavender, Grace Edwards and Zarko Alfirevic

HIV and Midwifery Practice by Jane Bott

Maternal and Infant Nutrition and Nurture: Controversies and challenges edited by Victoria Hall Moran and Fiona Dykes

Perineal Care: An international issue edited by Christine Henderson and Debra Bick

Psychology for Midwives by Ruth Paradice

Coming soon:

Supervision for Midwifery Practice: A resource for midwives

Student Midwife Survival Guide

Sociology for Midwives

Series editor: Tina Lavender

Challenges for midwives

volume two

edited by

Yana Richens

QUAY
BOOKS

A division of MA Healthcare Ltd

Quay Books Division, MA Healthcare Ltd, St Jude's Church, Dulwich Road,
London SE24 0PB

British Library Cataloguing-in-Publication Data
A catalogue record is available for this book

© MA Healthcare Limited 2007
ISBN-10 1 85642 295 X
ISBN-13 978 1 85642 295 6

Printed in the UK by Athenaeum Press Ltd, Dukesway, Team Valley, Gateshead, NE11 0PZ

Contents

List of contributors

Shamoly Ahmed is a Research Officer, City University, St Bartholomew School of Nursing and Midwifery, London

Khalida Ashrafi is Research Officer, University of Leeds

Karl Atkin is Senior Lecturer, Department of Health Sciences, University of York

Sue Battersby is Independent Midwifery Researcher/Lecturer, Sheffield

Jacqueline Baxter is Research and Development Midwife, University College London Hospitals NHS Foundation Trust, London

Kay Bennett is BIBS Midwife, Sure Start Foxhill and Parson Cross, Sheffield

Cliff Cunningham is Visiting Professor, Liverpool John Moores University

Dawn Edge is Research Fellow, School of Nursing, Midwifery and Social Work, University of Manchester

Josephine Green is Professor of Psychosocial Reproductive Health, Mother and Infant Research Unit, University of York

Angie Hart is Principal Lecturer in Healthcare Policy and Practice, Centre for Nursing and Midwifery Research, University of Brighton

Joy Hastings is a Sure Start Breastfeeding Co-ordinator in East London

Janet Hirst is Lecturer in Midwifery, School of Healthcare, University of Leeds

Kath Jones is Community Midwife at the Wrexham Maelor Hospital, NE Wales NHS Trust, Wrexham

June Keeling is Lecturer, School of Nursing, Arrowe Park Hospital, Wirral, Merseyside

Mussarat Khan is Director of Advocacy and Interpreting Services, Leeds

Elaine Lee is Lecturer in Midwifery, School of Nursing and Midwifery, University of Dundee

Rachael Lockey is Research Fellow at the Centre for Nursing and Midwifery Research, University of Brighton, and Midwife, Brighton and Sussex Universities Hospital Trust

Alison Macfarlane is Professor of Perinatal Health, City University, St Bartholomew School of Nursing and Midwifery, London

Faye McCrory is Consultant Midwife, Manchester Specialist Midwifery Service, Zion Community Resource Centre, Manchester

Stella McKay-Moffat is Senior Lecturer Midwifery, Edge Hill College, Liverpool

Jenny McLeish is Co-ordinator of the National Teenage Pregnancy Midwifery Network, and Project Officer on the Reaching Out Project

Cathie Melvin is Midwifery Research Co-ordinator, East Lancashire Hospitals NHS Trust

Jo Naylor is a Sure Start Breastfeeding Co-ordinator in East London

Denise Pemberton is Registered Midwife/International Board Certified Lactation Consultant, Nottingham

Karen Sabin is BIBS Midwife, Sure Start Foxhill and Parson Cross, Sheffield

Debrah Shakespeare is Head of Midwifery, Gynaecology and Sexual Health, Northern Lincolnshire and Goole NHS Trust

Debbie Singh is Independent Researcher and Evidence Analyst, London

Hora Soltani is Senior Lecturer in Midwifery, Faculty of Health and Wellbeing, Sheffield Hallam University, formerly Lead Research Midwife, Derby Hospitals NHS Trust.

This book is dedicated to my mum, Helen Theresa Aslam,
who I miss more every day

Foreword

Inequalities in health and access to health care are not just a matter of political correctness – even in the UK in the 21st century, inequalities kill mothers and babies.

An independent inquiry into inequalities in health chaired by Sir Donald Acheson made 39 recommendations in 1998. It found that these inequalities ranged across geographical areas, social class, gender and ethnicity. The report recommended that the needs of pregnant women, young families and infants should be a high priority for efforts to reduce inequalities in health, and to ensure a healthier nation. Reports from the Confidential Enquiry into Maternal and Child Health (CEMACH) such as *Why Mothers Die* provide stark evidence of inequalities in maternity care. Women from the most disadvantaged groups of society were about 20 times more likely to die than women in the highest two social classes. Their babies are more than twice as likely to die. Inequalities affect a large proportion of women – over one-third of mothers in the UK receive benefits. The drive to reduce health inequalities has a direct impact on the role of midwives and all those involved with women.

The key issues that challenge midwives about addressing inequalities in their everyday practice are:

- Minimizing the effects of inequalities is an integral part of maternity care, not an optional extra.

All professional and lay workers involved in any work or contact with pregnant women (whether working for the NHS, social services, or in other public sectors such as education, the police, prison services, probation or voluntary agencies) should treat women with respect and parity to other clients regardless of the carer's own feelings about that woman and her family. Clinicians, carers and health care commissioners cannot decide that they want to ignore services for vulnerable, socially excluded, disadvantaged or just down right 'difficult' women.

- Minimizing the effects of inequalities involves looking at individuals rather than disadvantaged groups.

Care needs to be individual, flexible and personal for each woman with consideration of her circumstances. Carers should not jump to conclusions and make assumptions from a woman's appearance, ability to communicate, past history, culture or religion. It can be unhelpful to identify groups of women who are 'unequal' as this view does not respect women as individuals but encourages stereotyping.

The purpose of this book is to signpost and inform midwives how they can engage with women and families from different backgrounds in a more effective evidence-based way. The authors are all experts in their own fields and offer sound and very practical thoughts on the way in which the experience of women can be improved significantly if midwives identify the obstacles that women may encounter and rise to the challenge of overcoming them in partnership with the woman and her community.

Topics include involving women in strategic decisions about their own care and ensuring that the voices of disadvantaged women are heard both in health care planning and on an individual basis, such as providing a postnatal listening service for minority ethnic women.

There are several chapters on issues that cause difficulties both for individual women and midwives that help to provide ways to solve them – domestic violence, providing healthy eating advice or recognizing that postnatal depression is not restricted to White women. Other chapters look at how service providers need to discuss and plan particular services for women who do not fit into conventional stereotypes of families – lesbians, women with disabilities, travellers, teenagers and substance abusers. There are chapters on breastfeeding – using peer support to increase breastfeeding for longer and looking at the views of Bangladeshi women on feeding their babies.

There are two chapters addressing areas where professional concerns may cause conflict for a midwife over what is 'right' for the woman – requesting an elective caesarean section and tackling the apparent conflicts in information recently surfacing through concern about links between a mother sleeping with her baby to make breastfeeding easier and a possible increased risk of sudden infant death as a result.

The key message of this book is that each and every pregnant woman wants safe, high quality care regardless of ethnicity, background, physical disability, age, sexual orientation or cultural needs. It gives practical advice on seeing services from the user point of view. The provision of safe, high quality care is the challenge for all engaged in the delivery of maternity services – woman-centred care looks beyond the label society puts on a woman to the individual underneath.

Jean Chapple is Consultant in Perinatal Epidemiology/Public Health
Medicine, Westminster Primary Care Trust, London

Introduction

Yana Richens

Midwives today face very different challenges to providing woman-centred care than their predecessors 100 years ago. Today we meet and care for women with a raft of different problems, some old, some new. Teenage pregnancy is age-old and midwives continue to work with this group. More modern concerns include caring for women presenting for antenatal care from different ethnic or geographic origins. They may be refugees, traumatized, or have undergone female genital mutilation.

Midwives may encounter mothers who express a wish to have their baby by caesarean section or women who make the choice to have a baby and raise the infant with another woman as their partner. Breastfeeding remains an issue.

A hundred years ago, pregnant women had dietary issues and suffered from anaemia. Today pregnant women from disadvantaged backgrounds may face obstacles in following dietary advice. These topics are still current – maybe not much has changed, except that it is within the gift of most practising midwives to identify vulnerable mothers.

The aim of this book is to remind midwives and those involved in the care of women to be aware of the issues and challenges that are likely to present in delivering care to women in today's diverse society.

I would like to thank the contributors for sharing their ideas on ways to improve care for all women.

CHAPTER I

Women's involvement in health care: A practical model for maternity services

Hora Soltani

Core concepts

Patient and public[1] involvement (PPI) is a relatively new concept, introduced to the NHS through the national directives. Other terms used, often interchangeably in this concept, are service users or consumers. Consumers are defined as 'patients, carers, long-term users of services, organizations representing consumers' interests and members of the public likely to be the target of health promotion programmes' (Steel, 2002).

It is becoming increasingly explicit that the commitment to build a health service that is sensitive and responsive to patients', carers' and the wider public's needs, is an integral part of national health services today. Many initiatives and key public documents repeatedly emphasize the essential role of PPI as a catalyst for a high quality health service. The frequently cited importance of PPI is encapsulated within the following documents:

- *Patient Partnership: Building a Collaborative Strategy* (NHS Executive, 1996).
- *The New NHS, Modern and Dependable: A National Framework for Assessing Performance* (Department of Health, 1997).
- *A First Class Service: Quality in the New NHS* (Department of Health, 1998).
- *Patient and Public Involvement in the New NHS* (Department of Health, 1999).
- *The NHS Plan* (Department of Health, 2000).
- *Delivering the NHS Plan* (Department of Health, 2002).
- *Patient and Public Involvement in Health: The Evidence for Policy Implementation* (Department of Health, 2004a).

[1]*The term 'patient(s) and public' refers to patients, users (consumers), carers and the public. More specifically, in this chapter, it includes women and their relatives, when taking about maternity services.*

The principle message coming out of all these publications, is to 'give greater voice and influence to users of NHS Services and their carers...' (NHS Executive, 1996) and also the NHS commitment to 'shape its services around the needs of different groups and individuals within society ... patients and citizens will have a greater say in the NHS, and the provision of services will be centred on patients' needs' (Department of Health, 2000).

The recognition of this concept has however had a deeper root and an older history in the maternity services. The *Changing Childbirth* report (Department of Health, 1993) highlighted the importance of 'woman-centred care' several years ago. The promotion of informed choice and the encouragement of patient autonomy has been the centre of debate within maternity care for many years. More recently, the *National Service Framework (NSF) for Children, Young People and Maternity Services* (Department of Health, 2004b) also re-enforces this same vision through a cultural shift to promoting services that are around the needs of women (children and their families) rather than the needs of organizations. How maternity services compare with the other areas in terms of achieving objectives of user involvement however, needs to be examined separately and is beyond our discussion in this chapter.

A great deal of effort has gone into elaborating the significance of engaging patients and public in their care. However, on a practical level, specially at earlier stages, there seemed to be a lack of clear structure as to how, when and where to involve health service users. This in turn had a knock on effect on the velocity of the implementation process and led to a considerable variation in the extent to which different units adopted the initiative. On the other hand, it gave a certain range of flexibility which could promote creative ways of involving patients and their carers in service development. This is, nevertheless, evolving and more clarifications on the support mechanisms and models of engagement are becoming available to health services. This chapter presents a discussion of patient (women) involvement in the context of clinical governance, strategies, support mechanisms and expected challenges with some practical examples specifically focused on maternity services.

Why patient and public involvement is important

One of the primary purposes of modernizing the NHS is to 'rebuild public confidence in the NHS as a public service, accountable to patients, open to the public and shaped by their views' (Department of Health, 1997). Involving patients/women in service development can help to achieve the above objectives at different levels:

- At an individual level: there is growing evidence that involving patients in decision making can improve satisfaction with their care and enhance the effectiveness of their treatment (Department of Health, 1999). Providing opportunities to make decisions and giving sufficient and appropriate information are key to active involvement of women/patients in their care. Women feel better about themselves and the services provided if they are listened to and given choices in making decisions about their care. A systematic review of involving patients in health care (Crawford et al., 2002) suggests that involving patients has contributed considerably to changes in service provision, nevertheless, an evidence base for the effect of those changes in terms of use of services, quality of care and satisfaction needs further evaluation.

- The notion of the 'expert patient' is another way of utilizing patient experiences towards improving care and services. Some may argue that this is not quite relevant to maternity as it specifically relates to patients with chronic conditions such as diabetes. On the contrary, the length of time that women experience maternity care for each birth and the fact that quite often there are repeated pregnancies, makes this most relevant as 'expert mothers'. Women's experiences can be effectively drawn on, at a personal level or collectively in antenatal education or in the form of birth stories, to be shared with expectant mothers. It can also be beneficial for practitioners in identifying what they do well and where there is room for improvement. In addition, in chronic conditions such as diabetic pregnancies or in women with high blood pressure or even women in special situations such as drug users or teenage pregnancies, their involvement could be equally beneficial in service improvement.
- It provides a convenient opportunity to establish a two-way communication between care providers and service users.
- It offers an opportunity for health carers to enhance and demonstrate accountability to their clientele.
- Involving users at different stages, from planning through to delivering care, reduces the risk of providing services that are not suitable and enhances the chance of provision of quality care in the way that is acceptable to patients/women.
- Consulting users' views is central to the definition of clinical governance, and can help to improve standards of care in many different aspects, such as:

    Day-to-day care and service provision.
    Access to facilities.
    Preferences for different types of care.
    How care has been delivered ranging from staff's attitude to physical environment and provided facilities.
    Information and support.

A recent report by the Department of Health (2004a) gives an in-depth account of supporting evidence for patient and public involvement. The report is based on the findings from 12 projects as part of a larger health research programme called *Health in Partnership*. Some of the areas identified within this document are represented above.

Support mechanisms

The NHS is progressively promoting patient/woman-focused care, emphasizing that it is not only about structure but also about change of culture (Department of Health, 2004c). It is widely recognized that in addition to transformation of ethos of thinking, a robust infrastructure should be in place to re-enforce cultural and behavioural changes. Hence, support for operational mechanisms is gradually introduced into the system. From January 2003, it is a legal duty to involve and consult the public (Department of Health, 2004c). Since then, more documents have been published to guide establishment, implementation, monitoring and outcome evaluation of this exciting initiative. The infrastructure has been steadily built up at several layers within the health service including strategic health authorities, primary care trusts and local NHS trusts. At a corporate level, these include (Department of Health, 2004c):

- Commission for Patient and Public Involvement in Health (CPPIH): This is an independent body that primarily sets up, funds and manages the performance of Patient and Public Information Forums and also monitors the Independent Complaints Advocacy Service (ICAS). As part of a Department of Health review, this is going to be abolished and replaced with new plans.
- Independent Complaints Advocacy Service (ICAS): This service provides support and help to patients and their relatives who wish to make a complaint about the care they receive.
- Patient Advice and Liaison Services (PALS): With a substantial input from users, these are established in every local NHS trust and act as a primary contact between patients and public and the organization. They are at the forefront of the organization with the aim of building a strong and reliable relationship with patients and to provide them with advice and guidance as and when required.
- Overview and Scrutiny Committee (OSC): This committee is responsible for scrutinizing health service programmes by monitoring their impact on local people using performance management data and reports from PALS and ICAS.
- Patient and Public Involvement Forums (PPI Forums): These are now set up in all NHS trusts and their primary mission is to gather patients' and public views and communicate them to relevant bodies for action. They

should take a proactive role and refer matters of concern to the OSC, CPPIH or Strategic Health Authorities for final resolution.

It is interesting to see that in a relatively short period of time, since the concept of PPI has been established within the NHS, a variety of supporting structures have been introduced. It is expected that all the above committees and forums will functionally interlink, with the aim of demonstrable improvement in patient experiences. Since all the processes are new, it is important to know that they are not static and will evolve. At the same time, some were abandoned in a short period of time and this may be concerning in terms of the impact of continuous alterations on forward planning. Unless there is a dramatic u-turn in implementation of this initiative (due to change of political flow), small adjustments and alterations are expected to be beneficial and constructive rather than fundamentally disparaging.

Awareness of such existing mechanisms in support of PPI is of crucial importance in setting up local user groups within maternity or any other units. It facilitates the development of a framework that is beyond local practice and explores other avenues that may help to link the voice of carers and caregivers through appropriate channels to the relevant bodies. Although superficial acceptance and employment of the PPI concept has the risk of adding another layer of bureaucratic exercises to the system, implementing this initiative can be tremendously helpful in moving health services forward.

Dimensions, approaches and challenges of PPI

Dimensions

Provision of high quality services is at the heart of the clinical governance agenda. Clinical governance encompasses several dimensions including research, audit, clinical guidelines, clinical risk and complaint management. To enhance efficiency, it is recommended to establish a partnership with the patients and public in all aspects of clinical governance and service development. The main focus of this chapter is PPI in service development which is extensively discussed in other sections. A brief representation of different stages at which research can benefit from PPI is represented in *Figure 1.1*. The principles shown in *Figure 1.1* could also be applicable to audit and to some extent to risk assessment exercises. For all these activities, it is of fundamental importance that the involvement should commence right at the beginning, in a way that leads to improvement and influences decision making. A great example of user involvement in the research process is the consumer panel participation in the Cochrane pregnancy and childbirth group which has added value to the development of systematic reviews from the early stage of protocol design to the final stages of writing up and dissemination of the reviews.

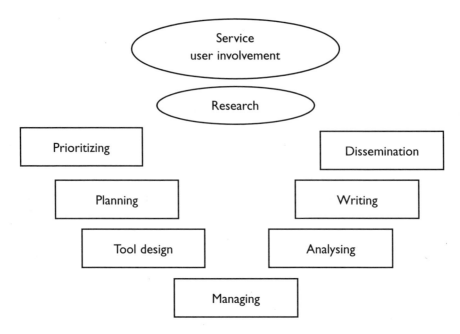

Figure 1.1. Stages in which health service consumers can effectively participate in research activities (Steel, 2003).

PPI approaches

The approach can be mainly in two forms; either at an individual level or collectively as in a group consultation. The approach at the individual level, the value of which is extensively recognized, may be harder to achieve. In maternity services this is particularly important, as women are faced with several choices from the start of pregnancy to birth and the postpartum period including numerous screening tests, models of care, type of birth and place of birth as well as various prophylactic interventions for them and their babies. The strategies for these should be embedded in everyday practice and are of great significance in relation to the provision of information and the decision making process. It requires a genuine willingness, appropriate training, adequate resources and time to enable maximum effectiveness. This is the most sensitive element of PPI in delivering its objectives in its real term. It could potentially help in empowering women and advocating autonomy in decision making. It is the cornerstone of PPI and yet the most challenging aspect of it.

Collective approaches mainly use methods such as surveys, patient diaries, in-depth interviews or focus groups. These are useful methods of gathering patient/public perspectives and views on existing services and possible alterations that are needed to improve services. It should be remembered that these methods are not just to identify problems but also could identify areas where good practice is in place. In contrast to critical perceptions, this could be a positive, rewarding and encouraging exercise which can help to improve the morale of the work environment.

The presence of patients/public representatives at meetings where decisions about service development are made, is another way of involving people in service development which is of crucial importance. There may be some concerns about breaching confidentiality if patients are involved in developmental meetings. This of course depends on appropriate handling of sensitive matters by coding and avoiding revealing any names.

Areas such as access, waiting times, safety, environment and cleanliness and care quality can be best monitored and evaluated through such collective methods.

Challenges

The major challenges that may be encountered in the process of implementing public and patient involvement include:

- *Recruitment*: How and where to recruit volunteers is the key stage in this whole process. Public awareness is crucial to ensure health service users know their rights and the opportunities available to them, how to get involved and what the benefits of engagement in service development are. They need to be reassured that changes will be made and their participation will have an impact on the many aspects of care provision that matters to them. Possible routes of raising awareness and recruiting service users include national and local media, posters in wards, clinics and other public places as well as specific open days and patient education forums (e.g. antenatal classes). People who have had a complaint or a less positive experience from the services, are usually more proactive in trying to get engaged and quite often see this as an opportunity to communicate their concerns more effectively. This is a constructive way of engaging this group of people, it is comforting to them that they are listened to and that they have a way to share their experiences with others and hear from others who may have had more positive experiences.
- *Membership*: To ensure a balanced reflection, the user group should include a wide range of clients and minority groups. The user group co-ordinator (being a current or former client her/himself) should be sure to approach as many hard to reach groups as possible as well as mainstream clients for inclusion in the group. Sometimes subgroups can be organized to make it more convenient and to keep the options open for those who cannot participate regularly but would like to be in touch, get informed and have a role from a distance. This is of course not always easy and can be frustrating and time-consuming.

- *Time and workload*: This applies to volunteers from the public and patients as well as to health care professionals. In maternity, in particular, women and their partners, in their roles as new parents (or quite often with having previous children) it is difficult to fit in any other activities. It takes a high level of commitment and motivation to become proactively engaged. There is a need for appropriate support and adequate resources (e.g. child care reimbursement of expenses and training where appropriate) to encourage and promote service user involvement.
- *Maintenance*: Another challenge is to sustain the group and maintain it in an active format. Maintenance of the group depends on the level of commitment and motivation of the participants as well as on the support they receive from local and central organizations and, above all, on the results of their contribution. Changes to national directives, initiatives and supporting mechanisms are also major barriers that directly affect the sustainability of the involvement of the user group in service development.
- *Isolation*: Unless there is a high level of interest, a strong belief and commitment from the service providers, the service users can be isolated and therefore not effectively influence service changes. There should be a robust two-way communication between the health carers and users to ensure voices are heard and actions are made towards bettering the services.

Finally, it should be emphasized that a spirit of collaboration and partnership as well as provision of adequate resources and appropriate training for users in particular, are essential in maintaining an effective contribution by health service consumers towards reforming the health care setting.

Developing a model to involve maternity user groups

A demonstration of user group settings in different health service units and how they contribute to service development can be seen in a Department of Health document called *Getting over the Wall: How the NHS is Improving the Patient's Experience* (2004d). A local example of maternity user involvement is the Southern Derbyshire Maternity User Group (SDMUG) which was established in 1997 as a subcommittee of the local Maternity Services Liaison Committee (SDMSLC). It ran successfully for a period of time after which there was some fluctuation in its membership, and it was left with just one member by 2002. Since then, having obtained external funding to support the group activities (to cover expenses such as child care and travelling, time compensation and appropriate training), and the proactive member taking the role of co-ordinator, the group was revitalized and widened its scope of involvement. The group works and liaises closely with the maternity research department. The range of activities undertaken by the maternity user group includes:

- Proactive recruitment and consultation of women and their families who are or have experienced local maternity services. This is often done by setting stands in the market or popular shopping areas, where parents/ families are asked to fill a brief questionnaire to explore their views and comments on the local maternity services. Awareness is also raised in terms of opportunities for members of the public to join the maternity user group.
- Involvement in different meetings such as research, audit and labour forums in which different relevant issues are discussed and decisions are made. The group comments on draft versions of guidelines and patient information leaflets.
- An innovative approach used by this group is involvement in collective analysis of complaints and thank you cards as well as comments collected through suggestion boxes in antenatal and postnatal wards and the labour ward. The result of this analysis was an independent report, made by the group, reflecting areas in which improvement is needed and also areas of good practice. The local PALS practically supports the whole process, especially in collecting and posting the comments from the suggestion boxes to the maternity user group co-ordinator for further processing. Involving the user group in all aspects, particularly through complaint handling is strongly recommended by the *National Service Framework (NSF) for Children, Young People and Maternity Services* (Department of Health, 2004b).
- Currently the group consists of eight members who meet regularly and produce quarterly newsletters. Subgroups have also been established for breastfeeding and caesarean sections. It is also planned to visit specific hard-to-reach groups such as the deaf community and has approached Sure Start projects for further expansion and inclusion of a wider range of women into the group.
- The group is also in the process of developing a specific page within the local NHS trust website. This is hoped to improve recruitment and communication to a wider group.
- To make sure the loop is closed and suggestions made by the group are taken on board, a strategy has been developed to facilitate a two-way communication between the MUG and maternity health service providers/ staff. This can be seen in *Figure 1.2.*

In conclusion, although having all the above infrastructure at various levels is helpful, it should be remembered that while the culture is shifting, and the concept of PPI, in its real terms, is being established, there is a risk of an oversight to the proper use of such valuable resources by being either taken for granted or worse used merely for the purpose of 'ticking the

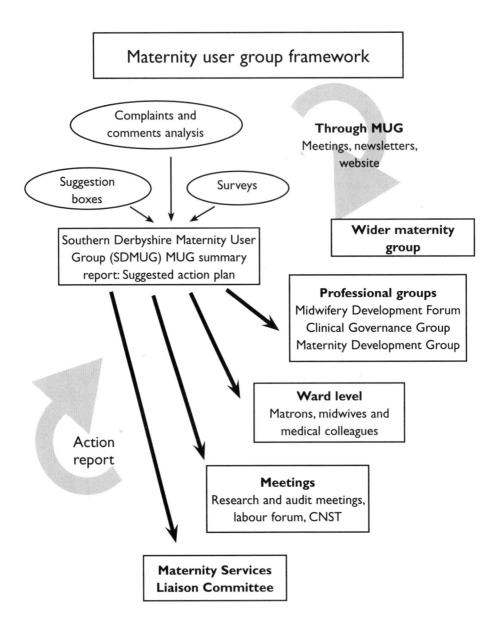

Figure 1.2. Communication plan between the maternity user group and heath care providers.

right boxes'. To avoid these unhelpful outcomes, an appropriate evaluation system should be in place to ensure closure of the loops, continuing effective communication and regular monitoring of the outputs of user involvement in service development.

Acknowledgement

Many thanks to Lisa Wood for sharing her experiences of co-ordinating the Southern Derbyshire Maternity User Group and for her valuable comments on this chapter.

References

Crawford MJ, Rutter D, Manley C, Weaver T, Bhui K, Fulop N, Tyrer P (2002) Systematic review of involving patients in the planning and development of health care. *Brit Med J* **325**: 1263.

Department of Health (1993) *Changing Childbirth: Report of the Expert Maternity Group* (Cumberlege Report). The Stationary Office, London.

Department of Health (1997) *The New NHS, Modern and Dependable: A National Framework for Assessing Performance*. The Stationary Office, London.

Department of Health (1998) *A First Class Service: Quality in the new NHS*. The Stationary Office, London.

Department of Health (1999) *Patient and Public Involvement in the New NHS*. The Stationary Office, London.

Department of Health (2000) *The NHS Plan*. The Stationary Office, London.

Department of Health (2002) *Delivering the NHS Plan*. The Stationary Office, London.

Department of Health (2004a) *Patient and Public Involvement in Health: The Evidence for Policy Implementation*. Available from http://www.dh.gov.uk [Accessed 9 October 2006].

Department of Health (2004b) *National Service Framework for Children and Young People. Standard 11, Maternity: 27*. The Stationary Office, London.

Department of Health (2004c) *Legal Duty: Patient, Public Involvement: A Brief Overview*. Available from: http://www.dh.gov.uk/PolicyAndGuidance/OrganisationPolicy/PatientAndPublicInvolvement/InvolvingPatientsPublicHealthcare/InvolvingPatientsPublicHealthcareArticle/fs/en?CONTENT_ID=4000457&chk=V44bEb [Accessed 1 February 2005].

Department of Health (2004d) *Getting Over the Wall: How the NHS is Improving the Patient's Experience*. Available from: http://www.dh.gov.uk/PublicationsAndStatistics/Publications/PublicationsPolicyAndGuidance/PublicationsPolicyAndGuidanceArticle/fs/en?CONTENT_ID=4090841&chk=hvlEoY [Accessed 1 February 2005].

NHS Executive (1996) *Patient Partnership: Building a Collaborative Strategy.* NHS Executive Quality and Consumers Branch, Leeds.

Steel R (2002) *A Guide to Paying Members of the Public Who Are Actively Involved in Research: For Researchers and Research Commissioners (Who May Also Be Consumers).* INVOLVE Publications, Hampshire.

Steel R (ed.) (2003) *Involving the Public in NHS, Public Health and Social Care Research: Briefing Notes for Researchers* (2nd edn.) INVOLVE Publications, Hampshire.

CHAPTER 2

Improving consultation with disadvantaged service users

Rachael Lockey and Angie Hart

Introduction

This chapter looks at two major policy drives: (1) consulting and involving service users in health care research, planning and provision and (2) addressing inequalities in health, in relation to the actual practice of consulting 'disadvantaged' service users in research. Drawing on the findings of a research project previously undertaken by the authors we look at the researchers' experience of consulting 'disadvantaged' service users. While 'disadvantaged' service users may be the most hard to involve, because of practical and/or social barriers as well as the extra time and expertise needed by researchers, these services users must be involved in order to inform research, policy and service delivery.

Within the health arena we have seen a development in Government policy that indicates service user involvement and consultation is now required of those planning and delivering services.

Documents such as the *NHS Plan* (Department of Health, 2000) and *Involving Patients and the Public in Healthcare: A Discussion Document* (Department of Health, 2001) clearly indicate that service user involvement, feedback and consultation when planning and delivering health services is a requirement. The latter document gives some instruction on how to involve and consult service users. Some scholars have critically reviewed these kinds of policy visions and how they are carried out (Grant-Pearce et al., 1998; Harrison and Mort, 1998; Johnson, 2001; Ling 1999).

The degree to which service users are involved will vary greatly and we suggest it may be conceptualized as being a continuum with 'consultation' at one end and user 'involvement' at the other (Cornwall and Jewkes, 1995). Thus 'consultation', which we discuss in depth in this article, may be seen as the 'soft' end of service user involvement, where the service user's views and opinions are sought.

Whether or how this then shapes future planning and provision will depend on a commitment to see such consultation impact on policy and practice. 'Involvement' then, at the other end of the continuum, would involve service users in planning, research and delivery of services at varying degrees.

Within the maternity services there is a relatively long history of service user involvement and consultation. A 'select' committee, which included service users, was responsible for the *Changing Childbirth* (Department of Health, 1993) report. Well-established organizations such as the National Childbirth Trust (NCT) and the Association for the Improvement in Maternity Services (AIMS) have grown out of service user campaigns to bring about a change in the maternity services. Representatives from these organizations are now present on many boards and committees relating to the maternity services at both national and local level, such as Maternity Select Liaison Committees.

Such involvement has been invaluable in giving the public a voice in service development. It is important, however, to consider which service users are involved. We suggest it is certainly easier to involve the more pro-active, articulate and empowered service users. Such people might be termed 'professional' service users who have become familiar with a committee/formal setting. Previous work concluded that this was largely the case with service user involvement in *Changing Childbirth* (Hart, 1997).

Alongside policies which assertively promote service user involvement, there has been an expressed commitment on the part of the current Labour Government to address inequalities in health and the still widening gap between rich and poor, the greatest contributing factor to which remains socioeconomic deprivation (Benzeval et al, 1995). Policy documents, including the Acheson Report (Department of Health, 1998) and the *NHS Plan* (Department of Health, 2000) state that services must address inequalities and that practitioners need to target clients who experience inequalities in health and health care.

How this is done is rarely specifically expanded on in policy documents and service providers and individual practitioners are often left to develop, or not, their own means by which to address inequalities (Hart and Lockey, 2002).

Considering both of the above then; (1) the increased commitment to consult with and involve service users and (2) the tackling inequalities agenda, it is necessary to consider how to consult and involve service users who are 'disadvantaged', and as a consequence may be hard to reach, hard to engage or unpopular. While it is important to see people as individuals, from our research data we identified some very broad categories of 'service user' and we explore this within this chapter.

There are many reasons why a particular service user might be hard to reach or difficult to engage and the different types are outlined in *Table 2.1*. These might be very practical ones such as not having access to a telephone, not speaking or understanding English or being homeless.

There may also be 'unpopular' clients whose voices and opinions may not be considered important or valid, including people who experience prejudices and discrimination, such as pregnant women who use drugs and women in prison. We found in practice that consulting with 'disadvantaged' service users

Table 2.1. Disadvantaged service user types	
User type	Definition
Hard to reach	There may be difficulties in accessing people who experience inequalities such as a language barrier or homelessness.
Difficult to engage	Some service users had no views or feedback regarding the care they had received. A one-off interview may not always be adequate enough to engage some service users
Unpopular	Certain service users may experience prejudice and discrimination, such as pregnant women who misuse substances and women in prison. The views of these people may not always be seen as equally important. However they may experience some of the worst inequalities in health and health care provision

often requires a lot of time, flexibility and specific skills such as outreach techniques and working with translators.

In the following section we draw on our own experience of consulting disadvantaged service users in order to inform a national research project we undertook looking at midwifery education and services in relation to inequalities (Hart et al., 2001). We also draw some parallels between our experiences as researchers of engaging disadvantaged service users and the experiences of midwives.

Consulting disadvantaged service users

Our research project, Addressing Inequalities in Health: New directions in midwifery education and practice (Hart et al., 2001) was commissioned by the English National Board for Nursing, Midwifery and Health Visiting (ENB). Our work explored the needs of disadvantaged service users and the role of midwifery services and education in meeting them.

As well as an extensive literature review and a national survey of pre- and post-registration midwifery education courses and curricula, the research included three in-depth case sites, each lasting three months, in different locations across England. The three case sites were selected, using the Jarman index particularly in relation to socioeconomic deprivation.

Two of the case sites had relatively high levels of socioeconomic deprivation and one of these had a diverse Black and minority ethnic population including refugees and asylum seekers. In this chapter we draw on some of the data collected from these case sites. For more details on the actual research see Hart et al. (2001).

The project design drew on stakeholder analysis (Stake, 1980). At each case site service users, educators, managers, practitioners and, where applicable, bilingual health advocates were interviewed about their role. For service providers the interview focused on their own understanding of inequalities in health, as well as how the local maternity services and education were tailored to address inequalities. For people using services we carried out an in-depth semi-structured interview, firstly exploring their life history followed by their experience of using maternity services. This included their own perceived needs, the expectations of midwives and other practitioners, and whether or not these needs were met.

During interviews the practitioners were asked to think about people on their caseload who they felt may experience inequalities in health and tell us how they had provided care for them. We then asked the practitioner to contact the woman on our behalf to gain permission to interview her. In total we interviewed 15 service users at each case site giving a total of 45. We paid each woman £10 to take part in the research in recognition of their expertise as service users.

The range of service users we interviewed as a result of this 'referral' process was diverse. People's experiences included the following issues: living in poverty, teenage parenting, substance misuse, domestic violence, homelessness, physical disability, learning difficulties, poor obstetric histories, refugee and asylum status people and women for whom language was a barrier. The contacting and consulting of the service users to inform our research reflected some of the difficulty practitioners' described in providing maternity care for disadvantaged clients. These included practical issues such as a woman having no phone or no fixed abode. In some cases there was also unwillingness on behalf of the woman to be met by yet another 'professional', although this was surprisingly rare.

The interviews took place in the woman's home or a venue that suited her. The time varied from half an hour to three hours, as determined by the service user herself, and interviews were largely taped (always with written consent), for transcription and analysis later. We have chosen three interview examples. Each one is chosen to illustrate the broad themes identifiable in our research data: (1) hard to reach, (2) hard to engage, and (3) unpopular.

Interview 1: Zahra – Hard to reach

Background
Zahra had been living in England for several years; she had come as a refugee because of the war in Somalia. She had several children, a partner who was unable to live with her in this country and an extended family living locally.

Zahra was referred to us by a bilingual health advocate who had worked with her during her recent pregnancy and postnatal period. The same bilingual health advocate acted as translator for us during this three-way interview. We also had research information translated into Zahra's language in order to gain her full consent to participate in the project.

Interview
We met with Zahra at her home with her children and several female relatives. She was happy to be interviewed and had lots to say. Zahra chose not to be tape-recorded during the research interview, her reason for this was that tape recordings had been used as evidence against people during the Somalian civil war.

Experiences
Zahra told us that her experience of hospital care was largely negative. During the postnatal period she developed a contagious disease and was isolated. At this time she felt that she was treated, 'like a dog, they used to push the plate at me.' However she describes one particular midwife whom she found caring and kind:

> *'She was compassionate, she had an open face. She used to know I was in pain, she'd say, "You go and relax and I'll bring you something [for the pain]"'*

Comments
In contrast to this Zahra's case highlights many incidences where lack of communication between staff meant she received poor care:

> *'The senior midwife wrote instructions and notes for the night midwives but nobody used to bother [looking at them].'*

Some of the problems that she experienced were related directly to poor communication not resources:

> *'There was no communication between doctors and midwives. A lot of this [problems with her care] could have been prevented.'*

When asked how the services might be improved Zahra had the following to say:

> *'The midwife sister has to know who is bad and who is compassionate. Rotten midwives should go, why should women have to change hospital? There are one or two good midwives but most you thought you had killed their relatives the way they treated you.'*

Feeding back

Interview data of this nature bring up very sensitive issues that are often difficult to feed back, especially to staff directly involved, who may feel defensive.

Conclusion

Zahra was hard to reach due to a language barrier that existed for both her and the researcher. A third person was needed throughout the whole process of identifying and reaching Zahra as well as during the interview, and this reflects her needs when receiving maternity care. She expressed some frustration at the bilingual health advocacy service being available only during the hours of 9 to 5.

Interview 2: Eleanore – Hard to engage

Background

Eleanor, aged 17, and baby Jade who was a few months old were living with Eleanor's mum and dad, two sisters and a brother. Eleanor's mum had an 18-month old toddler and they had both had the same midwife whom they spoke of very highly. Housing conditions were crowded and the family lived on state benefits but family support was evident.

Interview

The reason for looking at this interview is to give an example of someone who might be considered 'hard to engage'. Eleanor agreed to be interviewed and was happy for a researcher to come to the house, however it was a difficult interview as she had little to say or to feed back to us about her experiences of services. The interview lasted half an hour and the following extract occurred towards the end of this time:

> Interviewer: What is it like being a mum?
> Eleanor: Good.
> Interviewer: Did you think it would be like this?
> Eleanor: No.
> Interviewer: How did you think it would be?
> Eleanor: I thought she would scream all the time but she doesn't.
> Interviewer: Is there anything else you want to tell me about?
> Eleanor: No.
> Interviewer: It sounds as if you have been happy with all the people involved in your care. What's Clare [the midwife] been like?
> Eleanor: She's been good.
> Interviewer: Is there anything that could have been done differently?
> Eleanor: No.

Findings

The issues arising in this interview may be mirrored in practice. Firstly, low expectations of services may mean some people can be undemanding compared to articulate and informed service users. Secondly, lack of time and continuity, preventing us from engaging in peoples lives, may prohibit the development of a meaningful relationship. This has important implications for how we provide midwifery care. More time, effort and understanding may be required in order to begin to address inequalities.

Conclusion

Interviews like these were not uncommon, despite the interviewers having diverse experience in fieldwork and interviewing techniques. We termed this as participants who were 'hard to engage', as in they were fairly easy to reach but difficult to then engage beyond a superficial level. Such interviews are characterized by a kind of flatness. We reflected that this could be that the subject material just is not of interest to the respondent, that some people's expectations of services are very minimal or that the use of one-off interviews is not appropriate as no time for trust or understanding has developed. At times we considered that a more ethnographic approach, where the researcher undertakes participant observation and becomes more embedded in people's lives, would possibly elicit more views and opinions. Both of us had previous experience of this approach and had found it helpful in enabling people to engage with the research (Hart, 1998).

Interview 3: Nicola – Unpopular

Background

Nicola was a 19-year-old mum with her first baby who was eight months old at the time of this interview. Mandy, her midwife, put us in touch with her. The researcher met with Nicola and her partner Alan at their next-door-neighbour's flat. The flats were in an area of a city that had high levels of socioeconomic deprivation. Many of the surrounding houses were boarded up and no longer lived in. Nicola had a history of using drugs and alcohol, she had also been homeless during the pregnancy with a change of address several times. She now lived quite far from the team of midwives she booked with. However, the midwives had continued to visit her despite having to travel to the other side of the city. In an interview the midwife looking after Nicola explained that she and Nicola had developed a relationship and that she wanted to use this in order to ensure Nicola got as much care as possible.

Interview

During this interview, which lasted a couple of hours and involved cups of tea, cigarettes and 'spliffs' (marijuana), Nicola was able to tell a lot of her own life story. She swore a lot and spoke of things some people might find unacceptable such as drugs and stealing baby milk and towels from the ward.

Relationship with midwife

During the interview Nicola spoke very highly of her named midwife, she said she 'made you feel at ease, talked to you like you were normal like'. This was very important for Nicola who had been brought up in care and had a sequence of difficult events in her life including being 'kicked out of care' on her 17th birthday in the middle of winter. Having a midwife who she could relate to and felt understood her a bit was very important to her:

'I grew up in care and I'm sort of funny with different people if you know what I mean...'

She then went on to say about Mandy, her named midwife:

'I didn't trust any of them at first but Mandy, she made me feel dead comfortable.'

Discrimination

Nicola was very reflective during the interview and talked about how she might be on the receiving end of discriminatory attitudes and prejudices about people who use drugs. She said of doctors:

'I don't associate with doctors because they didn't listen to us. No one listens to me.'

One of the things she felt most strongly about was the way the hospital midwives looked at her:

'It was the hospital I didn't like when they were all staring at us. When you go into maternity there is reception and all the midwives are sitting round gawping at you.'

Nicola talked about how she felt uncomfortable when she went off the ward for a cigarette, because of the looks the midwives gave her. She talked openly throughout the interview about depression, drug use and on what occasions she might 'use'. When asked who she might speak to if she started feeling depressed again she said:

'I wouldn't go to no-one. I'd just end up ... there's a rave over at (names place) I would go there and get myself a couple of pills and go and jump about, strobe lights, and it's all better.'

Hospital midwives

In our study, hospital midwives were more likely to be experienced as unkind and uncaring than were community midwives (Hart et al., 2001). Hospital midwives, however, may have less opportunity to be able to develop such a relationship given the short period of contact time and lack of continuity, and thus may be at risk of focusing on the negative.

Findings

What was clear was that Nicola had had a hard life and had had to fend for herself from a very young age. In such circumstances a health practitioner needs to be able to spend some time with Nicola, as Mandy was able to do. Nicola was very appreciative of this, it had made a difference to her. Furthermore, it may be no coincidence that Mandy herself came from a background of relative poverty in childhood, which may have increased her capacity to empathize and not judge.

Conclusion

When caring for people such as Nicola practitioners might draw on their imagination to enhance their ability to provide good quality care that is culturally appropriate and non-judgemental. In our research we called this an 'inequalities imagination' and developed a learning tool/model to encourage people to strengthen their 'inequalities imagination' (Hart et al., 2001).

People like Nicola might be 'unpopular' because of their drug use, aggressive language and for having little respect for institutions. Furthermore, engagement in services may be sporadic as other factors may take precedence, such as homelessness. As providers of care we may feel rejected or affronted by her. For us, interviews like Nicola's enriched our research data.

Findings

Our most consistent finding was that women wanted a midwife who was nice to them, kind, had a sense of humour and made them feel at ease.

This was talked about far more commonly than issues to do with clinical skills. All these issues revolve around communication and this finding is similar to other midwifery research where the views of service users were sought (Hart, 1997).

General conclusions

Current Government policy advocates that we address inequalities in health and consult and involve service users in planning, research and delivery of services. In this chapter we have highlighted some of the difficulties and rewards of bringing these two policy visions together in practice by seeking the views and experiences of disadvantaged women. We looked in depth at three women's experiences. Zahra was hard to reach because of a language barrier existing between her and the researcher. For Zahra this paralleled communication problems that became evident in her care. Eleanor had no strong views or opinions on her care. The research method applied, that of a one-off interview, may have been an inadequate tool in order to understand her. Lastly, Nicola had plenty to say but her views may not always have been sought or welcome.

It is important for researchers and health practitioners to feel comfortable about working with people from a wide variety of backgrounds, and to adopt a positive attitude towards the research participant/client, otherwise they risk compounding the difficult experiences some people spoke of in relation to health care professionals.

The complexities of undertaking these interviews were vast, ranging from practical issues such as homelessness, to ethical dilemmas around 'disadvantage' and how we define people. However, these complexities mirror those faced by the midwife, or other health professional, who, in order to provide care to those who need it most, will need extra time and skills. The development of an 'inequalities imagination' might help practitioners to provide good quality care that is empathetic and not judgemental.

Lastly, a great effort is needed on behalf of researchers and service providers to ensure that the views and experiences of socially excluded and disadvantaged woman are sought in order to inform research, planning and delivery of services. Most of all, if we are to undertake service user consultation and involvement, we must ensure that it is actually used, and not just shelved somewhere as a consultation document.

References

Benzeval M, Judge K, Whitehead M (eds.) (1995) *Tackling Inequalities in Health: An Agenda for Action.* King's Fund, London.

Cornwall A, Jewkes R (1995) What is participatory research? *Soc Sci Med* **41 (12)**:1667–76.

Department of Health (1993) *Changing Childbirth Part 1: Report of the Expert Maternity Group.* HMSO, London.

Department of Health (1998) *Independent Inquiry into Inequalities in Health Report* (Chaired by Sir Donald Acheson). HMSO, London.

Department of Health (2000) *The NHS Plan.* HMSO, London.

Department of Health (2001) *Involving Patients and the Public in Healthcare: Response to the Listening Exercise.* Opinion Leader Research, London.

Grant-Pearce C, Miles I, Hills P (1998) *Mismatches in Priorities for Health*

Research Between Professionals and Consumers. PREST, Manchester University.

Harrison S, Mort M (1998) Which champions, which people? Public and user involvement in health care as a technology of legitimation. *Social Policy and Administration* **32(1)**: 60–70.

Hart A (ed.) (1997) *An Evaluation of Team Midwifery: The Impact on Women, Practitioners and Practice*. Brighton Health Care NHS Trust, Brighton.

Hart A (1998) *Buying and Selling Power: Anthropological Reflections on Prostitution in Spain*. Westview Press, HarperCollins, Boulder, Colorado.

Hart A, Lockey R (2002). Inequalities in health care provision: Contemporary policy and practice in the maternity services. *J Adv Nursing* **37(5)**: 1–9.

Hart A, Lockey R, Henwood F, Pankhurst F, Hall V, Somerville F (2001) *Addressing Inequalities in Health: New Directions in Midwifery Education and Practice*. English National Board for Nursing, Midwifery and Health Visiting, London.

Johnson S (2001) *Managed Empowerment in the Modernised National Health Service*. Unpublished D.Phil Thesis, University of Sussex.

Ling T (ed.) (1999) *Reforming Healthcare by Consent*. Radcliffe Medical Press, Oxford.

Stake R (1980) Programme evaluation, particularly responsive evaluation. In WB Dockrell, D Hamilton (eds.) *Rethinking Educational Research*. Hodder and Stoughton, Sevenoaks.

CHAPTER 3

Volunteers and users' views of a postnatal listening service for minority ethnic women

Janet Hirst, Josephine M Green, Khalida Ashrafi, Mussarat Khan and Karl Atkin

Introduction

Listening to people and ensuring their views inform health and social care provision has been a policy goal for over 10 years. Unfortunately, policy makers and practitioners still remain unclear about how best to engage with the communities they serve. This has particular implications for minority ethnic populations. At best, this means their perspectives and needs do not adequately inform service delivery. At worst, it means service support is informed by racist myths and stereotypes.

Despite considerable research activity we still have little indication about what types of policies and interventions actually work when providing accessible and appropriate support for minority ethnic people. Examples of good practices, for instance, are rarely disseminated and seldom subject to rigorous evaluation, which would help us understand why they work. Accounts of the experience of minority ethnic populations tend to focus on the unfair structuring of opportunities and on unmet needs. The critical emphasis of the literature is perhaps understandable and has successfully highlighted the negative consequences of racism, marginalization and unequal treatment. Constantly highlighting the negative consequences of service provision, however, does little to advance thinking and practice. There is, therefore, a need to develop a strategy that enables us to explore interventions that meet the needs of minority ethnic populations.

This chapter presents an evaluation of a listening service for South Asian women, following the birth of a child, and contributes to these debates. This innovative service, with its emphasis on listening to the voice of mothers makes an important contribution to understanding how services can best meet the needs of such women. Issues are raised within the chapter around the importance of investing in capacity building among community organizations to ensure they can deliver appropriate support.

This chapter makes an important contribution to tackling health inequalities and draws attention to the points that focusing on the needs of minority ethnic populations is not the same as meeting their needs and that documenting disadvantage is no longer enough; a commitment to change and action is necessary. To help achieve this, it is important to understand, explore and disseminate potential strategies that could improve the delivery of health and social care to minority ethnic groups. It is within this context that the value of the evaluation really lies.

The story started in 1998 with talks between the two parties about topics of common concern. From this emerged a shared interest in women's well-being after birth and embryonic plans were made for a postnatal listening service that would be provided by the community group and evaluated by the researchers. It was recognized from the beginning that the lessons that would be learnt from the evaluation would be about process as much as about outcomes.

Background

Giving birth is a major life event, one in which women are likely to experience extreme emotions and, at times, are vulnerable. Most women in the UK give birth in hospital and for many, this will be their first experience of hospitalization. However, giving birth is not just about interactions with the health services. It is also (and perhaps primarily) a family event, one that is likely to cause rearrangements of family dynamics, roles and relationships.

Many women experience emotional turmoil in the immediate postnatal period. In most this resolves, but others experience varying degrees of postnatal depression. There is little consensus about the causes of postnatal depression, but it is clear that socio-economic adversity, low self-esteem and social isolation, which are associated with depression in general, are similarly relevant to women who have recently given birth. An additional element, which has been implicated, is what Affonso (1977) called 'missing pieces': a need to integrate and understand the experiences of labour and birth. This has led some health professionals to establish 'birth afterthoughts' listening services (Charles and Curtis, 1994; Friend, 1996; Westley, 1997) where women are given the opportunity to talk through their experiences and make sense of them.

Bowes and Domokos (1996) suggest that childbirth may be especially traumatic for women with limited English in an English speaking culture. Firstly, they are likely to have less idea about what is happening to them and why. Secondly, the limitations on communication with their caregivers makes it less likely that either party will feel that a relationship has been formed, so the woman will probably receive less emotional support. In addition Bowler (1993a, b) has shown that women may not be offered appropriate care because of the stereotypes their caregivers hold, for example, not being offered pain relief because it is thought they are 'just making a fuss'. These stereotypes are an issue for all Asian women irrespective of their ability to speak English (Bowes and Domokos, 1996; House of Commons Health Committee, 2003). When listening services exist in a locality, Asian women are likely to feel excluded from these because of language and cultural barriers. Thus Asian women are likely to be trebly disadvantaged: many live in poor socio-economic circumstances; they are more likely to have unsatisfactory birth experiences; and they are less likely to have access to someone to talk to about these afterwards.

The Advocacy and Interpreting Service

The Advocacy and Interpreting Service (AIS) is a voluntary organization in the north of England working with Asian women in the context of health and social services. It works primarily with Pakistani, Bangladeshi and Chinese women, many of whom have a very limited command of English. Most of the bilingual development co-ordinators and volunteers who work for the service are women of childbearing age who are themselves from those communities. The AIS operates in an area with the highest local concentration of people from these ethnic groups. This area is served by a large teaching hospital where most of the women from these communities give birth.

Why a postnatal listening service?

For some time the AIS had been concerned at the postnatal unhappiness of some of the women that it encounters, which may not have been recognized by health care workers as norms of behaviour are different in different cultures. Asian women who are depressed are more likely to present with somatic symptoms rather than psychological ones, because of the stigma attached to mental illness, and this may not always be recognized by health professionals (Thompson, 1997; Fuggle et al., 2002). There are also erroneous beliefs about people from non-Western cultures, for example, that they do not experience depression as a psychological condition, or that they have no need of outside assistance because they 'look after their own' (Commission for Racial Equality, 1993).

The AIS workers concluded that many of the women they saw would like someone with whom they could talk through their birth experiences, but that the women's circumstances did not permit this, particularly if this meant admitting to relatives that they were having difficulty coping. Social isolation could be a particular problem for women who do not speak English, and for those who may be more assimilated, there may be complementary problems such as lack of nearby supportive relatives. A new 'postnatal listening service' for women from Pakistani, Bangladeshi or Chinese backgrounds, irrespective of the woman's level of fluency in English, was launched to try and address such issues.

The postnatal listening service

The service was offered from July 2000 until February 2002 and was available free of charge to any Pakistani, Bengali and Chinese woman in the area who had recently had a baby. It consisted of a single home visit from a lay volunteer from the new mother's own ethnic community group. The visit was conducted in whatever language the mother preferred. The aims of the listening service were: to provide an opportunity for women to talk about health and social issues around pregnancy and childbirth; to obtain broad documentation about what those issues were; and to provide an avenue for women to seek assistance if they needed to do so.

Unlike the 'Birth Afterthoughts' services, volunteers were not health professionals. They were specifically instructed about the limits of their role; in particular they were not allowed to offer medical or legal advice, but they were able to refer women back to AIS for professional help and support if needed. The training covered both offering and delivering the listening service and emphasized confidentiality and active listening skills, drawing on the work of Culley (1996), Dufresne (1996) and Kacperek (1997). Initially (July 2000–June 2001) target women were told about the service by volunteers when they attended for their routine scan at about 18–20 weeks gestation, and this was followed by a home visit to give more information. From July 2001 until February 2002 the system changed and women were told about the service on the postnatal ward. Some of the latter women chose to have their 'listening visit' while they were still in hospital.

This service was the first of its kind and, thus, there was no directly related literature to draw on. There were, therefore, many questions to be addressed about how women and their families would respond to such a service, and whether a single visit would be seen as beneficial. There were also organizational issues around the delivery of the project; this latter point is addressed elsewhere (Hirst et al., 2002).

Methods

The evaluation as a whole had the following aims:

1. To monitor the implementation of the new postnatal listening service.
2. To obtain women's views about the postnatal listening service.
3. To obtain the service providers' views about the postnatal listening service.
4. To obtain women's views about their childbearing experiences more generally, and about the services that they would find helpful.
5. To train volunteers from the communities to assist in carrying out the research.
6. To feed back the findings of the study to the volunteers, the communities, the relevant statutory and voluntary services and to the readers of academic and professional journals.

The research was to address two compatible agendas. The first was the evaluation of the new postnatal listening service. The second was to give a voice to Asian women to talk about the issues that were of most importance to them around childbirth. This was felt to be particularly important for groups who have few other ways of making their views known, those with 'muted voices' (Bowes and Domokos, 1996; Ardener, 1997). It was important for us as researchers to be aware of the two agendas in order that we clearly conveyed to the women that their views were important to us even if they did not want to talk about the listening service.

Ethical clearance for the evaluation was obtained from the local research ethics committee and access to women was approved by the NHS service provider. A researcher visited women who had received the service at home approximately six weeks later to conduct an evaluation interview. The researcher was fluent in English and Urdu and had an understanding of a range of Pakistani dialects. For women with other preferred languages an interpreter was used. Volunteers were interviewed at the end of the project.

Data collection and analysis

The primary source of outcome data was face-to-face interviews using semi-structured interview schedules. Different schedules were developed for the volunteers and for recipients of the service (See *Boxes 3.1 and 3.2*). Additional, anonymous, data were collected on volunteers' perceptions of their organization, management and support mechanisms and the appropriateness of their training. All interviewees were asked for their permission to tape-record the interview and recorded interviews were transcribed. Content analysis of the interview data enabled illumination of volunteers' and women's views and experiences, although there were insufficient data to conduct any within or between group analysis. In reporting the results, every effort has been made to maintain confidentiality and anonymity of volunteers and women; hence, quotations are individually numbered rather than being ascribed to individuals.

Recruitment

Women were told about the evaluation at the time of being offered the service, and gave consent to participate at this time. They were reminded about the evaluation interview at the end of the listening visit, and an appointment was made at this time for the researcher to visit. The research team wrote to all volunteers requesting an interview at the end of the evaluation period. By this time many were no longer within the organization.

Box 3.1: Interview guide for volunteers

Service delivery:
- How did you feel about approaching women in the scan clinic?
- How did you feel about going out in the community to women's homes? What safety precautions did you take?
- How did you feel about going onto postnatal wards?
- What was it like to give listening visits?
- How did you feel as the listener?
- Looking back is there anything that would have made delivering the listening service any easier for you as a volunteer?
- Did you always deliver the service as you were trained to?
- Is there anything you particularly liked/disliked about being a volunteer?
- Do you feel you have gained anything by being part of this process, if yes, what? If no, what might you have liked to gain for yourself?
- Was there anything that surprised you?

Volunteer support:
- Were you already a volunteer at AIS or were you specially recruited for this service?
- Did you have someone to share your experiences of being a volunteer with for this service, if you wished to do so?
- Who if anyone did you seek advice from if you needed it regarding the listening service?
- If there was ever an occasion where you needed de-briefing after a listening visit, who would you approach? Did you ever need to?
- What support have you received as a volunteer for PNLS? Do you feel it was enough? Could anything else have made it better?

Results

Volunteers

Eighteen volunteers were trained to offer and/or deliver the listening service and eight actually did so. Six volunteers were interviewed by the research team and the interviews lasted between 1 and 1½ hours. The volunteers represented the Pakistani, Bengali and Chinese communities; were all female and aged between 20 and 45. Not all were mothers themselves and some were unmarried; all were bilingual or multilingual. Most agreed to being tape-recorded but one interview was conducted in Urdu, and handwritten notes taken in English.

Box 3.2: Interview guide for recipients of the service

General
- Pregnancy and childbirth experiences – how has life been since the birth?

About the listening service
- What was it like to have someone come and listen to you?
- Was it easy for her to talk to this person; did you have enough time with the listener?
- Was the listener appropriate in terms of age, gender, ethnicity and social networks?
- Was there anything you particularly liked about the listening service?
- Was there anything that you didn't like about the service?
- What would you have liked instead or done differently?
- Did the listening service make any difference, e.g. in terms of how you were feeling? If so, what?

At the end of the interview, structured questions were also asked about living arrangements and proximity of family; availability of a confidante; employment outside the home; age; education; and length of residence in the UK.

Offering the service

A wide range of experiences were described both within and between volunteers, when offering the service. For some volunteers, the experiences were enjoyable and empowering but others felt cautious as they did not know how women or their families would react. Where there were negative responses, volunteers sometimes felt unprepared for the challenge. As might be expected, the presence of family members often altered the social interaction between the woman and the volunteer, and some volunteers found this difficult. However, family members were not always suspicious of the service, and volunteers became aware that the way in which they initially approached women would influence whether they would want the service, and that confidence, cheerfulness and mindfulness of the woman's needs were important:

'I enjoyed it to start with, telling people about something that will benefit them, and I enjoyed meeting new people and explaining the benefits of this new service to them. I felt quite confident and enjoyed it and I think this made quite a good impression. I think it's possible that if you do not feel confident that you convey this in your message and it has a negative effect.' (Q-7).

'I had a negative experience of recruiting a young mother. Her mother, who was with her, was extremely cautious and wasn't in favour – she said, "We don't need any information." In the end I managed to explain about this service, and she felt more trusting and agreed. She told me that initially she thought that this service might be something to do with social services, and talking might get them into trouble. Her view on social services was "vo ghar tabbah kurtai hain" [they destroy households].' (Q-11).

'I spoke to a lot of women in the scan clinic and they seemed really happy to speak to me, we talked about things like children, Eid, Ramzan, etc., and I think by doing this they really felt I as one of them and they could relate to me. One elderly Pakistani woman said to me, "She is one of us, we must see her again."'(Q-16).

Listening visits

One of the biggest challenges for volunteers was dealing with the negative impact that other family members had during the listening visits, which affected volunteers' confidence in visiting women at home and their performance while they were there. It was evident that some families were suspicious and hostile to the service and attempted to restrict access to women or monitor the listening visit by repeatedly interrupting the process. It is difficult to know whether such interruptions were prompted out of benign curiosity; a means to report the content to other family members, or as a means to control disclosure. It was apparent that one woman could have disclosed family secrets, which could have brought shame upon the family.

'... the listening visit kept being interrupted by the sister-in-law and the aunts. I was there nearly two hours because of all the interruptions. Then the woman told me that the other family members had been keeping an eye on her because her husband treated her very badly, and they were worried it might get out.' (Q-22).

It was also apparent that it was difficult for the recipients of the service to dissipate suspicion and reassure the family of the purpose of the listening visit, what it was for and why they needed it, as they were uncertain too (see below).

Problems encountered

It was anticipated that some of the volunteers and women would know each other from the community setting but we were not sure whether this would be beneficial or a disadvantage. One of the volunteers reported that she knew one of the women and, at first, this was a problem as the woman associated the volunteer with someone she did not like. The problem was resolved through explanation and friendly discussion. Important issues were also raised around the safety of the volunteers as some felt unsafe walking around particular areas of the city and if they were away from the office for a longer duration than normal that there was no means of making contact. Two of the volunteers commented that they addressed this by working in pairs.

Benefits to the volunteers

The postnatal listening visit was a new and innovative service and many of the volunteers gained personally by taking part. They all believed that they were offering something that was needed by women and that they benefited on a personal level as they felt valued and important; possibly raising their personal status and their status within the wider group of volunteers at AIS:

> 'Well, the whole process widened my experience, communication skills, confidence and social skills, having met so many mothers to be, mother-in-laws, sister-in-laws, etc... I also gained some experience in offering options to women when they felt there was an issue they needed to talk about. I would say it also improved my listening skills from the training. I'm quite an impatient person, but I think this training and the service has helped me become more patient.' (Q-35).

There were of course aspects of the service that the volunteers did not like such as women refusing to take part and family members interrupting or being overly curious. However, in addition to volunteers gaining personally from providing the service, the service gained from the personal attributes of the volunteers. In particular, the volunteers had a range of language skills and transferable skills associated with motherhood, culture and religion that enabled them to discuss issues knowledgeably. However, perceived similarities between the listener and a woman meant that some assumptions were made, by the listener, about a woman's view of the world:

> 'We speak the same language ... it was helpful because we both have children, we are both mothers, just by speaking a little, and we were able to understand. No need to explain, because we have the same background.' (Q-43).

Recipients

We are not able to report the total number of women who were approached by the volunteers (at any venue), or how many actually wanted the listening visit after hearing about it as the data collected were unreliable; one of several training and management issues identified by volunteers. Data were available for 54 women who were offered the listening service and who commented that they either wanted to hear more about it or that they wanted to receive it (37 Pakistani, 17 Bangladeshi, no Chinese women). We also know that 37 out of the 54 women were first met at the scan clinic, 11 on the postnatal wards and 6 through other AIS contacts. Nineteen women actually received the listening service (13 Pakistani and 6 Bangladeshi) between July 2001 and March 2002. Four women withdrew after requesting the service (2 Pakistani and 2 Bangladeshi) and 31 women either wanted to hear more about the listening service or wanted to receive it but did not. This mainly occurred during the first year when the number of suitably trained volunteers was unstable as they often left in preference for paid employment, to further their education or to respond to other social demands. The impact of having raised women's expectations in this way cannot, unfortunately, be assessed.

Twelve women out of a potential 19 (8 Pakistani and 4 Bengali women) took part in the evaluation interview in their home between 3 and 17 weeks after they had received the postnatal listening interview. These interviews were conducted in English, Mirpuri, Punjabi, Urdu or Bangla, or a mixture, as appropriate. Overall, 9 interviews with women were interpreted to some extent (5 Pakistani and 4 Bangladeshi women) using three different, formally trained interpreters. The interviews lasted between 40 and 130 minutes. All the women declined to be tape-recorded. This inevitably affected the quality and depth of the data obtained, as did the context in which the evaluation interviews took place as some were in a relaxed and calm atmosphere, others were more chaotic.

Recipients' characteristics

Full demographic data were available for 7 of the 12 women interviewed (there was insufficient opportunity to obtain such data for 5 women). All were full-time housewives living in inner city terraced housing. Ages ranged from 22 to 32 years and they had been living in the United Kingdom between 3 and 32 years (two had lived in the UK all their lives). Three women had attained educational qualifications (1 matriculation in Bangladesh; 1 inter-matriculation in Pakistan; 1 GCSEs grade C or above) and three did not appear to have attended any formal and regular education either in the UK or abroad. Only 3 women felt that they had someone to talk to who was supportive; these were all Pakistani women.

Response to being offered the service

The place where women were informed of the service had no discernable effect upon their initial impression. In general, they were curious, cautious and sceptical that it would in fact be of any personal benefit (whether it was their first or subsequent baby). Since there were no other similar services available for them to relate to, or people to ask, they could not seek the experiences of others:

'I was introduced to this new service after my son had been born, when I was on the postnatal ward. I was told about it by one of the volunteers from the service. I was not sure what to expect, this was my first baby, and I'm still fairly new in this country, so hmmm, I wasn't sure what it was about. But I thought it might be helpful.' (Q-50).

Response to the listeners

The subgroup of volunteers who delivered the listening visit (listeners) were matched with the recipients in terms of ethnicity and language but the pool of volunteers was not large enough to permit matching by other characteristics such as age or motherhood. We had thought that having a listener who was younger than the woman and/or who was not herself a mother might be a problem, and recipients were asked specifically about this. It appeared that this was not in fact perceived to be a problem as women observed other qualities in their listener such as maturity and having the ability to make them feel at ease. Overall, women said that they found their listener easy to talk to, considerate and easy to get on with. Other valuable characteristics of listeners were that they shared cultural knowledge and women trusted them with confidential information. For many women sharing the same language outweighed characteristics such as age and motherhood:

'She [the listener] didn't rush me, was there till I wanted her to be ... we spoke in both languages [English and Mirpuri] but mainly in English. I think background and language makes a lot of difference. Having the same culture means you can say what the thing is without having to explain it every time ... So long as what is discussed stays between you and that person, it doesn't matter whether that person is local or from outside the area.' (Q-67).

Women valued the listener as someone who was interested in them, who was outside of the family and who had the ability to explain issues and suggest access to other resources and to whom they could speak easily and freely. This was particularly the case for women who did not speak English:

'I was so glad to speak to [the listener], I couldn't speak to anyone at the hospital, because of language ... it felt really easy to speak to her, I felt "shaanti" [at peace, peaceful]. I think we spoke for three-quarters of an hour to an hour, it was enough time, but I wish we could have spoken again; it was difficult to talk in the hospital.' (Q-74).

Venue, frequency and content of listening visit

The venue and frequency of the visits were particularly mentioned as aspects that women would want to change; some women wanting more visits, some the home setting and others the hospital. Some women were clearly not aware that they could access ongoing social support, interpreting and advocacy through AIS even though these were not features of the listening service:

> 'I think the service was fine but I didn't need it that much … the only problem I have is that I don't know English, I could have done with some help in filling out passport forms when I had to apply for nationality.' (Q-90).

Practical help within the home was also mentioned as a potential development although this would be beyond the scope of both the listening service and AIS.

Inevitably, some women remained ambivalent about the service and did not think it was useful or would only be so for women who had 'problems'.

Psychological benefit

We were interested to find out if women felt that receiving the postnatal listening service had psychological benefit. A number volunteered that the process of talking to the listener had relieved anger and tension, particularly if they had no one who spoke their language at the hospital. Comments such as feeling 'comfortable', 'shaanti' [peaceful, at ease] and 'feeling good' were mentioned:

> 'I felt that after talking to [the listener] about the birth and other things, that dil hulka hogya [my heart felt lighter, meaning I felt I got a load off my mind, or I got it off my chest]. Also speaking to someone knowing that it's not going any further is really reassuring … Yes, it helped me feel better; talking to [the listener] made me feel less angry, before it was on my mind a lot.' (Q-97).

The data were checked to see if the women who valued the service less were English speaking, but this was not the case. Similarly, the data were checked to see if those who had difficulties, either socially or with the health service, were all non-English speakers, but they were not. It was also found that women valued the service whether or not they had someone supportive to talk to.

Experiences of maternity care

One of the aims of providing the listening service was to give women the opportunity to voice their views about any issues around their maternity experiences and women disclosed both positive and negative dimensions relating to the quality of their maternity care. Any woman who indicated that she was distressed and wanted to complain about her care (whether or not she had accessed the resource provided for Asian women at the maternity unit) was offered a referral to a member of staff at AIS by their listener and by the researcher. One woman's response demonstrates both positive and negative aspects. She commented that she really appreciated the nurses and felt very pampered as she was able to stay on the postnatal ward an extra two days. However, she then went on to recount her experience of the birth process:

'I told her, don't send me home, listen, I've had six others, and I know when I'm in labour and I am in labour so don't be sending me home ... I felt the student midwife was more concerned than the actual midwife ... I didn't want an epidural, just wanted some gas, then I was so sleepy I didn't want to push ... My sister made me push, and talked me through the whole process but the midwife was no help.' (Q-105).

Women considered that being able to speak and communicate in English within the hospital setting was an important attribute in achieving a positive experience. The maternity service concerned provided an internal interpreting service for women who did not speak English but accessing it when needed was clearly a problem:

'You see if you go the doctors they have people to interpret for you ... they asked [at the hospital] "Can't your husband come?" ... I said no, that he was at work ... then [at hospital] I needed help with the form ... but I can't read or write so I couldn't fill in the form so at the first mealtime I just said I wasn't hungry, then in the evening the relative of the lady in the next bed to me helped me fill it in.' (Q-109).

Not all of the participants had negative experiences. For those who did, and who felt strongly enough to disclose it, we can conclude that their experience was profound. Other researchers have reported that women comment upon aspects of maternity care that are either profoundly good or profoundly poor (Proctor and Wright, 1998; Hirst and Hewison, 2002). It is difficult to judge, therefore, where the quality of care was 'good enough'.

Discussion

This chapter has presented the views and experiences of the volunteers and recipients of an innovative postnatal listening service for Pakistani, Bangladeshi and Chinese women. Because this service was the first of its kind, there is no literature directly related to lay postnatal listening services for Pakistani and

Bangladeshi women for us to compare our findings with. Most of the literature around professional postnatal listening is embedded among professional debriefing, the benefits of which are still unclear (Charles and Curtis, 1994; Lavender and Walkinshaw, 1998; Small et al., 2000; Gamble et al., 2002).

There is, however, a broader literature on volunteering and some specific reports of volunteers in the context of families with young children (e.g. Hiatt et al., 2000; Taggart et al., 2000; Attree, 2004). These other projects have all been based around an ongoing volunteer commitment, rather than a single visit, as in our case, and so some different issues arise. Nevertheless, common themes are notable, especially the beneficial effects on volunteers' own self-esteem. These studies also draw attention to the ways in which volunteer input may be seen as more acceptable than that from professionals and to the importance of cultural matching.

Although volunteers made positive comments about the process of delivering the service they also identified a number of shortcomings in their training, such as dealing with unexpected hostile behaviours from members of the families; and management issues, such as security arrangements. Developments in the programme could address the training needs although the time needed to train should not be underestimated nor the need for resourcing training through adequate and legitimate mainstream funding. Addressing security issues for female volunteers working alone was problematic. Working in pairs, providing secure transport and using mobile phones effectively are simple measures; but protecting volunteers in the community was an issue that was not adequately addressed. Delivering the service in a hospital setting minimized most of the security issues and limited the effect of the wider family.

During interviews, Bowes and Domokos (1996) recommend that we should respect women's silences but sometimes the listeners were under the impression that women's silences were under duress rather than choice. It could be that we were expecting too much of women as some often relied on their husband and other family members for interpreting and dealing with the outside world on a day-to-day basis. It was possible, therefore, that in asking women to express their own views we were asking them to do something that they were unaccustomed to doing. Perhaps this too could explain why women refused to be tape-recorded and were hesitant in disclosing 'too much' information, although more confident English speaking women also refused. It is unlikely that we can attribute this refusal entirely to cultural diversity, as other studies have found Pakistani women who are willing to be tape-recorded and interviewed in-depth (Ahmed et al., 2002) and confirms that language may not be the overriding barrier as others have suggested (Hunt and Bhopal, 2003).

The study found that a listening service provided by volunteers has the potential to provide benefit for both recipients and volunteers. Women who received this postnatal listening service were able to disclose psychological benefits such as, 'my heart felt lighter', I could 'throw out all my anger', I 'got it out of my mind', 'it was more comforting for me', and 'I felt peaceful, at ease'. Women benefited regardless of being able to speak English or whether or not they had someone close to talk to. In addition, it was clear that women who had difficulties in the family or health care setting valued a listener to confide in, support her and lead her to other services. Even women who did not reveal any problems enjoyed having a 'chat' with someone, although others were clearly ambivalent about the value of the service. Volunteers benefited from providing the service and the service benefited from the life experiences of volunteers. This reciprocal arrangement should be harnessed and this pioneering work taken forward and explored in other settings.

It is been reported that women from minority ethnic communities receive poorer maternity care (Audit Commission, 1997; Bulman and McCourt, 1997; House of Commons Health Committee, 2003) although comparative studies between ethnic groups have shown that neither a good nor a poor quality of maternity care can always be attributed to ethnicity (Hirst and Hewison, 2001, 2002). However, some women in this study did receive poor care that they attributed to their inability to speak clear English, their ethnicity and/or their cultural practices. These findings have been reported to the participating trust for inclusion into their strategy for managing diversity. Towards the end of the project arrangements were made with the local provider of maternity services and AIS to strategically plan the incorporation of the listening service into mainstream services. Currently, the service has not become operational, although we understand that it has, independently, been taken up by a local Surestart initiative.

Acknowledgements

The evaluation was funded by the National Lottery Charities Board for its first year, thereafter by the University of Leeds; the service delivery was also supported in part by a Health Action Zone grant.

The grant holders were Mussarat Khan, Jo Green and Janet Hirst; the research officer was Khalida Ashrafi and the advisory group, Karl Atkin, Kuldip Bharj and Fran Dargen.

References

Affonso DD (1997) 'Missing pieces'. A study of post-partum feelings. *Birth and the Family Journal* **4(4)**: 159–64.

Ahmed S, Green J, Hewison J (2002) Thalassaemia carrier testing in pregnant Pakistani women: Perceptions of 'information' and 'consent'. *Eur J Hum Genet* **10(Suppl 1)**: 309.

Ardener E (1997) Belief and the problem of women and the 'problem' revisited. In Ardener S (ed.) *Perceiving Women*. Dent, London.

Attree P (2004) 'It was like my little acorn, and it's going to grow into a big tree': A qualitative study of a community support project. *Health and Social Care in the Community* **12(2)**: 155–61.

Audit Commission (1997) *First Class Delivery. Improving Maternity Services in England and Wales*. Audit Commission, London.

Bowes AM, Domokos TM (1996) Pakistani women and maternity care: Raising muted voices. *Sociology of Health and Illness* **18(1)**: 45–65.

Bowler IMW (1993a) Stereotypes of women of Asian descent in midwifery: Some evidence. *Midwifery* **9(1)**: 7–16.

Bowler I (1993b) They're not the same as us': Midwives' stereotypes of South Asian descent maternity patients. *Sociology of Health and Illness* **15(2)**:157–77.

Bulman KH, McCourt C (1997) *Report on Somali Women's Experiences of Maternity Services*. Thames Valley University, London.

Charles J, Curtis L (1994) Birth afterthoughts; setting up a listening service. *Midwives Chronicle* **107**: 266–8.

Commission for Racial Equality (1993) *The Sorrow in My Heart ... Sixteen Asian Women Speak about Depression*. Commission for Racial Equality, London.

Culley S (1996) *Integrative Counselling Skills in Action*. Sage Publications, London.

Dufresne R (1996) Listening to Narcissus. *Br J Psychoanalysis* **77**: 497–508.

Friend B (1996) Thoughts after birth. *Nursing Times* **92(36)**: 24–5.

Fuggle P, Glover L, Khan F, Haydon K (2002) Screening for postnatal depression in Bengali women: Preliminary observations from using a translated version of the Edinburgh Postnatal Depression Scale (EPDS). *J Repro Infant Psychol* **20(2)**: 71–82.

Gamble JA, Creedy DK, Webster J, Moyle W (2002) A review of the literature on debriefing or non-directive counselling to prevent postpartum emotional distress. *Midwifery* **18**: 72–9.

Hiatt SW, Michalek P, Younge P, Miyoshi T, Fryer E (2000) Characteristics of volunteers and families in a neonatal home visitation project: The Kempe community caring program. *Child Abuse and Neglect* **24(1)**: 85–97.

Hirst J, Green J, Khan M, Ashrafi K, Mortimer J (2002) *Evaluation of a Postnatal Listening Service for Pakistani, Bangladeshi and Chinese Women. Internal Report*. Mother and Infant Research Unit, University of Leeds.

Hirst J, Hewison J (2001) Pakistani and indigenous 'white' women's views and the Donadebian-Maxwell grid: A consumer-focused template for assessing the quality of maternity care. *International Journal of Health Care Quality Assurance* **14(7)**: 308–16.

Hirst J, Hewison J (2002) Hospital postnatal care: A comparison of Pakistani and indigenous 'white' women's views. *Clinical Effectiveness in Nursing* **6**: 10–18.

House of Commons Health Committee (2003) *Inequalities in Access to Maternity Services*. The Stationery Office, London.

Hunt S, Bhopal R (2003) Self reports in research with non-English speakers. *Br Med J* **327**: 352–3.

Kacperek L (1997) Non-verbal communication: The importance of listening. *Br J Nursing* **6(5)**: 275–9.

Lavender T, Walkinshaw SA (1998) Can midwives reduce postpartum psychological morbidity? A randomized trial. *Birth* **25**: 215–21.

Proctor S, Wright G (1998) Consumer responses to healthcare: Women and maternity services. *International Journal of Health Care Quality Assurance* **11(5)**: 147–55.

Small R, Lumley J, Donohue L, Potter A, Waldenstrom U (2000) Randomised controlled trial of midwife led debriefing to reduce maternal depression after operative childbirth. *Br Med J* **321**: 1043–7.

Taggart AV, Short SD, Barclay L (2000) 'She has made me feel human again': An evaluation of a volunteer home-based visiting project for mothers. *Health and Social Care in the Community* **8(1)**: 1–8.

Thompson K (1997) Detecting postnatal depression in Asian women. *Health Visitor* **70(6)**: 226–8.

Westley W (1997) 'Time to talk' listening service. *Midwives*, **110:** 30–1.

CHAPTER 4

Intimate partner abuse

June Keeling

Introduction

Domestic abuse can be defined as 'any violence between current or former partners in an intimate relationship, wherever and whenever the violence occurs'. The abuse can include physical violence, sexual violence, or emotional or financial abuse (Department of Health, 2000). For an individual to be at risk of experiencing domestic abuse, the single most important risk factor is being a woman (Department of Health, 2000).

The pandemic problem of domestic abuse is well documented and high prevalence rates are cited (Basile, 2002; Bradley et al., 2002; Bacchus et al., 2004) with a known deleterious effect on the mental (Dienemann et al., 2000) and physical (Coker et al., 2000) health of an individual. Some authors suggest that the absence of a strategic screening programme for women experiencing domestic abuse has a negative effect on disclosure (Edin and Hogberg, 2002; Shadigian and Bauer, 2004). Although this might predominantly be the main factor in the reluctance of survivors to disclose, it is apparent that there are a plethora of other issues that also contribute to this reluctance. Following a review of some of the international literature on this subject, it is evident that the choice to disclose intimate partner abuse is a significantly more complex issue. There are many quantitative and qualitative methods employed to encourage disclosure of abuse. The success of implementing these methods may depend upon the interpersonal skills of the health care professional.

Impact on health

Domestic abuse is recognized as having a detrimental effect on the mental and physical health of an individual. In addition to the physical injury, many abused women also experience psychological problems including low self-esteem, anxiety and depression, passivity and learned helplessness (Stewart and Cucutti, 1993). It will affect a woman's physical, psychological and sociological health and may affect her decision making abilities, erode her self-esteem or increase the risk of drug and alcohol dependency.

Women in such abusive relationships are at risk of sexual violence including forced anal, oral and vaginal intercourse and in extreme cases, enforced prostitution (Friend, 1998). This may manifest as sexual dysfunction (Becker et al., 1984). Sexual abuse may include rape, forced participation in extreme sexual acts, pornography and prostitution, and the use of a weapon resulting in injuries to the genital tract (Schei and Bakketeig, 1989). The perpetrator may question the woman's sexual integrity although he may have other physical relationships. Consequently, there is an increased risk of sexually transmitted diseases. Previous studies have demonstrated the association between domestic abuse and gynaecological complaints. This association has been identified as increasing the likelihood of gynaecological morbidity (Campbell, 2002). An abused woman may have damage to the vagina and rectum, trauma during vaginal examination, and pelvic pain of unknown origin (Campbell and Soeken, 1999). Sexual assault or rape by the partner may lead to health risks related to sexually transmitted disease. Women may find it difficult to be intimately examined by a doctor. The anxiety and fear resulting from the intimate abuse may inhibit the attendance at the cervical screening programme (Ussher, 2000). Gynaecological symptoms are more common in abused women, including pelvic pain, dyspareunia and pelvic inflammatory disease (Schei and Bakketeig, 1996; Friend, 1998). It has also been reported that abused women have more pelvic operations than non-abused women (Drossman et al., 1990)

The deleterious effects of abuse make it a significant contributing factor to women accessing the health care system. Women may present to health professionals complaining of somatic complaints, as a direct result of the abuse they have experienced from their intimate partner.

During the author's work as a domestic violence co-ordinator a qualitative study was made to examine the prevalence and nature of domestic abuse. One comment made by a woman demonstrates the deleterious effects of domestic abuse:

> *'My first husband abused me, mainly mentally, sometimes physically. I now have no confidence and feel so insecure. I wish I could talk to someone about all this because it is with me every day, but I wish I could just walk in somewhere without having to be referred by my doctor because wrongly there is a feeling of shame. Good luck in your work towards helping many women – maybe even me!'*

Impact on pregnancy

Pregnancy has been identified as a particularly high risk period for women, when the physical violence often begins or intensifies (CEMACH, 2004) with prevalence rates cited as being between 2.5% (Mezey et al., 2001) and 33.7% (Huth-Bocks et al., 2002). The nature of the blows are often directed at the women's abdomen and breasts (Berenson et al., 1994; Bacchus et al., 2004). This violence poses a significant threat to the health and well-being of both the woman and her unborn child and may adversely affect the outcome of the pregnancy. Pregnancy is a particularly high-risk life event for domestic abuse with actual physical violence initiating or escalating in pregnancy (CEMACH, 2004). It is estimated that up to 30% of the abuse commences in pregnancy (Royal College of Gynaecologists, 2001). Many women do not require medical assistance in early pregnancy therefore it could be assumed that this percentage is not a true figure. Many will remain at home undetected. Rarely does the abuse diminish. The effects of the abuse can result in long-term psychological and physical morbidity and have a direct impact on the pregnancy. Higher rates of miscarriage have been identified in women who are experiencing domestic abuse (Schei et al., 1991). Of pregnant women who died in the United Kingdom between 2000 and 2002, 14% had self-reported experiencing domestic abuse within the home. For 12 women their deaths resulted directly from domestic abuse (CEMACH, 2004). Domestic abuse in pregnancy can result in immediate or long-term complications.

Child protection

There is an increased risk of child abuse when the child is at home with a mother who is being abused (World Health Organization, 2001; CEMACH, 2004). Children growing up in an abusive environment may demonstrate a range of challenging behaviours including aggression, disruptive behaviour, sleep disturbances, lack of emotional attachment and have suicidal tendencies (Shankleman et al., 2001). If any concern arises about the child's welfare, it is paramount that the midwife adheres to the local child protection guidelines. The Department of Health (2004) states that the safety of children is paramount. It is preferable to work with the mother under these circumstances and ensure relocation of mother and children rather than removing the children from her care. A shift of responsibility from the perpetrator to the mother may occur if a child is removed from the mother as she has 'failed' to maintain the child's safety (New Zealand College of Midwives, 2005). It is crucial to lay the blame at the door of the perpetrator.

The Royal College of Midwives (2004) advocates:

'...a clear need for the appointment of midwife specialists with specific responsibilities for the protection of vulnerable children. The establishment of specialist link/child protection midwife posts provides all midwives with a clear line of communication for relaying information and concerns regarding children at risk and enables midwives to engage effectively with other professionals working with vulnerable children.'

Similar to the role of the domestic violence co-ordinator, each maternity unit would have a named child protection midwife responsible for the provision of statutory education and training of all midwives and for liaising with the multi-professional team. This midwife would take the lead in child protection issues while maintaining her clinical skills.

A rapid response from the judicial profession, with immediate and compulsory attendance on relevant programmes for the perpetrator is essential. This should be coupled with the multi-agency approach necessary to ensure the effective safety of the woman and her children. It important to realize that the most dangerous time for a woman and her children is at the time of separation (New Zealand College of Midwives, 2005).

Professional responsibilities

It is not acceptable to assume that someone else will deal with the problem. It is the health professional's duty to listen effectively to a survivor of domestic abuse and be able to offer appropriate support. The initiation of statutory and voluntary agencies to provide support remains the choice of the survivor, however we must firstly be aware of whom these agencies are, and the support they provide. Multi-agency communication with the establishment of policies and protocols may help in the health service providing a consistent approach.

In association with this is the significant deleterious effect on the psychological and physical health of children witnessing this abuse within the home. Community health care providers such as district nurses, practice nurses and general practitioners are in close contact with the family and can observe the family dynamics. However, we all have a professional remit to inform the child protection team if we consider that a baby/child is at risk of mental or physical harm. It is crucial to work with the mother when there are children involved. Our message should be that we want the mother and child to stay together, but remove the person causing the distress and harm to the child.

It would be incorrect to assume that we are managing the woman's social problems or indeed diverting away from midwifery. We are becoming holistic practitioners, able to work within an effective multi-agency team in providing care for a woman throughout pregnancy, childbirth and postnatally. Midwives are often the only health care professional to build a rapport with families. Consequently a survivor of domestic abuse may confide in them, enforcing the midwife to play a pivotal role in the initiation of essential support services. The Royal College of Midwives has recently detailed that the House of Commons Health Committee (2003) should recommend that women should be encouraged to contact midwives as their first contact point when they are pregnant, and the Department of Health has accepted this recommendation (Department of Health, 2003).

A referral strategy and support network for all staff must be in place prior to health professionals asking clients about their past or present experiences of domestic abuse. The author recommends all hospitals have a designated domestic violence co-ordinator to establish protocols and provide support for midwives and other health professionals ensuring a co-ordinated and effective response. The Royal College of Midwives (1999) Position Paper *Domestic Abuse in Pregnancy* clearly states that 'Maternity services should be active in developing a multi-agency, inter-disciplinary approach in local procedures and services, to ensure a seamless and effective response to a woman seeking help'. However, a survey of National Health Service trusts and health authorities found that only 27% and 29% respectively, had a written policy for responding to domestic abuse (Barron, 2001). The responsibility to educate and train midwives is within the remit of individual trusts, thus there is great variation in practice nationally.

To ensure a national and consistent high standard of training for all midwives, professional organizations could work together to produce a recognized training programme that is compulsory for all registered midwives to attend. Using a 'train the trainer' approach and utilizing agencies such as the Women's Aid organization, local and relevant information in conjunction with professional education and training would ensure a consistent approach throughout the country.

What midwives should do

1. Midwives must be fully informed and aware of the implications of domestic abuse and be competent to offer appropriate support to a woman who chooses to disclose a violent relationship.
2. The physical and behavioural signs of domestic abuse are well documented. Why do we look for these alone? All women have the right to be asked if they feel safe with their partner. Domestic abuse is a public health issue as well as a personal one. Sensitive and routine enquiry about domestic abuse is appropriate for all pregnant women assuming that midwives are knowledgeable in the support services available. If you do not know this information, go and find out today.
3. All women should be seen at least once (preferably two or three times) *on their own* in pregnancy and in the postnatal period. This should be a right for every woman.
4. If English is not a first language *do not* ask the woman about domestic abuse using a family member to interpret. They could be the abuser. Arrange for the woman to return for another appointment with an external interpreter present.
5. Always communicate with the child protection team regarding children/babies.

6. Your own safety is paramount. Never place yourself in danger by asking about abuse in the presence of a partner or where you can be overheard.
7. Obtain the woman's consent prior to documentation. Remember, if the perpetrator reads this information, the woman's life may be in danger.

One woman was severely physically assaulted in her first pregnancy which resulted in the birth of a stillborn baby. The midwife providing care for the woman at this time documented the abuse in the hospital records. The woman requested to meet with me when her second child was 12 months old. She had decided to leave her abusive partner and wanted information about safe housing and legal support. The catalyst for her decision was that her partner had assaulted her after the baby's birthday party. She now feared for her baby as well as herself. However, the overriding concern for this woman was the possibility of losing custody of her child as she had a medical and psychiatric history. However the abuse was well documented and resulted in the mother having sole custody of the child.

Discussion

Approximately one in four women have experienced domestic abuse at some stage in their lifetime (Friend, 1998; Bradley et al., 2002; Bacchus et al., 2004). Domestic abuse accounts for one quarter of all violent crime in the UK (Friend, 1998) while approximately 1.4 million women have experienced domestic abuse in the USA (Abbey et al., 1994). This abuse usually involves financial abuse, physical violence, sexual assault and psychological abuse.

Universally, the sequalae of domestic abuse have a devastating impact on the lives of the survivors and their families. Often women remain in these violent relationships for years, living in fear. After leaving the abusive partner, many women express regret for their acquiescent approach to the relationship (Fry and Barker, 2001).

Perhaps the most significant deterrent for disclosing domestic abuse may be a deficiency in the interpersonal skills of the health care professional due to the lack of knowledge and understanding of the issues surrounding intimate partner abuse which may result in them appearing insincere, ineffectual and even a danger for the abused to disclose to (Chambliss et al., 1995; Hathaway et al., 2002). It is generally accepted that the implementation of an educational programme specific to the dynamics of domestic abuse is beneficial to health professionals and it is suggested that these changes would have a positive influence over rates of disclosure (Mezey and Bewley, 1997; McGuigan et al., 2000; Keeling, 2002). Other barriers to asking clients about domestic abuse that have been identified by health care professionals include lack of time in clinical situations, inadequate training and fear of offending (Hathaway et al., 2002; Keeling, 2002). However, in a recent study when women were asked anonymously, 'Do you think it is appropriate for staff to ask patients questions about domestic violence?' over 80% agreed with being asked (Keeling and Birch, 2004). The author has also identified the necessity for the use of printed information about domestic abuse to raise awareness of these issues and the positivist action of leaving abuse, the importance of the patient/health provider relationship, the patients' readiness for disclosure, and ways to ask about domestic abuse (Hathaway et al., 2002; Shadigian and Bauer 2004).

The gender of the health professional appeared to make a difference as to whether survivors of abuse disclose, with one study identifying that 16% of women in a study felt that it would be easier to disclose to a female health care provider (Hathaway et al., 2002), whereas the specialty of the heath professional did not appear to differentiate between the rates of disclosure (Warshaw, 1989). However, many survivors of abuse have reduced contact with the health service thereby minimizing their opportunity to disclose (Shadigian and Bauer, 2004).

It has also been clearly identified that intervention by a non-family member may act as a significant factor in a woman leaving an abusive partner (Helton and Snodgrass, 1987).

All experiences of domestic abuse may be affected by recall bias, as some experiences are too traumatic to recall, and some women may not associate their experiences as domestic abuse. Some women may minimize their injuries, be in denial or accept their treatment as a 'cultural norm'. However, for all abused women contemplating disclosing abuse there is a plethora of issues surrounding her decision. Almost a third of women in a study were fearful of disclosing abuse (Hathaway et al., 2002). A perceived lack of confidentiality may adversely affect disclosure (Hathaway et al., 2002). Other factors identified include lack of time or perceived rush to be seen/treated (Hathaway et al., 2002), shame and embarrassment (Parsons et al., 1995) and not being aware of any help being available.

This raises the question of whether or not men should accompany women when attending for any intimate female examination. The gradual acceptance of men to accompany their female partner during an intimate examination has denied women the opportunity to disclose abuse and to access the vital support that may be offered by the health care provider. Physical violence is often accompanied by psychological abuse and sexual violence, which tends to intensify over the course of a pregnancy, therefore the earlier the abuse is detected, the less risk is posed to the pregnant woman and fetus because the empowerment process can commence earlier.

The acceptability of being asked about experiences of domestic abuse, coupled with the known deleterious effects of abuse, support the argument for the inclusion of routine questioning of the presence of domestic abuse in a woman's life (Keeling and Birch, 2004; Tacket et al., 2004). The pivotal reason for abuse intervention is to promote the safety of the woman. All health professionals must be fully aware of the resources available to survivors of abuse and be able to provide effective support to the woman as part of the empowerment process for that woman.

Conclusion

There appear to be several factors that inhibit a survivor's opportunity and desire to disclose abuse. It is imperative that, as health professionals, we are aware of the implications of abuse, and able to offer effective support to those who choose to disclose (Keeling, 2004).

Women will rarely volunteer their experiences of abuse. To ensure that all health professionals are skilled at empowering survivors of domestic abuse when they choose to disclose, education of the health care professional should be considered an essential component of any educational health programme (McFarlane et al., 1991; Keeling, 2002).

Due to the unproven effect of implementing routine screening for domestic abuse (Davidson et al., 2000; Ramsay et al., 2002; Richardson et al., 2002) and the knowledge that women are more likely to disclose abuse if asked (Richardson et al., 2002), a paradox exists. However, the author suggests that by assimilating the factors identified in this chapter, and utilizing these skills towards increasing the knowledge and efficacy of domestic abuse programmes within the health service, morbidity and mortality due to the causative effects of abuse might be reduced, in conjunction with reducing health costs.

From the comments offered by women, the experiences of domestic abuse are profound and devastating. As health care professionals we are responsible for the provision of holistic care. The nature of the health service today and the often ever-present partner can make addressing the issue of domestic abuse extremely difficult. Thus as a profession we should now consider providing all women with an opportunity to see a health professional on their own at regular intervals throughout their childbirthing experience.

It is essential that all midwives and student midwives receive training to recognize and respond effectively to a woman who chooses to disclose domestic abuse and be able to use multi-agency collaboration.

Acknowledgements

The author would like to thank all the women who have shared their experiences, often in great detail, in order that information and understanding about intimate partner abuse can be gained.

References

Abbey BB, Constance MW, et al. (1994) Perinatal morbidity associated with violence experienced by pregnant women. *Am J Obstet Gynec* **170(6)**: 1760–9.

Bacchus L, Mezey G, et al. (2004) Domestic violence: Prevalence in pregnant women and associations with physical and psychological health. *Eur J Obstet Gynaec Repro Biol* **113**: 6–11.

Barron J (2001) *Health and Domestic Violence Survey 2000. Summary of Findings*. WSAFO, Bristol.

Basile CK (2002) Prevalence of wife rape and other intimate partner sexual coercion in a nationally representative sample of women. *Violence Vict* **17(5)**: 511–24.

Becker JV, Skinner LJ, et al. (1984) Sexual problems of sexual assault survivors. *Women's Health Issues* **9**: 5–20.

Berenson AB, Wiemann CM, et al. (1994) Perinatal morbidity associated with violence experienced by pregnant women. *Am J Obstet Gynec* **170**: 1760–9.

Bradley F, Smith M, et al. (2002) Reported frequency of domestic violence: Cross sectional survey of women attending general practice. *Br Med J* **324(2 February)**: 271–3.

Campbell J (2002) Health consequences of intimate partner violence. *Lancet* **359(9314)**: 1331–6.

Campbell J, Soeken K (1999) Forced sex and intimate partner violence. Effects on women's risk and women's health. *Violence Against Women* **5(9)**: 1017–35.

CEMACH (2004) *Why Mothers Die 2000–2002. Confidential Enquiry into Maternal Deaths in the United Kingdom*. RCOG, London.

Chambliss LR, Bay RC, et al. (1995) Domestic violence: An educational imperative? *Am J Obstet Gynec* **172(3)**: 1035–8.

Coker AL, Smith PH, et al. (2000) Physical health consequences of physical and psychological intimate partner violence. *Arch Fam Med* **9(5)**: 451–7.

Davidson L, King V, et al. (2000) *Reducing Domestic Violence. What Works? Health Services. Policing and Reducing Crime*. Home Office Research Development and Statistics Directorate, London.

Department of Health (2000) *Domestic Violence: A Resource Manual for Health Care Professionals*. HMSO, London.

Department of Health (2003) *Building on the Best: Choice, Responsiveness and Equity in the NHS*. HMSO, London.

Department of Health (2004) *National Service Framework for Children, Young People and Maternity Services*. HMSO, London.

Dienemann J, Boyle E, et al. (2000) Intimate partner abuse among women diagnosed with depression. *Issues in Mental Health Nursing* **21**: 499–513.

Drossman D, Leserman J, et al. (1990) Sexual and physical abuse in patients with functional or organic gatrointestinal disorders. *Ann Intern Med* **113**: 828–34.

Edin KE, Hogberg U (2002) Violence against pregnant women will remain hidden as long as no direct questions are asked. *Midwifery* **18(4)**: 268–78.

Friend JR (1998) Responding to violence aginst women: A specialist's role. *Hosp Med* **59(9)**: 678–9.

Fry PS, Barker LA (2001) Female survivors of violence and abuse. Their regrets of action and inaction in coping. *Journal of Interpersonal Violence* **16 (4)**: 320–42.

Hathaway JE, Willis G, et al. (2002) Listening to survivors' voices. *Violence Against Women* **8(6)**: 687–719.

Helton AS, Snodgrass FG (1987) Battering during pregnancy: Intervention strategies. *Birth* **14(3)**: 142–7.

House of Commons Health Committee (2003). *Choice in Maternity Services*. HMSO, Norwich.

Huth-Bocks AC, Levendosky AA, et al. (2002) The effects of violence during pregnancy on maternal and infant health. *Violence Victims* **17**: 169–85.

Keeling J (2002) Support and education: The role of the domestic violence co-ordinator. *Nursing Times* **98(48)**: 34–5.

Keeling J (2004) A community-based perspective on living with domestic violence. *Nursing Times* **100(11)**: 28–9.

Keeling J, Birch L (2004) Asking pregnant women about domestic abuse. *British Journal of Midwifery* **12(12)**: 746–9.

McFarlane J, Cristoffel K, et al. (1991) Assessing for abuse: Self-report versus nurse interview. *Public Health Nurse* **8**: 245–50.

McGuigan WM, Vuchinich S, et al. (2000) Domestic violence. Parents' view of their infant and risk for child abuse. *J Family Psychol* **14(4)**: 613–24.

Mezey G, Bacchus L, Bewley S, Haworth A (2001) *An exploration of the Prevalence, Nature and Effects of Domestic Violence in Pregnancy*. ESRC/Violence Research Programme, London.

Mezey G, Bewley S (1997) Domestic violence and pregnancy. *Br J Obstet Gynaec* **104**: 528–31.

New Zealand College of Midwives (2005) *Family Violence Education for Midwives*. New Zealand College of Midwives, New Zealand.

Parsons LH, Zaccaro D, et al. (1995) Methods of and attitudes toward screening obstetrics and gynecology for domestic violence. *Am J Obstet Gynec* **173(2)**: 381–7.

Ramsay J, Richardson J, et al. (2002) Should health professionals screen women for domestic violence? Systematic review. *Br Med J* **325**: 314–18.

Richardson J, Coid J, et al. (2002) Identifying domestic violence: Cross sectional study in primary care. *Br Med J* **324**: 274–7.

Royal College of Gynaecologists (2001) *Confidential Report into Maternal Deaths in the United Kingdom (1997–1999)*. Royal College of Gynaecologists, London.

Royal College of Midwives (1999) *Domestic Abuse in Pregnancy. Position Paper No.19a*. Royal College of Midwives, London.

Royal College of Midwives (2004). *Response to Chief Nursing Officer's Review of the Nursing, Midwifery and Health Visiting Contribution to Children at Risk*. Royal College of Midwives, London.

Schei B, Bakketeig L (1989) Gynaecological impact of sexual and physical abuse by spouse. A study of a random sample of Norwegian women. *Br J Obstet Gynaec* **96**: 1379–83.

Schei B, Bakketeig L (1996) Gynaecological impact of sexual and physical abuse by spouse. A study of a random sample of Norwegian women. *Br J Obstet Gynaec* **96**: 1379–83.

Schei B, Samuelson SO, et al. (1991) Does spousal abuse affect outcome of pregnancy? *Scan J Soc Med* **19**: 26–31.

Shadigian EM, Bauer ST (2004) Screening for partner violence during pregnancy. *Int J Gynaec Obstet* **84**: 273–80.

Shankleman J, Brooks R, et al. (2001) Children resident in domestic violence refuges in Cardiff: A health needs and healthcare needs assessment. University of Cardiff, Department of Child Health, Cardiff.

Stewart D, Cucutti A (1993) Physical abuse in pregnancy. *Can Med Assoc J* **149**: 1257–63.

Tacket A, Beringer A, et al. (2004). *Tackling Domestic Violence: Exploring the Health Service Contribution*. Faculty of Health, Home Office, London.

Ussher JM (2000) *Women's Health: Contemporary International Perspectives*. British Psychological Society Books, Leicester.

Warshaw C (1989) Limitations of the medical model in the care of battered women. *Gender Soc* **3**: 506–17.

World Health Organization (2001). *Putting Women First: Ethical and Safety Recommendations for Research on Domestic Violence Against Women*. World Health Organization, Geneva.

CHAPTER 5

The challenge of providing dietary advice to disadvantaged pregnant women

Jenny McLeish

Giving basic dietary advice is an established part of antenatal care. It may take the form of going through a list of foods to avoid when pregnant, or a recommendation to eat more iron-rich foods, or it could be a leaflet given out at the booking visit. There is considerable evidence that this type of generalized directive advice is of very limited value to disadvantaged pregnant women. This chapter identifies the type of obstacles disadvantaged women face to following dietary advice, and explores some ways in which midwives can meet the challenge of giving 'healthy eating' advice and support more effectively. Effective dietary advice is particularly important in the context of the new Healthy Start scheme, complementing food vouchers for disadvantaged women.

Why does pregnancy nutrition matter?

Inadequate diet during pregnancy is the second most important cause (after smoking) of low birth weight (World Health Organization, 1992). Low birth weight is associated with infant mortality and an increased risk of disabilities, brain damage, poor language development, special educational needs, and, in later life, coronary heart disease, hypertension and diabetes (British Medical Association, 1999).

Poor nutrition during pregnancy can also permanently alter the baby's blood pressure and metabolism even where fetal growth is not affected. A 'healthy' diet in pregnancy may therefore reduce the baby's long-term risk of cardiovascular disease even where there is no measurable impact on birth weight (British Medical Association, 1999).

The mother's body mass index (BMI) – weight in kilos/height in metres^2 – also affects the baby's development. The babies of women who are excessively thin are at increased risk of prematurity, low birth weight, coronary heart disease, non-insulin dependent diabetes and raised blood pressure. Babies of overweight mothers are at increased risk of coronary heart disease and non-insulin dependent diabetes (British Medical Association, 1999).

Sometimes nutritional advice for pregnant women seems to imply that all the attention is on eating well for the sake of the baby, and the advice-giver is not interested in the mother. In fact, of course, a healthy diet for pregnancy is little different from a healthy diet for normal adult life. If a woman can be supported in making sustainable improvements to her diet during pregnancy, and encouraged to think of them as worth maintaining after pregnancy for her own sake, these will have a positive impact on her own long-term health.

What do disadvantaged pregnant women eat?

Women living on state benefits generally eat a less varied diet than women not on benefits (Dowler and Calvert, 1995), including less fruit and vegetables, less fish and less high fibre breakfast cereals, but more sugar, sweets, whole milk, burgers, kebabs and pasties (Food Standards Agency, 2002).

The same pattern is found in the diets of pregnant women. One survey of the diets of pregnant women in East London found that the most disadvantaged pregnant women had the least nutrient-dense diets, consuming the same amount of energy but with significantly lower intakes of protein, seven nutrients and six B-vitamins than women in higher social classes (Wynn et al., 1994). These findings were confirmed in a large cohort study which found that of 20 nutrients, only three were unaffected by financial difficulty (Rogers et al., 1998).

A significant proportion of adolescent girls have an inadequate intake of key pregnancy nutrients, including vitamin A, folate, zinc, iron and calcium (Food Standards Agency, 2000). Teenagers are particularly likely to have a low body mass index at the start of pregnancy and many have erratic and unhealthy eating patterns (Garcia et al., 1999). Most pregnant teenagers under 18 are not eligible for social security benefits until the last 11 weeks of pregnancy and are particularly at risk of poor diet in pregnancy, especially if they do not live with their parents (Burchett and Seeley, 2003).

There are also significant variations in diet between minority ethnic groups. For example, Chinese women eat the most fruit and vegetables of any minority group, Bangladeshi women eat the most red meat and fatty foods but the least fruit, and Pakistani women eat the least vegetables (Erens et al., 2001). Studies of local populations of pregnant Asian women have found them to be particularly vulnerable to vitamin D deficiency (Eaton et al., 1984; Abraham et al., 1987), especially if they eat a vegetarian diet and keep their skin covered.

Obstacles to healthy eating

Research has repeatedly found that traditional antenatal dietary advice, including classes and leaflets, may slightly increase a disadvantaged woman's nutrition knowledge but is generally ineffective in changing what she eats (Alley et al., 1995; Anderson et al., 1995). There is also no good evidence that dietary counselling alone can affect pregnancy outcome or birth weight (Van Teijlingen et al., 1998; Bull et al., 2003).

Even though pregnant women are usually considered to be particularly motivated to make positive lifestyle changes, there are in fact many potential obstacles to following 'healthy eating' advice. These obstacles may be associated with pregnancy, with poverty, or with the format in which the advice is conveyed. It is essential that midwives understand these obstacles in order to give effective nutritional advice.

Pregnancy and obstacles to healthy eating

Irrespective of financial circumstances, physical reactions such as nausea, pregnancy sickness, heartburn and cravings for particular foods may have a greater impact on what a pregnant woman eats than theoretical knowledge about what she 'should' eat. Making lifestyle changes requires energy as well as motivation, and this may be lacking for women experiencing extreme tiredness in early and late pregnancy.

Advice on foods to avoid during pregnancy is subject to change as new evidence becomes available, and it varies between countries. Women often therefore receive conflicting messages from different health professionals, from their mothers and from the media which emphasizes current health 'scares', and can become sceptical of all advice. In addition, some women report much more emphasis on being told what they 'should not' eat during pregnancy than on what they 'should' eat, with the alarming negative messages drowning out the positive.

Poverty and obstacles to healthy eating

Disadvantaged pregnant women often face formidable additional obstacles to following 'healthy eating' advice.

Lack of money

Women who are dependent on means-tested benefits for any length of time find it virtually impossible to follow an adequate pregnancy diet that meets basic social and cultural norms. To eat a 'modest but adequate' diet that meets all the nutritional requirements for pregnancy would cost a pregnant woman an estimated £25.63 a week if she had access to a wide range of foods at current average prices (Dallison and Lobstein, 1995; McLeish, 2005). For a pregnant woman on income support, who receives between £33 and £56 a week depending on her age (women under 25 receive a lower rate and some women under 18 receive even less), this represents an impossibly high proportion of her income.

Instead, money for food is often seen as the 'elastic' item in a tight budget – it is whatever is left over when the non-negotiable bills such as utilities have been paid. Research into the diets of pregnant women receiving income support has found that they were only spending on average £16.50 a week on food (Dallison and Lobstein, 1995, uprated to current prices) – just £2.36 a day.

When money is short and the pregnant woman or her children are hungry, the logical response is to buy foods that fill up the family most cheaply and that are unlikely to be rejected. The cheapest calories come from nutrient-poor fatty foods that are often high in sugar and salt – in terms of calories per penny, chips are about half the price of carrots. A diet of biscuits, sweet tea, white bread, hard margarine and meat products can provide all the calories needed at an affordable price (Lobstein, 1997). Such a diet also incurs minimal fuel costs which may be a significant obstacle to preparing 'cheap' nutritious food (e.g. baking a potato). Retailers do little to address this problem: the majority of supermarket 'economy' or 'value' lines are for fatty or sugary foods. Healthier options (e.g. wholemeal bread, lean mince) cost on average 50% more than less healthy alternatives (Food Commission, 2001).

Lack of knowledge

Much antenatal dietary advice assumes the problem is one of ignorance, but in fact, pregnant women living in poverty have been found to have a fairly high awareness of the main constituents of a healthy diet (Dallison and Lobstein, 1995). Some disadvantaged women, especially, for example, younger women, may have less knowledge of what they 'should' be eating, but these women are also likely to lack the skills to prepare more nutritious food. As in the case of advice to give up smoking, theoretical knowledge alone is not the key to behavioural change.

Lack of cooking skills

Many disadvantaged women are very resourceful cooks but some (like some women in all sectors of society) will have grown up without having been taught cooking skills either at home or at school. Women with families may lack the confidence to try out new foods when they cannot afford an alternative if they make a mistake or the food is rejected by family members. There is some evidence that families living on low incomes often rely on convenience foods

(Dowler and Calvert, 1995). This is not only because they are quick and easy to prepare but also because they are relatively cheap, popular with children, come in regular portion sizes and there is no waste.

Lack of budgeting and shopping skills
To eat well on a low income needs considerable budgeting and shopping skills. While many women living in poverty develop effective strategies for managing their limited food budget and finding the cheapest bargains, some lack the literacy or numeracy skills for the kind of detailed planning and label reading necessary.

Lack of cooking equipment
Some women have no cooking facilities at all, or very limited access to a shared kitchen, for example if they are homeless or living in temporary accommodation. Appliances may be dirty or unsafe, and there may be no storage space for food. The floor may be too dirty to put a baby down while cooking. Some women have little or no cooking equipment.

Lack of access to shops selling fresh, affordable and high quality food
With the trend towards out-of-town supermarkets designed for car users and the collapse of small independent food shops, people living in poor neighbourhoods without access to a car increasingly have very limited access to affordable fresh foods. Local corner shops are usually an expensive option – basic foods can be up to 60% more expensive in local shops than in supermarkets (Piachaud and Webb, 1996). Small shops often stock a very limited range and in poor areas are particularly unlikely to stock healthier options such as semi-skimmed milk (Consumers' Association, 1997). Where there is a local discount store it may have cheaper prices but typically stocks little fresh produce and few of the healthier options (Food Commission, 2001).

A trip to the supermarket may, however, be uneconomic, because of having to pay the bus fares or (if there is too much to carry) taxi fares home. The physical difficulty of the trip may be overwhelming for a pregnant woman with other children as well as the shopping to carry. The problems of transportation may also make it impossible to take advantage of bulk-buy supermarket promotions such as '3 for the price of 2'.

Lack of control over meals
Some pregnant women, especially teenagers and women living in extended families, do not have any control over shopping or cooking, and are dependent on the nutrition decisions of someone else, usually their mother or mother-in-law. The same applies to women living in residential settings such as young women in care.

Putting others first

A common coping strategy for women in poor families, especially lone parent families, is to feed their children while skipping meals themselves, sometimes using cigarettes to suppress their appetite. A woman expecting her second or subsequent child is therefore particularly likely to economize on her own food and to experience feelings of guilt were she to prioritize the nutritional needs of her unborn child (Dobson et al., 1994; Middleton et al., 1997).

Social norms

Food is, of course, not just about nutrition. It also has an important role in socializing, cultural identity, and as a source of pleasure and comfort. If a woman has a poor diet which is the same as her peer group (e.g. teenagers eating takeaways) it may be very difficult to change that diet without feeling isolated from the group. If a woman is stressed or unhappy she may find it very hard to replace 'comfort foods' with healthier options. If a woman is primarily concerned about body image and minimizing weight gain, she may be reluctant to increase her energy intake when she is pregnant.

Women with families are often very concerned to protect their children from the stigma of poverty and may prioritize foods such as crisps or chocolate for them to take to school as a way of participating in conventional behaviour (Joseph Rowntree Foundation, 1994). They may also struggle to continue eating what they consider to be a 'mainstream' diet, by eating cheaper (and thus often less healthy) versions of conventional foods, rather than risking radical change which the children might reject, as there is no margin for waste.

Other priorities

Some families that spend very little on food may spend comparatively large amounts of money on cigarettes. In one study, working class mothers reported that cigarettes were their only luxury, their only leisure activity, their only item of personal expenditure, and were a quick and easy way of coping with stress (Graham, 1993). Physical and psychological addiction may therefore mean that for the woman concerned, smoking is a higher priority than nutrition.

Obstacles to following written nutrition advice

Lack of relevance

If written materials contain lifestyle advice which seems entirely irrelevant to the reader because she would never do it anyway (e.g. a disadvantaged young woman who lives on fast food being told to avoid brie), she may draw a more general conclusion that 'this is not for me'. There is a similar problem if the text and pictures do not reflect her community's normal diet. Generalized nutritional messages that fail to take account of a woman's financial situation are perceived as impossible and are ignored.

Unfamiliar concepts

Leaflets often talk about numbers of servings of foods but this is not usually how people think about what they eat. Likewise many women will find it difficult to analyse their food in terms of 'nutrients'.

Low literacy levels and women who do not speak English

Women whose first language is not English may not be able to understand the information in standard leaflets. Some English-speaking disadvantaged women have very low literacy levels or may be illiterate (Office for National Statistics, 1997), but due to the stigma attached to illiteracy are unlikely to admit this to health professionals. They may be put off by leaflets which seem dauntingly long, or where there is a lot of text and not much white space or pictures.

Special diets

Women may choose a particular diet because of personal preference or ethical beliefs, e.g. vegetarian (no meat or fish), vegan (no meat, fish or animal products including milk, eggs and honey), or choose to avoid red meat but eating poultry and fish. General leaflets do not always give specific guidance on achieving the 'balance of good health' while taking account of dietary restrictions.

The impact of 'Healthy Start'

The Welfare Food Scheme has been replaced by Healthy Start. The new scheme offers low income pregnant women and young children food vouchers worth a fixed amount of money – £2.80 a week, and £5.60 a week for children under one – rather than (as under the Welfare Food Scheme) a fixed quantity of milk or infant formula. The Healthy Start vouchers can be spent on fruit and vegetables, liquid cow's milk, and cow's milk-based infant formula, and this list may be extended in the future. The intention is that women receiving Healthy Start vouchers will also receive advice and support from health professionals, tailored to their needs and local circumstances. To apply for Healthy Start vouchers, the pregnant woman must get her application form countersigned by a health professional, who must confirm that the woman has been given health-related advice.

Although Healthy Start will contribute to a disadvantaged woman's food budget in a very limited way, meeting little over 10% of the estimated cost of a

---

Box 5.1. 24-hour recall of food intake

The client is asked to make a list of everything she ate and drank the previous day, with prompts, e.g. 'What was the first thing you ate or drank when you got up?', 'Did you have a snack in the morning?', 'Did you eat lunch?'.

Advantages:
- The client is asked to talk about food in 'real' terms, i.e. meals and snacks she has eaten, rather than more abstract terms of portions.

Disadvantages:
- It can be difficult to remember a whole day's meals, snacks and drinks. This can be helped by linking food/drink to what the client was doing that day.
- The day may not be typical.

'modest but adequate' pregnancy diet, the scheme has been repeatedly heralded in Government papers as a key policy to overcome health inequalities. Schemes in the US and Canada have found that counselling linked to extensive food voucher support can reduce the incidence of low birth weight (Abrams, 1993; Buescher et al., 1993; Wigda and Lewis, 1999), but there is no evidence that vouchers at the low level of Healthy Start will have this effect. This creates an even greater challenge for midwives to offer pregnant women the best possible dietary advice and support.

Good practice in giving nutritional advice

The most effective advice intervention for changing pregnant women's diets is one-to-one nutritional counselling (Widga and Lewis, 1997), or counselling in tiny groups (Hermann et al., 2001). In contrast, there is no evidence that written information or large group sessions have much impact on pregnant women's diets (Anderson et al., 1995; Alley et al., 1995). Nutritional advice has the best chance of success if it is:

- Personal (to the woman herself, her concerns and her abilities).
- Relevant (to her age, culture, and existing diet).
- Realistic (fully understanding any obstacles she may face).
- Practical (helping her to find ways around those obstacles to achieve specific improvements).
- Grounded in a relationship of trust and respect.

The following eight steps to effective nutritional counselling are adapted from Story and Stang (2000)

Box 5.2. Food frequency questionnaire

The client is asked how many servings of particular foods or food groups she typically consumes. This can be a fairly detailed list, or based on general questions.

Advantages:
- This method can give a more rounded picture of overall diet.

Disadvantages:
- The client has to remember and analyse her meals into components and servings, which she may find difficult.
- This may not be suitable for women with very erratic diets.

Example of food frequency 'general questions'
> How many meals or snacks do you eat most days?
> How often do you eat meat or lentils/beans/soya?
> How often do you eat vegetables/fruit?
> How often do you eat takeaways?
> How often do you drink milk or eat yoghurt/cheese?
> How often do you snack on biscuits/chocolate/crisps?

Step 1: Listen attentively and non-judgementally
The foundation of giving realistic, practical advice is to listen to the client's own nutritional concerns and her perception of the obstacles in her life to achieving a better diet.

Step 2: Gather information about the client's diet
This could be done by using a simple 24 hour recall (see *Box 5.1*) or a food frequency tool (see *Box 5.2*). The aim is to get a general picture of what the client eats, so you know what issues to target – for example, that she never eats fruit, or rarely eats foods high in calcium or iron.

Step 3: Give positive feedback
Emphasize the positive: highlight what is good in the client's current diet before discussing needed improvements.

Step 4: Focus your information and advice on up to three key points
Key points are something you hope the client will remember or do. They should be simple and specific, and should suggest small and realistic changes based on the information you have about her current diet. The aim is not to change her whole diet or lifestyle, but to help her change aspects of her diet where she is lacking nutrients or consuming excessively.

Step 5: Help the client to set small, achievable, specific goals

The client is much more likely to change her behaviour where she has a specific plan (e.g. 'I'll eat an apple every day', 'I'll have cereal and milk for breakfast', 'I'll take a piece of fruit in my bag when I go out').

Step 6: Help the client in a problem-solving approach

Show that you understand the obstacles she perceives, share what has worked for others, and facilitate her own problem-solving. Encourage her to think about what she will buy with the Healthy Start vouchers.

Step 7: Use leaflets wisely

Avoid overloading the client with leaflets. What you give her should be able to go on the refrigerator as a reminder of what you talked about. If you give her a leaflet, mark the most important parts for her.

Step 8: Refer the client to other sources of support

The client may not be receiving all the benefits she is entitled to. She can get advice from a Citizen's Advice Bureau or the Maternity Alliance.

In addition:

- Check that the client is receiving Healthy Start vitamins.
- Refer her to a dietitian if appropriate and available.
- Refer her to any local groups or classes on cooking or nutrition.
- Give her the contact details of any local food projects.

Women from minority ethnic communities

To be appropriate to the individual client, advice should take account of cultural and religious influences or restrictions on her diet, ensuring that she is able to eat the recommended foods. It is, of course, essential not to make assumptions that an individual of any particular background will follow traditional practices; for example British-born ethnic minority women may also be strongly influenced by mainstream culture.

Where nutrition leaflets or posters are felt to be a valuable resource it is important to have versions available in key local community languages. A word-for-word translation is not appropriate where the minority community has different dietary traditions and the text and images should be adapted to reflect the normal diet of that community.

It must be remembered that women from minority communities are not necessarily literate in their mother tongue. Where there is a combination of low English and mother tongue literacy, and a strong oral culture in the particular ethnic group, resources may be better spent on bilingual health professionals spreading messages by word of mouth (Doff, 2004).

Other useful resources

- Pictures or posters of nutritious foods and snacks, relevant to local cultures.
- Recipe cards for easily prepared, inexpensive, nutritious snacks and meals, with costs.
- Examples of what the Healthy Start vouchers could be used to buy locally and what could be done with those foods.
- Videos and audiotapes.
- Offering a nutritious snack (e.g. fruit) to women at antenatal visits can reinforce the messages being taught.

Practical activities

The maternity services can be a gateway to practical activities that increase a participant's nutritional knowledge and skills, by making direct links with local food projects or alternatively developing some activities as part of antenatal education.

Many disadvantaged areas have some kind of community food project aiming to overcome some of the barriers to healthy eating. These often address access to affordable food, and/or enhancing cooking and shopping skills. They include food co-operatives, community cafés, transport to supermarkets, cooking clubs, lunch clubs, schemes to lend or give disadvantaged women a start up pack of cooking equipment, and one-to-one support from home visitors including bilingual community nutrition workers. They may be provided for example by a neighbourhood regeneration scheme, a Sure Start local programme, or a children's centre. Pregnant women will not necessarily know about local projects and will benefit from signposting. Local food projects may also benefit from having input from the maternity services as some do not target pregnant women and may lack understanding of their needs.

To find out about projects in your area, contact the Health Promotion Team, Sure Start local programmes, community dietitians, the Food and Low Income Database (Tel: 020 7413 1995), the Scottish Community Food Database (Tel: 0141 226 5361), or the Community Transport Association (Tel: 0161 367 8780).

Conclusions

It is easy to give disadvantaged pregnant women the type of directive, general nutritional advice that has little impact on their diets. The challenge for midwives is to change the style of nutritional counselling, so that it becomes much more personal, relevant, realistic and practical. Rather than trying to change a whole lifestyle, this style of nutritional counselling treats each woman as an individual and supports her in making specific, modest but achievable changes to her diet.

References

Abraham R, Campbell-Brown M, North W, McFadyen R (1987) Diets of Asian pregnant women in Harrow: Iron and vitamins. *Hum Nutr: Appl Nutr* **41A**: 164–73.

Abrams B (1993) Preventing low birth weight: Does WIC work? *Ann the NY Acad Sci* **678(3)**: 306–16.

Alley H, McCloud-Harrison J, Peisher A, Rafter J (1995) Expectations may be too high for changing diets of pregnant teens. *J Extension* **33(1)**. Available from: http://www.joe.org/joe/1995february/rb1.html [Accessed 13 October 2006].

Anderson A, Campbell D, Shepherd R (1995) The influence of dietary advice on nutrient intake during pregnancy. *Br J Nutr* **73**: 163–77.

British Medical Association (1999) *Growing Up in Britain: Ensuring a Healthy Future for our Children.* BMJ Books, London.

Buescher PA, Larson LC, Nelson MD Jr, et al. (1993) Prenatal WIC participation can reduce low birth weight and newborn medical costs: A cost–benefit analysis of WIC participation in North Carolina. *J Am Diet Assoc* **93**:163–6.

Bull J, Mulvihill C, Quigley R (2003) *Prevention of Low Birthweight: Assessing the Effectiveness of Smoking Cessation and Nutritional Counselling Interventions.* Health Development Agency, London.

Burchett H, Seeley A (2003) *Good Enough to Eat? The Diet of Pregnant Teenagers.* Maternity Alliance/Food Commission, London.

Consumers' Association (1997) *The Food Divide: Eating on a Low Income.* Consumers' Association, London.

Dallison J, Lobstein T (1995) *Poor Expectations: Poverty and Undernourishment in Pregnancy.* Maternity Alliance/NCH Action for Children, London.

Dobson B, Beardsworth A, Keil T, Walker R (1994) *Diet, Choice and Poverty: Social, Cultural and Nutritional Aspects of Food Consumption among Low Income Families.* Loughborough University of Technology, Centre for Research in Social Policy, Loughborough.

Doff S (2004) *Local Food Policies and Cultural Diversity in London.* Government Office for London, London.

Dowler E, Calvert C (1995) *Nutrition and Diet in Lone Parent Families in London*. Family Policy Studies Centre, Oxford.

Dubois S, Coulombe C, Pencharz P, Pinsonneault O, Duquette MP (1997) Ability of the Higgins Nutrition Intervention Programme to improve adolescent pregnancy outcome. *J Am Diet Assoc* **97(8)**:871–3.

Eaton PM, Wharton PA, Wharton BA (1984) Nutrient intake of pregnant Asian women in Sorrento Maternity Hospital, Birmingham. *Br J Nutr* **52**: 457–68.

Erens B, Primesta P, Prior G (2001) *Health Survey for England. The Health of Minority Ethnic Groups '99*. The Stationery Office, London.

Food Commission (2001) Healthier diets cost more than ever. *Food Magazine* **55**: 17.

Food Standards Agency (2000) *National Diet and Nutrition Survey of Young People Aged 4–18 Years*. The Stationery Office, London.

Food Standards Agency (2002) *National Diet and Nutrition Survey: Adults Aged 16–64* (Vol 1). The Stationery Office, London.

Garcia J, France-Dawson M, Macfarlane A (1999) *Improving Infant Health*. Health Education Authority, London.

Graham H (1993) *When Life's a Drag: Women, Smoking and Disadvantage*. HMSO, London.

Hermann J, Williams G, Hunt D (2001) Effect of nutrition education by paraprofessionals on dietary intake, maternal weight gain and infant birthweight in pregnant Native American and Caucasian adolescents. *J Extension*, **39(1)**. Available from: http://www.joe.org/joe/2001february/ rb2.html [Accessed 13 October 2006].

Joseph Rowntree Foundation (1994) Eating on a low income. *JRF Social Policy Research Findings 66*. Joseph Rowntree Foundation, York.

Lobstein T (1997) *Myths about Food and Low Income*. National Food Alliance, London.

McLeish J (2005) *Talking about Food: How to Give Effective Healthy Eating Advice to Disadvantaged Pregnant Women*. Maternity Alliance, London.

Middleton S, Ashworth K, Braithwaite I (1997) *Small Fortunes: Spending on Children, Child Poverty and Parental Sacrifice*. Joseph Rowntree Foundation, York.

Office for National Statistics (1997) *Adult Literacy in Britain*. Office for National Statistics, London.

Piachaud D, Webb J (1996) *The Price of Food: Missing out on Mass Consumption*. London School of Economics, London.

Rogers I, Emmett P, Baker D, Golding J and the ALSPAC Study Team

(1998) Financial difficulties, smoking habits, composition of the diet and birthweight in a population of pregnant women in the South West of England. *Eur J Clin Nutr* **52**: 251–60.

Story M, Stang J (eds.) (2000) *Nutrition and the Pregnant Adolescent. A Practical Reference Guide.* University of Minnesota, Minnesota.

Van Teilingen ER, Wilson BJ, Barry N, Ralph A, McNeill G, Graham W, Campbell DM (1998) *Effectiveness of Interventions to Promote Healthy Eating in Pregnant Women and Women of Childbearing Age: A review.* Health Education Authority, London.

Widga AC, Lewis NM (1999) Defined, in-home, prenatal nutrition intervention for low-income women. *J Am Diet Assoc* **99(9)**: 1058–62.

World Health Organization (1992) *Low Birth Weight. A Tabulation of Available Information.* World Health Organization/UNICEF, Geneva.

Wynn M, Wynn AM, Crawford MA (1994) The association of maternal social class with maternal diet and the dimensions of babies in a population of London women. *Nutrition and Health* **9**: 303–15.

Further reading

McLeish J (2005) *Talking about Food: How to Give Effective Healthy Eating Advice to Disadvantaged Pregnant Women.* Maternity Alliance, London.

CHAPTER 6

Lesbian users of maternity services: Challenges in midwifery care

Elaine Lee

Numerous attempts have been made, not always successfully, to improve levels of equality for ethnic minorities and the many different religious groups which form the make-up of the United Kingdom's eclectic and ever diversifying society. However, within this social imperative of equality, sexuality and sexual orientation seem less important. The prejudice, both individual and institutional, against this significant minority group is pervasive and it also appears to be considered socially acceptable (Walton, 1994; Kent, 2000). The impact of legislation such as the Employment Equality (Sexual Orientation) Regulations 2003 and Civil Partnerships Act 2004 is not yet known, although these formal provisions provide important legal protections and raise the status of this substantial group. However, it is undeniable that homosexuality is still abhorrent to most religions and cultures, and its incidence can result in 'media outrage' which in turn fuels personal bias (Salmon and Hall, 1999).

Many lesbian women become pregnant and have families. Midwives must develop an understanding of this group of women so that they can be given care, advice and support according to individual needs. The aim of this chapter is to address the issue of the treatment of lesbian users of maternity services. The intention is not only to look at the specific needs of lesbian mothers and their partners, but also to identify midwifery responses to this client group and suggest ways to improve the experience of lesbian users of maternity services.

Woman-centred care: The rhetoric of inclusion

In 1993 the House of Commons Expert Maternity Group (Department of Health, 1993) set out to explore the important issues surrounding current maternity care provision and the improvements which could be made within it. The group specifically approached the report from the needs of clients rather than simply the perspective of those working within the maternity services. The phrase 'woman-centred care' is used throughout the report, and this is a phrase which can be heard within the corridors of maternity hospitals throughout the country and underpins much midwifery education. However, to be meaningful, women-centred care must exist in actions and not just in conversation. Words without action become rhetoric, and rhetoric does not bring about meaningful change.

The report (Department of Health, 1993) stated that:

> *'Every woman has unique needs. In addition to those arising from her medical history, these will arise from her particular ethnic, cultural, social and family background. The services provided should recognize the special characteristics of the population they are designed to serve. They should also be attractive and accessible to all women, particularly those who may be least inclined to use them.' (p.5)*

The *Standards of Proficiency for Pre-registration Midwifery Education* (Nursing and Midwifery Council, 2004a) set out the outcomes for programmes of preparation for practice, including 'practise in a way which respects, promotes and supports individuals' rights, interests, preferences, beliefs and cultures' (p.7). The promotion of non-discriminatory practice is also part of this. This includes consideration of lesbian women who are affected by a range of social, political and cultural factors, as well as rights and interests that derive from their personal culture and family structures. Such family structures are open to scrutiny and disapproval, both public and personal, which runs counter to the principles of woman-centred care.

The prevalence of homosexuality in the population at large is virtually impossible to ascertain owing to degrees of homosexual behaviours and reluctance to 'come out' (Kinsey, 1948, 1953). However, a proportion of women in the UK who are lesbian will either be or wish to become mothers. The exact number of lesbians who are already or are hoping to be mothers is unknown (Wilton and Kaufmann, 2001). This does not only apply in the UK, but in all other countries and this is hardly surprising. The last UK census in 2001 included categories of married couple, cohabiting couple and lone-parent households but does not include information of the sexual orientation of the adults involved (Office for National Statistics, 2001). Census data is not currently sensitive enough to identify more complex family structures and lesbian mothers will be included in either the figures for lone parent households or the category of cohabiting couples. Following the Civil Partnership Act (2004) the next UK census will presumably contain statistics that relate to civil partnership households. This might go some way to making the census data collection more sensitive to variations in relationships, both between couples and the children within the family. It might also provide some indications of the potential number of women in this group.

However, figures relating to the prevalence of lesbian motherhood are also problematic because lesbian motherhood does not only exist in same-sex relationships. A significant number of lesbians become mothers while in a marriage or other heterosexual relationship (Saffron, 2001). Also, heterosexist assumptions within maternity care lead to the failure to ask questions regarding sexual orientation during the childbearing process, thus rendering this client group less visible.

Lesbian mothers and invisibility

Failure to ask women about their sexual orientation in the belief that it is irrelevant inhibits the ability of midwives to provide individualized, woman-centred care because providing such care for any woman requires rapport and open channels of communication. It is this failure that returns as a recurrent theme within the evidence surrounding this subject area, even though that evidence within midwifery is scant. The needs of the individual are not being recognized and acknowledged because lesbian mothers remain invisible within health care provision (Royal College of Midwives, 2000). When their existence is acknowledged in health care, this often relates to sexual health and disease. The more positive aspects of adult life such as having children and creating families do not seem to attract the same interest.

Invisibility, as opposed to anonymity, surfaces as one of the most significant areas within the literature on lesbian motherhood. This invisibility can be legal, where previously partners were not considered next of kin (Foster, 1995; Beresford, 1996); deliberate, through ignorance; or well meaning, through a denial of its relevance (Platzer and James, 2000). If a whole subgroup of the women accessing maternity services are not being adequately acknowledged, then their individual problems, concerns and needs will not be acknowledged either (Brogan, 1997). If midwives do not give appropriate care to lesbian women throughout pregnancy, the intrapartum period and postnatally then they cannot be said to be fulfilling their professional obligations (Nursing and Midwifery Council, 2004b). The simple issue of offering contraceptive advice becomes problematic. It may appear common sense that a woman who is lesbian does not need advice on contraception or safe sex. However, assumptions and stereotyping of this sort can lead to such a need being missed; some lesbian women do have sex with men (Saffron, 2001). Unless the midwife identifies the particular needs of each individual woman care cannot be individually appropriate. The key issue is that all women have their own needs which relate to their own personal set of life circumstances. It is only by asking what these needs are that a midwife can meet them.

Beresford (1996) complains that the role of motherhood has been so closely associated with heterosexuality that the 'lesbian mother' has become an oxymoron. Society arguably does not have the terms with which to assimilate lesbian motherhood, and so it is rendered invisible. Beresford

(1996) is particularly concerned with legal definitions and how the lesbian mother must try to conform to norms of a heterosexual society in order to be seen. The author talks of the notion of the 'perfect woman' and how lesbian women have to put on the robes of conformity to prove themselves to be 'fit' to be mothers. Normalizing something that is viewed by many as something aberrant or deviant in a pejorative sense becomes important because it promotes safety by reducing scrutiny. This is similar to the process of 'covering' whereby lesbians and gay men hide their true sexual orientation for fear of censure (Ward and Winstanley, 2005).

This idea of 'fitness' is also discussed by Walton (1994). The author describes the fear that lesbians and gay men have of being declared unfit in whichever role they have, particularly where the care of children is involved (Walton, 1994). This fear not only exists in public roles, for example teaching, where parents fear the promotion of homosexuality as an acceptable way of life or even that their child may be at some physical risk, but also in private spheres of life, as lesbians face the fear of being declared unfit mothers. No other group of women has to prove that they are fit for motherhood before pregnancy (separate from issues surrounding adoption and fostering). Usually, social, political and legal structures only take an interest on an individual basis. The State does not wish to intrude on the private domain of the family, usually only doing so when given cause for concern such as the threat of physical abuse. But Walton (1994) states that this is not the case for lesbians wishing to become mothers. This fear of not being seen as fit for motherhood is what adds to the likelihood of lesbian mothers not declaring themselves as such, thereby perpetuating their invisibility (Brogan, 1997).

Brogan (1997) states that lesbian women are reluctant to reveal their sexual orientation to their health care professionals for fear of homophobic attitudes, physical or verbal abuse and inappropriate advice and questioning, as well as breaches of confidentiality. It cannot be assumed that because a lesbian reveals her sexual orientation to one midwife that she either wishes this to be recorded, or is happy for this information to be discussed between professionals (Platzer and James, 2000). This is a challenge in all aspects of health care where confidential information is passed between professionals for therapeutic and practical reasons. But for the lesbian woman who decides to disclose sexual orientation to her midwife, this decision may have been taken with a great deal of thought and for specific reasons. She may be very keen to remain in control of this process so midwives should be careful to ask consent to pass this information to others.

An important consequence of identifying herself as lesbian is that the woman may come to be viewed only in terms of her sexual practices (Platzer and James, 2000). This is important from the perspective of her midwifery care because the vast majority of midwives are women. If midwives see lesbian mothers only in terms of their sexuality then they run the risk of over-emphasizing this aspect and 'backing off' where they might normally develop a closeness, both physical and emotional (Harding and Corbett, 1994). Platzer and James (2000) argue that by focusing on the woman's sexuality we, consciously or unconsciously, assume them 'to be indiscriminately attracted to anyone of the same sex'. It is difficult to provide unbiased, woman-centred care if midwives cannot maintain the focus of the lesbian woman as a person and not simply a sexual orientation.

The Royal College of Midwives position paper *Maternity Care for Lesbian Mothers* (Royal College of Midwives, 2000) asserts that many of the problems related to lesbian parenting and midwives' perceptions of it can be improved with 'women-centred care'; that is, maintaining the woman and her individual needs as the focus of care. Importantly, the paper makes the point that for the midwife to argue that she or he treats all women equally and does not differentiate between groups, is to deny that specific problems exist for different client groups (Royal College of Midwives, 2000), a theme repeated by Platzer and James (2000). While it is certainly desirable to treat all women as equal, giving them respect, autonomy and empowering them through the childbearing process, the position paper (RCM, 2000) states:

'Working with diversity is not about categorizing people as "different", nor is it about treating them as special cases; it is about recognizing and understanding each woman's individual needs, so as to be able to provide the same high standard of care for everyone.' (p.1)

Lesbian mothers and maternity care: Where we are now

Some research has been undertaken in the area of lesbian experiences of maternity care. Studies by Platzer and James (2000) and Wilton and Kaufmann (2001) raise very similar points about lesbian women's experiences as they book for antenatal care or attend for treatment and encounter midwives (and other health care professionals) for the first time. While both allude to the problem of abuse and open hostility, one of the most important issues is that of inappropriate questioning. Maternity care is organized in such a way as to assume heterosexuality in the pregnant woman. Booking paperwork will ask for the name, age and occupation of the woman's partner, but does not ask for their sex. Midwives may have abandoned the use of the title 'Mrs' for all women regardless of marital status (Royal College of Midwives, 2000), and may even have become comfortable using the term 'partner' rather than 'husband'. However, this has probably come about as a result of the increasing number of couples having children outside marriage but still within a heterosexual relationship (Kent, 2000). Having said that, Platzer and James (2000) feel that the use of gender-neutral terminology such as 'partner' does work to enable lesbian women to identify themselves. It shows willingness on the part of the health care professional to acknowledge alternative relationships.

The same might be said of the new procedures for creating civil partnerships. The Civil Partnerships Act (2004) entitles all same-sex couples who register a civil partnership to the same legal protections enshrined within marriage. This has led to simplified rules regarding inheritance and next of kin which recognizes the level of commitment between the individuals concerned. This progressive piece of legislation also provides midwives and other health care practitioners with the means to facilitate supportive disclosure of sexual orientation through routine demographic information should the woman choose to disclose it. Adding 'civil partnership' to the list of possible relationships enables lesbian women to come out if they wish, assuming they are in a formal civil partnership. This legislation is very new and the numbers of women within civil partnerships is as yet very small but the very existence and acknowledgement of legally formalized same-sex relationships represents a step in the right direction for increasing visibility and representation of lesbian mothers.

Returning to the issue of questioning and information exchange, midwives and other maternity care practitioners may not only ask the wrong questions, but may ask questions that are irrelevant and also intrusive (Wilton and Kaufmann, 2001). For example, lesbian mothers have complained that they are asked how they became pregnant or what kind of relationship the genetic father will have with the baby (Wilton and Kaufmann, 2001). Instances were also noted where midwives took revelations about sexual orientation as an invitation to express personal disapproval and even refusal to provide care (Wilton and Kaufmann, 2001). It is an important part of midwifery practice that care to every woman should be provided in a way that does not discriminate on any grounds. This is a very practical issue and even a midwife with a philosophical objection to same-sex relationships can and must provide non-discriminatory care throughout the childbearing period. Even a deeply held belief need not be expressed in the care that is given. Every midwife has a professional and legal duty of care to women and their families, regardless of any extraneous factors.

Platzer and James (2000) suggest that when it comes to the taking of patient histories by health care workers, we should be more aware of the way in which questions are worded and the heterosexist assumptions that underpin them. They state 'the onus is on the health care professional to create an environment in which the patient feels safe enough to be open about the information that is relevant to her health care' (Platzer and James, 2000). If midwives are not clear in their own minds about why we ask certain questions, or whether these questions are loaded towards heterosexuality (next of kin being an important one), then we cannot be sure that lesbian women in our care feel 'safe' or trust that the care they receive is appropriate (Salmon and Hall, 1999). Being able to demonstrate an openness of attitude and recognition of the potential family structures that exist, may promote this feeling of safety. By asking only those questions that have a purpose or understanding the purpose behind every question midwives can maintain the integrity of care. And ensuring that the care that is given is congruent to the responses given by women enhances the quality of individualized woman-centred care. Women-centred care can go some way to reducing invisibility and providing a safe environment for lesbian users of maternity services.

Implications for care

In order to address the needs of lesbian mothers, midwives will have to be proactive. The bulk (and it is not a particularly substantial bulk) of the research which has been carried out in relation to lesbian motherhood has addressed the views of lesbian women about their midwifery care or care by other health professionals. There has been less of a focus on midwives' perceptions of lesbian mothers undergoing the childbearing process. It may be necessary to investigate this area further so as to improve the care of lesbian mothers.

A detailed exploration of this issue by midwives would be beneficial on several levels. Not only would it help individual midwives to recognize their own prejudices where these exist and to make them visible and thus able to be eliminated (Walton, 1994), but it would also lead to a better understanding of the specific needs of this group of women (Salmon and Hall, 1999). Improved understanding might lead to greater levels of communication – a vital tool for the midwife who wishes to practise truly woman-centred midwifery. This might be important when providing intrapartum care to a woman and her partner. This is a sensitive time in pregnancy where the support of the partner is important and the couple become a family. Intimacy between heterosexual partners is understood and accommodated well by midwives. The same degree of intimacy, such as hand holding, kissing and stroking, is just as important for same-sex couples.

It is important for the profession to stand back and identify examples of heterosexism in documentation. For example, asking the sex of a woman's partner or asking if the woman is in a civil partnership provides opportunities for a woman to come out if she feels safe and comfortable doing so. If it is possible to reduce the heterosexist assumptions that are so heavily interwoven throughout the profession, then lesbian women may feel less marginalized and, consequently, 'safer' in midwifery and maternity care. This will, hopefully, help to enable lesbian women to trust their midwives and feel more able to talk freely and openly, thereby making their specific needs clear (Brogan, 1997).

Midwives in all aspects of maternity care are likely to come into contact with lesbian mothers at some time, although, as we have discussed, they may not be aware of this (Brogan, 1997). If midwives are to help prepare this group of women for parenthood, then they need to inform themselves of all the issues surrounding lesbian motherhood. Homosexuality and being lesbian have come to be identified with sex and specific sexual acts (Harding and Corbett, 1994). The over-sexualization of lesbian mothers is a barrier to good quality care and midwives need to be aware that what they are encountering is simply another form of family organization (Symonds and Hunt, 1996). The literature points to midwives and others denying the family unit in lesbian relationships, imposing rules which exclude a female partner such as fathers-only visiting times, and failing to acknowledge the role of the partner as co-parent (Salmon and Hall, 1999). There is also the difficulty that maternity care structures have in incorporating the parental triangle, where the mother, her partner and the biological father all take a parental role. Introducing flexible interpretations of parenthood and acknowledging that changing family structures include those of homosexual couple households could facilitate a change in the way that non-normative families are integrated into clinical settings. Inclusiveness is the key to ensuring that all women of all backgrounds have the childbearing experience that they deserve and to which they are entitled.

A literature review by James et al. (1994) identified both positive and negative aspects of health care from the point of view of lesbian and gay clients. One of the factors identified as helpful was the creation of an atmosphere which promotes not only tolerance, but also acceptance of diversity. In such an environment, the client feels able to discuss this or her sexuality without fear of rejection or abuse. Indeed, such an open attitude was identified with good quality care which is, after all, what we strive to deliver as a profession.

Conclusions

Lesbian pregnancy, birth and motherhood is very much an issue for midwives and will undoubtedly continue to be in the coming years. Lesbian women becoming mothers, particularly for the first time, have all the same needs as any other woman who enters the maternity care system. However, they will also have their own set of needs particular to sexual orientation and family circumstances.

Lesbian women deserve, and are entitled to, the same quality of care that every other woman receives. Sexual orientation has no bearing on pregnancy or the type of mother a woman will be. It is relevant to her midwifery care because it may result in particular needs and worries. The lesbian mother should not be defined in terms of sexuality and this aspect of her personal life should not be over-emphasized. As Wilton and Kaufmann (2001) put it:

'Assessing the degree to which services meet the needs of lesbians test flexibility, responsiveness and woman-centredness of service provision as a whole, and should be regarded as an indicator of professional development by reflexive midwifery practitioners.'

Until lesbian women feel truly individual and accepted, and are given appropriate and relevant care, then midwives will have failed to fulfil the obligation to be 'with the woman'.

References

Beresford S (1996) Femininity, sexuality and identity in law. In: T Cosslett, A Easton, P Summerfield (eds.) *Women, Power, Resistance: An Introduction to Women's Studies*. Open University Press, Buckingham.

Brogan M (1997) Healthcare for lesbians: Attitudes and experiences. *Nursing Standard* **11(45)**: 39–42.

Department of Health (1993) *Report of the Expert Maternity Group – Changing Childbirth Part 1*. HMSO, London.

Foster P (1995) *Women and the Healthcare Industry: An Unhealthy Relationship?* Open University Press, Buckingham.

Harding JT, Corbett I (1994) Biased care? *Nursing Times* **90(51)**: 28–31.

Kent J (2000) *Social Perspectives on Pregnancy and Childbirth for Midwives, Nurses and the Caring Professions*. Open University Press, Buckingham.

Kinsey A (1948) *Sexual Behaviour in the Human Male*. WB Saunders, Philadelphia.

Kinsey A (1953) *Sexual Behaviour in the Human Female*. WB Saunders, Philadelphia.

Nursing and Midwifery Council (2004a) *Standards for Midwifery Pre-registration Education*. Nursing and Midwifery Council, London.

Nursing and Midwifery Council (2004b) *Midwives Rules and Standards* Nursing and Midwifery Council, London.

Office for National Statistics (2001) *UK Census 2001*. Available from: http://www.statistics.gov.uk/census2001/census2001.asp [Accessed 13 October 2006].

Platzer H, James T (2000) Lesbians' experiences of healthcare. *NT Research* **5(3)**: 194–203.

Royal College of Midwives (2000) *Position Paper 22 Maternity Care for Lesbian Mothers*. Royal College of Midwives, London.

Saffron L (2001) Decision-making among lesbians wishing to get pregnant. *Journal of Fertility Counselling* **8(2)**: 31–6.

Salmon D, Hall C (1999) Working with lesbian mothers: Their healthcare experiences. *Community Practitioner* **27(12)**: 396–7.

Statutory Instrument (2003) *Instrument No. 1661 The Employment Equality (Sexual Orientation) Regulations 2003*. HMSO, London.

Symonds A, Hunt S (1996) *The Midwife and Society: Perspectives, Policies and Practice*. Macmillan, London.

Walton I (1994) *Sexuality and Motherhood*. Butterworth-Heinemann, Oxford.

Ward J, Winstanley D (2005) Coming out at work: Performativity and renegotiation of identity. *Sociological Review* **53(3)**: 447–75.

Wilton T, Kaufmann T (2001) Lesbian mothers' experiences of maternity care in the UK. *Midwifery* **17**: 203–11.

CHAPTER 7

Supporting mothers who choose to breastfeed

Cathie Melvin

The majority of women in the United Kingdom (69%) breastfeed their babies at birth (Hamlyn et al., 2002). However, by six weeks of age, the majority are being bottle fed (Hamlyn et al., 2002). The British Government wants more women to breastfeed (Department of Health, 2002), and supports the World Health Organization recommendation that those who do should breastfeed for at least six months (Department of Health, 2004). Midwives are well placed to help achieve this aim.

The needs of breastfeeding mothers change over time, and vary according to their level of knowledge and skill, and the level of support around them throughout the time they are breastfeeding. This chapter focuses on the needs of mothers who have chosen to breastfeed, and addresses some of the challenges for midwives in supporting them.

All breastfeeding mothers need to know how breastfeeding works, and they need to learn the practical skills of positioning and attachment and hand expression (Henderson et al., 2000; Renfrew et al., 2000; Ingram et al., 2002; Dykes, 2003). Jamieson (1990) reported on the effectiveness of antenatal breastfeeding workshops in improving breastfeeding outcomes at the International Confederation of Midwives' Congress in Japan. The study was replicated several years later in the maternity unit of a large teaching hospital in Tasmania (Cox and Turnbull, 1998a, b). Results showed that the midwives who attended the workshop perceived an increase in their confidence level in supporting mothers to breastfeed, and that the women who attended the workshops were more likely to breastfeed for longer even though they experienced difficulties.

The use of a doll and model breast (or balloon) when showing mothers how to breastfeed and establish lactation is advocated during the Baby Friendly Initiative's three-day breastfeeding management courses (UNICEF UK Baby Friendly Initiative, 2005). In practice, some midwives may find it difficult to dedicate sufficient time to teach these skills well. Whether this is because existing antenatal education programmes do not lend themselves to the workshop style approach, or because the postnatal care of mothers and babies is compromised by low levels of staffing, it is essential that attempts are made to overcome such challenges. Dykes (2003) called for organizations providing support for women to address the reported inabilities of health professionals to provide sufficient time to breastfeeding women. Dykes (2003) emphasized that mothers' expectations of support from midwives should be met. For some midwives, acquisition of the necessary expertise through professional training may be required. Enlisting the support of student midwives, support staff, service users and health visitor colleagues, who may have undergone a programme of training in breastfeeding management (with the Association of Breastfeeding Mothers, Baby Friendly Initiative, Breastfeeding Network, La Leche League International, or National Childbirth Trust) may also be helpful.

Supporting breastfeeding mothers to avoid formula supplements, associated with early cessation of breastfeeding (Hamlyn et al., 2002), is a significant challenge, considering 28% of all breastfed infants are given formula while in hospital (Hamlyn et al., 2002). Many mothers seem to lack confidence in their ability, or their baby's ability, to breastfeed, and consequently, the typically frequent and irregular feeding patterns of breastfed newborns leads them to believe that their babies are not getting enough milk.

A longitudinal, phenomenological study by Dykes and Williams (1999) found that seven out of 10 primiparous breastfeeding mothers, interviewed at 6, 12 and 18 weeks after their baby's birth, became progressively less confident about breastfeeding, with six of them expressing concern that their breast milk was inadequate.

Unfortunately, it seems that it is not only mothers who question their ability to produce enough milk. Some health professionals do too. Midwives need to become more skilled in identifying and supporting those mothers and babies who have simply got off to a slow start and are experiencing a delay in establishing lactation, and those who are having pathophysiological, sociological and/or psychological difficulties. Commonly, mothers who have experienced long labours or operative deliveries, often followed by reduced maternal mobility, increased pain and tiredness, also experience a delay in establishing lactation (Dewey et al., 2003).

Those caring for these mothers need to adopt a consistent approach to breastfeeding management which enhances the mother's independence and confidence, in other words, enables the mother to do things for herself (hands off), while ensuring that unrestricted feeding is not freely practised until the basic skills of positioning and attachment have been acquired by the mother.

A non-randomized prospective cohort phased intervention study (Ingram et al., 2002) during which mothers were taught good breastfeeding technique by midwives in a 'hands off' style, which enabled mothers to position and attach their babies for themselves, concluded that breastfeeding rates increased and the incidence of perceived milk insufficiency decreased as a result. Having supportive health professionals who encouraged breastfeeding was also associated with successful breastfeeding.

An ethnographic exploration of the beliefs, expectations and experiences of breastfeeding mothers and health professionals in relation to the supplementation of babies in hospital (Cloherty et al., 2004), identified that many midwives felt they had a duty to protect new mothers from tiredness, distress and guilt. The study recognized the conflict that sometimes exists for midwives between wanting to alleviate a mother's immediate distress by resorting to supplements, and wanting to promote and facilitate effective breastfeeding by providing information on how breastfeeding works and offering help with positioning and attachment. Few of the staff participating in the study seemed aware that supplementation was associated with early cessation of breastfeeding, and only a minority of mothers seemed to be aware of the adverse effects of supplementing on their milk supply and on their chances of continuing to breastfeed successfully (Cloherty et al., 2004). Dykes (2003), in her evaluation of this study along with 78 other breastfeeding projects, suggested that reflective practice and related education could be used to ensure that midwives are supported in taking a longer term view.

Another particularly challenging aspect of providing breastfeeding support can arise for midwives when they themselves feel undermined by other midwifery or medical colleagues, or indeed, when they witness a breastfeeding mother being undermined. However, it is important to remain focused on providing skilled support to the mother, and to avoid being openly critical of others, as this may merely exacerbate feelings of doubt and inadequacy in an already vulnerable mother. At the same time, it is essential that practices detrimental to breastfeeding are addressed, and it goes without saying, that this is best done sensitively, and in a constructive and non-threatening manner.

Welford (1995) suggests that midwives' attitudes to breastfeeding are as varied as those of the rest of the population. The opportunity to review their own experiences of breastfeeding or of supporting mothers to breastfeed (good and bad) may be particularly valuable, especially when it comes to supporting women who are experiencing difficulties in establishing or maintaining lactation. Sue Battersby's (1999) two-stage descriptive, exploratory study of midwives' attitudes towards breastfeeding, derived from personal, educational and professional experiences of breastfeeding, and the role of midwifery education in promoting more positive attitudes, revealed evidence of suboptimal practices, and led her to recommend the inclusion of debriefing of midwives' own personal experiences of and attitudes towards breastfeeding within basic midwifery education, as well as mandatory breastfeeding updates for all qualified midwives.

In summary, the midwife's role in helping more mothers to breastfeed for at least six months, includes:

- Teaching optimal positioning and attachment for breastfeeding and hand expression techniques.
- Explaining to mothers the full implications of giving formula supplements to breastfed babies.
- Addressing sub-optimal breastfeeding practices among colleagues.
- Focusing support on women who are more likely to experience breastfeeding difficulties, early on.

It is essential that organizations support their midwives in achieving these goals, and that, where possible, midwives take the opportunity to reflect on their own experiences of and attitudes towards breastfeeding.

References

Battersby S (1999) Midwives' experiences of breastfeeding: Can the attitudes developed affect how midwives support and promote breastfeeding? *Proceedings of the 25th Triennial Congress of the International Confederation of Midwives*. Manila, Philippines.

Cloherty M, Alexander J, Holloway I (2004) Supplementing breast-fed babies in the UK to protect their mothers from tiredness or distress. *Midwifery* **20(2)**: 194–204.

Cox SG, Turnbull CJ (1998a) Developing effective interactions to improve breastfeeding outcomes. Part 1: Moving midwives towards mothers' autonomy in breastfeeding. *Breastfeeding Review* **6(2)**: 11–16.

Cox SG, Turnbull CJ (1998b) Developing effective interactions to improve breastfeeding outcomes. Part 2: Antenatal empowerment of mothers for postnatal success in breastfeeding. *Breastfeeding Review* **6(2)**: 17–22.

Department of Health (2002) *Improvement, Expansion and Reform – The Next 3 years: Priorities and Planning Framework 2003–2006*. HMSO, London.

Department of Health (2004) *Breastfeeding* (leaflet 31636). HMSO, London.

Dewey KG, Nommsen-Rivers LA, Heinig MJ, Cohen RJ (2003) Risk factors for suboptimal infant breastfeeding behavior, delayed onset of lactation, and excess neonatal weight loss. *Pediatrics* **112(3)**: 607–19.

Dykes F (2003) *Infant Feeding Initiative. A Report Evaluating the Breastfeeding Practice Projects 1999–2002*. Department of Health, London.

Dykes F, Williams C (1999) Falling by the wayside: A phenomenological exploration of perceived breast milk inadequacy in lactating women. *Midwifery* **15(4)**: 232–46.

Hamlyn B, Brooker S, Oleinilova K (2002) *Infant Feeding*. The Stationery Office, London.

Henderson AM, Pincombe J, Stamp GE (2000) Assisting women to establish breastfeeding: Exploring midwives practices. *Breastfeeding Review* 8(3): 11–17.

Ingram J, Johnson D, Greenwood R.(2002) Breastfeeding in Bristol: Teaching good positioning and support from fathers and families. *Midwifery* 18(2): 87–101.

Jamieson L (1990) Breastfeeding knowledge and skills shared in a midwife– mother partnership. A midwife's gift: Love, skill and knowledge. *Proceedings of the International Confederation of Midwives Congress 1990*. Kobe, Japan.

Renfrew M, Woolridge MW, McGill HR (2000) *Enabling Women to Breastfeed. A Review of Practices which Promote or Inhibit Breastfeeding – With Evidence-Based Guidance for Practice*. HMSO, London.

UNICEF UK Baby Friendly Initiative (2005) *Breastfeeding Management: A Modular Course*. UNICEF UK, London.

Welford H (1995) Breastfeeding: Promoting good practices. *Modern Midwife* 5(11) 29–30.

CHAPTER 8

Exploring the cost-effectiveness of a breastfeeding peer support programme

Sue Battersby, Kay Bennett and Karen Sabin

Introduction

Although many breastfeeding peer support projects have been initiated, evaluating their cost-effectiveness is difficult due to a paucity of data and relevant literature. However, from a review of the limited data it can be shown that breastfeeding peer support programmes can, by increasing the number of babies who are breastfed, make significant savings to the National Health Service (NHS). Other areas that could offer long-term savings to the NHS, but have not been fully analysed, include potential reductions in pre-menopausal cancers in mothers who have breastfed and reductions in childhood obesity, urinary tract infections and necrotizing enterocolitis (Pisacane et al., 1992; Department of Health, 1995; Von Kries et al., 1999; Weimer, 2001). Consideration of the value-added benefits that peer support workers offer to mothers and the community highlights the special value of breastfeeding peer support programmes and their role in meeting the five key outcomes presented in the Every Child Matters initiative (Department for Education and Skills, 2004).

Breastfeeding offers benefits to both mother and infant, yet the number of women breastfeeding in the United Kingdom (UK) remains low compared to many European countries at around 76%, with women in social class V (manual occupations) and those who have never worked having the lowest uptake rates at 65%, while social class I (managerial/professional) have the highest uptake at 88% (Bolling, 2006). The health benefits of breastfeeding are widely recognized and include reduced gastroenteritis, reduced respiratory tract, ear and urinary tract infections, and reduced susceptibility to diabetes. It also potentiates vaccination and immunity and reduces contamination of feeds and over/underfeeding for the baby (Heinig and Dewey, 1996). For the mother there is a reduced risk of pre-menopausal cancers of the breast, endometrium and ovaries (Heinig and Dewey, 1997). Other intangible benefits are emotional development and bonding.

The breastfeeding initiation rate increased between 2000 and 2005 with the greatest increase (13%) being among women who have never worked (Bolling,

2006). Various strategies have been implemented over the past five years to try and increase both the uptake and duration of breastfeeding, especially in socially and economically deprived areas where breastfeeding rates tend to be lower than the national average (Dykes, 2003). Breastfeeding peer support programmes are one such strategy. They offer the opportunity of contact over time with a woman who has successfully breastfed. These experienced and/or trained peers have been shown to increase the numbers of women breastfeeding (National Health Service, 2000).

The Breastfeeding is Best Supporters (BIBS) project is a breastfeeding peer support initiative that was funded by Single Regeneration Budget 5 (SRB5) monies, a fund administered by the Department of the Environment, Transport and the Regions, to take forward the work of two (amalgamated) breastfeeding peer support projects in North Sheffield. Two midwives run the project and supervise seven paid peer support workers and 27 volunteers. The project has now completed its fifth year.

Despite the wealth of research related to the benefits of breastfeeding, there is limited information on the cost-effectiveness of interventions to promote initiation of breastfeeding (O'Meara et al., 2000).

The aim of this chapter was to explore whether paid peer support workers were a cost-effective means to promote breastfeeding in a socio-deprived area. The stimulus and opportunity for this arose in the context of an evaluation of breastfeeding peer support work in the Sure Start Foxhill and Parson Cross Programme in Sheffield (Battersby, 2002).

It quickly became apparent, however, that due to limited data locally, nationally and internationally, and also the paucity of literature, a comprehensive assessment of the cost-effectiveness of breastfeeding was not feasible. Therefore within this chapter the limited literature available on the cost-effectiveness of breastfeeding has been considered and areas that have not been analysed, but that would provide added cost-effectiveness to breastfeeding, have been highlighted. Finally, the value-added benefits of peer support workers are explored.

Review of the cost-effectiveness of breastfeeding

The evaluation of the BIBS project identified that there had been an increase in the initiation rate of breastfeeding in the Sure Start Foxhill and Parson Cross area (one of the most deprived areas in the north of Sheffield) since the onset of a three-year breastfeeding peer support initiative to encourage local women to start and sustain natural feeding methods. This was achieved by the provision of high quality and consistent information-giving and peer support, the development of support networks and the creation or new role models for breastfeeding mothers. The initiation rate rose from the last recorded figures in

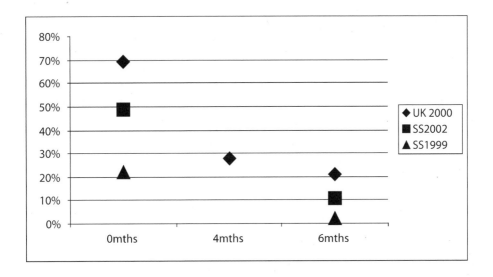

Figure 8.1: BIBS project closing the gap. Breastfeeding rates in the UK (Hamlyn et al., 2000) and in Foxhill and Parson Cross Sure Start 1999 and 2002.

1999 of 22% to 49% in 2002 when 103 babies, out of 210 births between April 2001 and March 2002, initiated breastfeeding (see *Figure 8.1*).Therefore 57 extra babies were breastfed in 2002 compared to 1999.

It has been calculated that in the first year of a baby's life, as a result of breastfeeding, the reduced incidence of gastroenteritis and admission to hospital alone produces financial gains to the NHS of £4000 per average health district for every 1% increase in breastfeeding (Department of Health, 1995). When calculating the health gains to the NHS within the Sure Start area it is necessary to calculate the saving per baby within the Sheffield area. In Sheffield, there are 7000 births per year (personal communication, Royal Hallamshire Hospital, Jessop Wing), therefore a 1% increase represents approximately 70 extra babies initiated; a saving of £57.10 saving per baby per year. There were 57 extra women who breastfed in the Sure Start area alone in one year with an expected saving to the NHS of £3254.7 (see *Table 8.1*).

However, when three illnesses are considered – gastroenteritis, respiratory infections and otitis media – Ball and Wright (1999) estimated that the cost of not being breastfed was £206–£296 per infant in the first year of life. When considering the Sure Start data, 57 extra babies were breastfed in the area which would give an expected average yearly saving of £11,742–£16,872 (see *Table 8.1*). This sum is roughly equal to the cost of the BIBS scheme.

The frequency of childhood insulin-dependent diabetes has significantly increased over the past years and Vaarala et al. (1998) identified a link between babies fed cow's milk formula and an increased risk of insulin-dependent

Table 8.1. Summary of the cost benefits of breastfeeding in the Sure Start area			
Study	Diseases	Estimated savings to NHS (per annum)	
		For all babies breastfed in Sure Start *n* = 103	For extra babies breastfed in Sure Start *n* = 57
Department of Health (1995)	Gastroenteritis	£5881.30	£3254.70
Ball and Wright (1999)	Gastroenteritis Respiratory infections Otitis media	£21,218–£30,488	£11,742–£16,872

diabetes. Consequently, there would be a further saving of approximately £10 to the NHS for every extra breastfeeding mother as a result of reductions in child onset diabetes mellitus. These savings however, lie in the future and are spread over many years of treatment of the condition (Department of Health, 1995).

Other areas of cost-effectiveness

Other areas that have not been analysed but would give added cost-effectiveness to breastfeeding include potential reductions in pre-menopausal cancers of the breast, ovaries and endometrium in mothers who have breastfed (Department of Health, 1995). The same would apply to the potential reduction in childhood obesity and urinary tract infections (Pisacane et al., 1992; Von Kries et al., 1999) as well as benefits for pre-term babies where breastfeeding promotes optimal neurological development and reduces the risk of necrotizing enterocolitis (Lucas and Cole, 1990; Lucas et al., 1992). These are not immediate savings but rather long-term savings, with the costs associated with treatment, surgery and care not being apparent until well after the initial breastfeeding episode.

Weimer (2001) analysed the cost-effectiveness of breastfeeding related to necrotizing enterocolitis (NEC) in the USA and deduced that the national savings from increased breastfeeding would be a minimum of £60,500,000. NEC is the pre-eminent gastrointestinal tract disease encountered in the neonatal intensive care unit. It is an important cause of neonatal deaths and 90% of cases affect premature babies. The incidence of NEC is 1% in exclusively breastfed premature low-birth weight babies compared to 7% in formula-fed premature low-birth weight babies. In the UK 7% of babies born fall into the low-birth weight category and in areas of social deprivation the level is even higher (Chapple, 2000). Although a direct comparison cannot be made with Weiner's (2001) study it is possible to surmize that similar substantial savings could be made to the NHS in the reduced incidence of NEC if more pre-term infants were exclusively breastfed.

It has been estimated that a 10–15% increase in breastfeeding throughout the whole of the UK could save the average health authority a total of £31,100 a year – £10,000 for averting two cases of insulin-dependent diabetes, £20,000 for averting four cases of neonatal necrotizing entercolitis and £1100 for averting three cases of pre-menopausal breast cancer (Woolridge, 1995).

As well as cost-savings to the NHS, there would be additional benefits from increased breastfeeding. These would include improved quality of life and increased life expectancy that would result from the reduction of illnesses and diseases. These would be particularly relevant when considering pre-menopausal cancers, and ill health and cardiac disease due to obesity.

The value-added benefits of the BIBS peer support workers

Alongside the cost-effectiveness and the health gains of breastfeeding there are many other value-added benefits of breastfeeding peer support workers within the BIBS project. This chapter demonstrates the value-added benefits gained over five years of the BIBS project using the five key outcomes from the Every Child Matters initiative (Department for Education and Skills, 2004). The key outcomes are:

- Improving health.
- Staying safe.
- Achieving economic well-being.
- Enjoying and achieving.
- Making a positive contribution.

Improving health

Health is the first key outcome and this has been achieved by the peer support workers promoting and supporting breastfeeding in the local community in order to enhance children's health, growth, development and emotional start in life. By achieving an increase in breastfeeding rates from 22% to 49% many infants and their mothers have been ensured of optimum health benefits.

Since the initial evaluation of the BIBS project the breastfeeding rate has fluctuated but has been sustained at around 46–49% although the true rate is difficult to assess because the project works across two Sure Start areas and has supported mothers out of area as far away as Australia, London, Scotland, Barnsley and as well as other areas in Sheffield.

Within the project area approximately 1500 mothers and their families have been informed about breastfeeding and supported across the Southey and Owlerton electoral ward in Sheffield, while 115 mothers have completed the La Leche League Breastfeeding Peer Counsellor Programme (LLLPCP) which is run by peer support workers and midwives. There were 62 mothers who breastfed during their training and 59 of those breastfed for over 6 months; 45 of them continued to breastfeed for over 12 months.

Staying safe

The second outcome, staying safe, was achieved by ensuring all families are secure, stable and cared for and safe from harm, bullying, prejudice and discrimination. As a direct result of the breastfeeding training 19 families received family support and 30 others completed the foundation Safeguarding Children course. All those who completed the peer support training (LLPCP) received information on confidentiality and awareness of safeguarding children and themselves.

Achieving economic well-being

Economic well-being was achieved by facilitating the women to engage in further education, employment or training, in order to support them to live in a sustainable community.

The BIBS project employs local people, thus generating an income into the community of £16,972 per year (which is the total salaries of the peer supporters for the year). The women who are employed have had their personal development enhanced with increases in self-esteem. Many of the peer supporters had never worked previously.

There have been 13 breastfeeding support workers who have either undergone or who are undergoing further education in health and social care working towards career changes, and all parents are supported in applying for training and employment. There are also many training opportunities within Sure Start including food hygiene, resuscitation and first aid, basic skills, and personal development and self-esteem training.

Mothers have also been encouraged by the peer support workers to access other Sure Start programmes which include La Leche League breastfeeding peer support training, child protection training, the parenting programme, self-defence training, community development training and cookery classes.

Enjoying and achieving

The fourth outcome has been achieved by enabling women and their families to achieve personal and social development and ensure that the children receive excellent child care in order for them to be ready for nursery and school.

As previously stated, 115 mothers have completed La Leche League training and this has resulted in mothers and their families increasing their self-esteem and confidence while making many long and lasting friendships.

Mother-to-mother support has led to a strong community network of breastfeeding mothers, and breastfeeding support groups have been developed, implemented and evaluated in the community. They provide an opportunity for mothers to talk about their experiences in a safe, welcoming, non-judgemental and safe place that is easily accessible.

Making a positive contribution

This final outcome has been achieved as a result of influencing and changing working practices for the benefit of the local community to elicit long-term cultural change in order that breastfeeding becomes the feeding method of choice. The peer support workers have undertaken a variety of voluntary activities out of hours and they act as role models within the community.

They are involved in other culturally-sensitive health-related areas, such as home safety, smoking, signposting, baby massage, nutrition and healthy lifestyles (e.g. advice on exercise is readily accepted by the local people when given by peer support workers) and advances have been made in these areas.

The peer support workers and volunteers have actively promoted breastfeeding within the community and the wider area by visiting and talking to children in nurseries and schools, speaking at conferences, both locally and nationally, and promoting the project at various health-related events. They have developed breastfeeding awareness-raising sessions for women, their partners and their extended families and also health professionals.

They have become advocates in the community to protect breastfeeding by lobbying both locally and nationally on breastfeeding issues, by raising awareness regarding breaking of the International Code of Marketing of Breast-Milk Substitutes (World Health Organization, 1981) to health professionals and others and by actively boycotting companies who break the code.

The peer support workers offer social support as well as breastfeeding support to mothers. They offer transport to mothers to enable access to support groups and help complete documentation (e.g. benefit forms, job applications, etc.). Social outings have been organized through breastfeeding support groups and have included both daytime and evening events. With assistance from the peer support workers mothers with older babies acquired funding and developed their own mother and toddler group.

The provision of social support in pregnancy has recognized benefits beyond increasing breastfeeding initiation rates. Oakley et al. (1990) found, in their randomized controlled trial, that when additional social support was given to mothers during in the antenatal period, this resulted in a reduction in low weight babies, an increase in spontaneous vaginal deliveries, and higher birth weight for term babies. They also found that, following birth, babies were healthier in the early weeks and needed less medical care (Oakley et al., 1990). The follow on study by Oakley et al. (1996) demonstrated seven years later that those who had been in the intervention group and had received extra social support were still reaping the benefits. Children suffered fewer serious accidents and increased sociability, while mothers were less anxious and had better relationships with their children.

The support of breastfeeding mothers takes time and many health professionals appreciate and value the assistance that is provided by the peer supporters (Battersby, 2002). An important aspect of the project has been that peer support workers offer a specific service to breastfeeding mothers, which is in addition to the support offered by health professionals.

Discussion

Although a comprehensive analysis of the cost-effectiveness of breastfeeding was not feasible, it can be seen from the review of the limited sources of data that savings to the NHS do result from an increase in the breastfeeding initiation rate. The reduction of gastroenteritis, respiratory infections and otitis media alone could actuate a cost saving of up to £16,872 per annum within Sure Start Foxhill and Parson Cross. This is approximately the cost of providing the peer support workers and therefore the service could be viewed as being self-funding.

There are other health benefits and health gains of breastfeeding that require further analysis. Without these data it is difficult to calculate the total cost-effectiveness of the project. Attempting to work out the cost-effectiveness without the data will result in unbalanced and inaccurate reports that may undermine or prevent the development of similar projects. This is an issue that needs to be addressed at a national level.

Taking a societal perspective highlights the extra value of a project such as the BIBS project, as the costs should be offset by the income and regeneration benefits to a deprived community. As the peer support workers in the BIBS project are selected from the local community, their salaries are added income to that community.

The added benefits of social support provided by the peer support workers cannot be underestimated in terms of reduction in low birth weight babies and the enhanced mother–child relationship, which could result in fewer childhood injuries and better socialization skills (Oakley et al., 1996).

The role of the peer support workers can also assist in achieving the five key outcomes laid down in the Every Child Matters initiative (Department for Education and Skills, 2004). Although their key role is to promote and support breastfeeding they can also influence many other areas. It can be seen through this discussion that support workers enrich the community, maximize opportunities and help to minimize risk.

Conclusion

Breastfeeding peer support programmes offer much more to a community than is measurable in terms of money.

With the limited data available, it can be demonstrated that the financial saving made to the NHS, by increasing the number of babies who are breastfed, is significant. These savings alone equate roughly to the costs of the intervention, which is employing the peer support workers. There are however, many other health benefits that cannot, with our present state of knowledge, be accurately costed.

This chapter has considered the many value-added benefits that peer support workers offer to both mothers and the community. It is these benefits in areas of socio-economic deprivation that give peer support projects special value.

In conclusion the BIBS project is certainly 'paying for itself' through calculable health savings but apart from these financial benefits it is also socially beneficial to the project area. Importantly it is assisting in achieving the key outcomes outlined in Every Child Matters.

References

Ball TM, Wright AL (1999) Health care costs of formula feeding in the first year of life. *Pediatrics* **103**: 870–6.

Battersby S (2002) *BIBS: An Evaluation of the Merged Breastfeeding Support Programmes. Foxhill and Parson Cross Sure Start.* Available from: http://www.sheffield.ac.uk/surestart [Accessed 11 October 2006].

Bolling K (2006) *Infant Feeding Survey 2005: Early Results.* Available from: http://www.ic.nhs.uk/pubs/breastfeed2005 [Accessed 23 August 2006].

Chapple J (2000) A public health view of maternity services. In: LA Page (ed.) *The New Midwifery: Science and Sensitivity in Practice.* Churchill Livingstone, Edinburgh: 141–53.

Department for Education and Skills (2004) *Every Child Matters: Change for Children.* DFES Publications, Nottingham. Available at: www.everychildmatters.gov.uk [Accessed 23 August 2006].

Department of Health (1995) *Breastfeeding: Good Practice Guidance to the NHS.* Department of Health, London.

Dykes F (2003). *Infant Feeding Initiative: A report Evaluating the Breastfeeding Practice Projects 1999-2002*. Department of Health, London.

Hamlyn B, Brooker S et al. (2002) *Infant Feeding 2000*. The Stationery Office, London.

Heinig MJ, Dewey KG (1996) Health advantages of breastfeeding for infants: A critical review. *Nutrition Research Reviews* **9**: 89–110.

Heinig MJ, Dewey KG (1997) Health effects of breastfeeding for mothers: A critical review. *Nutrition Research Reviews* **10**: 35–56.

Lucus A, Cole TJ (1990). Breast milk and neonatal necrotizing enterocolitis. *Lancet* **336**: 1519–22.

Lucas A, Morley R, Cole TJ, Lister G, Leeson-Payne C (1992) Breastmilk and subsequent intelligence quotient in children born pre-term. *Lancet* **339**: 261–4.

Oakley A, Hickey O, Rajan L, Hickey A (1996) Social support in pregnancy: Does it have long-term effects? *J Reprod Infant Psychol* **14**: 7–22.

Oakley A, Rajan L, Grant A (1990) Social support and pregnancy outcome: Report of a randomised controlled trial. *Br J Obstet Gynaec* **97**: 152–62.

O'Meara S, Sowden A, Richardson R (2000) Promoting the initiation of breastfeeding. *Effective Health Care* **6(2)**: 1–12.

Pisacane A, Graziano L, Zona G (1992) Breastfeeding and urinary tract infection. *J Pediatr* **120**: 87–9.

Vaarala O, Paronen J, Otonkoski T, et al. (1998) Cow milk feeding induces antibodies to insulin in children: A link between cow milk and insulin-dependent diabetes mellitus? *Scan J Immunol* **47**: 131–5.

Von Kries R, Kioletzko B, Sauerwald T, et al. (1999) Breastfeeding and obesity: Cross-sectional study. *Br Med J* **319**: 149–500.

Weimer J (2001) *The Economic Benefits of Breastfeeding: A Review and Analysis. Food Assistance and Nutrition Research Report No. 13.* Food and Rural Economic Division, Economic Research Service, US Department of Agriculture, Washington, DC.

World Health Organization (1981) *International Code for Marketing of Breast-Milk Substitutes*. World Health Organization, Geneva.

Woolridge M (1995) Calculating the Benefits of Breastfeeding for Purchasers and Providers of Health Care. Internal document produced for UNICEF UK's Baby Friendly Initiative. The UK Committee for UNICEF Baby Friendly Initiative, London. In: Royal College of Midwives (2002) *Successful Breastfeeding* (3rd edn.) Churchill Livingstone, Edinburgh.

CHAPTER 9

Breastfeeding, co-sleeping and the prevention of SIDS

Denise Pemberton

Introduction

This chapter describes the changes made following the discovery that there was a conflict in information which was being given to parents on co-sleeping and sudden infant death syndrome (SIDS). Co-sleeping had been encouraged, in particular in the hospital setting, to promote and support breastfeeding. The data collated on SIDS from regular audit of causes of death in infancy indicated that many of these deaths had occurred in a bed. There is an exploration of the issue of 'informed choice' for parents, with particular regard to working within the UNICEF UK Baby Friendly Initiative best practice standards in the UK. It concludes with a resume of the latest national recommendations.

The issue of sudden infant death and co-sleeping became prominent within the local area, where health professionals attending breastfeeding study days stated that they had been informed, in supervision, that parents were to be told not to co-sleep with their baby. This was because in the local area the majority of the 42 babies who had died in the past 5 years and whose deaths had been attributed to cot death had been in bed with a parent or carer, rather than in a cot, according to local data collated by Smith (2002).The cultural change towards the promotion of breastfeeding through co-sleeping and the encouragement of skin-to-skin contact and the local recommendations on reducing sudden infant death syndrome created a conflict for practitioners.

These findings suggested that it may have been that parents were co-sleeping with their infant without being given adequate information about the risks. This highlighted an urgent need to examine local guidelines, practice, and information given to parents, to ensure that all practitioners were giving consistent information based on nationally recognized evidence.

Promotion of breastfeeding

UK breastfeeding rates are among the lowest in Europe. Initiation rates are around 70% (Hamlyn et al., 2002), an increase of approximately 2% over the past 5 years, and 27% of mothers are still breastfeeding when the baby is 4 months old, a figure that has remained relatively unchanged over the same period of time. This is despite evidence of the health benefits of continued breastfeeding (Wilson et al., 1998), and the World Health Organization (Butte et al., 2002) recommendation of exclusive breastfeeding for around the first 6 months of life, and continuing up to the age of 2 years or beyond.

Co-sleeping and the promotion of breastfeeding

Co-sleeping has been associated with continuation of breastfeeding (McKenna et al., 1997). While many parents may not intend to co-sleep with their babies, Ball et al. (1999) state that most parents do it, at least partially, particularly when breastfeeding possibly because of frequency of night-time feeds. However some writers comment that bed-sharing (co-sleeping) may be an element within breastfeeding promotion that is missing (Ball, 1999).

There is evidence that breastfeeding mothers naturally adapt the sleep environment to their baby, by adopting a characteristic position, lying laterally facing the baby, with the upper arm above the baby's head, and the knees drawn up under the baby's feet, forming a 'C' shape. This positioning appears to facilitate breastfeeding while also protecting the baby from being rolled onto or moving up or down the bed (Blair et al., 1999; Ball, 2001a). This position has not been observed in mothers who are feeding their babies with breastmilk substitutes or with fathers (Ball, 2001a).

Prevention of SIDS

Following the Department of Health's two pronged 'Back to Sleep', and 'Feet to Foot' campaign, in 1991, deaths from SIDS reduced by around 70% within a year of the campaign, from 2 per 1000 live births to 0.8 per 1000, as stated by the Foundation for the Study of Infant Deaths (FSID, 2002a).

This campaign highlighted the dangers of babies sleeping prone, and recommended that babies' bedding be placed at the foot of the cot to prevent the danger of slipping under the covers and the baby becoming overheated. During the period 1991–2000 the neonatal death rate at 3.8 per 1000 live births has continued to decline. Over the same period the post-neonatal death rate at 1.8 per 1000 live births, has been relatively unchanged (Confidential Enquiry into Stillbirths and Deaths in Infancy, 2000). However there are still seven babies dying in the UK every week from SIDS (FSID, 2002a), making SIDS the leading cause of death in babies from one month to one year of age.

The FSID recommends that a newborn baby sleeps in the same room as his or her parents for the first 6 months of life (FSID, 2002a). It recognizes that co-sleeping occurs in parents' own homes; while not advocating co-sleeping they only give advice against co-sleeping where it is contra-indicated. They do however advise against co-sleeping in hospital, because of the presence of hard floors, narrow beds and newly delivered mothers who are extremely tired and may have had sedation during labour (FSID, 2002b).

Hospitals have a role to play in the reduction of cot deaths. In hospitals cot-sides have been used to prevent babies falling out of bed. These are no longer recommended due to the risk of entrapment (Medical Devices Agency, 2000). There are other issues within hospitals: a recent survey conducted by FSID (2002b), found that the temperature in 97.6% of maternity units is too hot for full-term babies; and furthermore up to 10% of babies may not be placed routinely on their back to sleep (FSID, 2002c).

The Avon Study into Infant Mortality (Blair et al., 1999), which was a 3-year multi-centre study following the deaths of 325 babies and 1300 control infants and which formed the basis for the Confidential Enquiry into Stillbirths and Deaths in Infancy (CESDI) recommendations, found that babies appear to have succumbed to SIDS both when sleeping in a cot, and when co-sleeping. Often SIDS occurred when there was a change in the normal place of sleeping, which may indicate a change in the baby's behaviour. The study found that there was insufficient evidence to point to a protective effect against SIDS from breastfeeding (Blair et al., 1999).

Risk factors for SIDS

The risk factors for SIDS include parents who are extremely tired, have consumed alcohol or are taking medication (FSID, 2002a). Illness of either the mother or the baby and a baby who is small or was born preterm (Barker, 1993) are also included. Sofas and water-beds should be avoided when co-sleeping with infants because of the dangers of suffocation. Pillows should be kept to a minimum and sheets and blankets should be used instead of duvets to avoid overheating.

The room temperature should be maintained around 18°C and the temperature adjusted with changes of lightweight bedding (Department of Health, 2000a). Bedding should not cover the infant's head, wherever he or she is sleeping (FSID, 2002a).

Another significant risk factor is smoking. The babies of mothers who smoke during pregnancy are up to 15 times more likely to die from SIDS than babies of non-smoking mothers (FSID, 2002d); yet only 9% of women surveyed in 1998 by the Department of Health knew that smoking in pregnancy increased the risk of SIDS (FSID, 2002d). The CESDI Sudden Unexpected Deaths in Infancy (SUDI) studies (2000) found that babies who died were twice as likely to have been exposed to tobacco smoke, with the risk increasing with the number of hours of exposure.

Box 9.1. Factors to minimize risks when co-sleeping

- The mattress on the bed should be firm. Co-sleeping should never take place on a water-bed or sofa, or old sagging mattress
- Ensure that there are no gaps for the baby to become trapped in, and that the baby cannot roll or fall out of bed
- The room should be maintained at a comfortable temperature, around 18°C
- In order to prevent overheating sheets and blankets should be used instead of a duvet. Do not allow bedding to cover the baby's head
- The baby should not be overdressed, or swaddled. Care should be taken to ensure that the baby cannot become entangled in loose ties from nightwear
- Pillows should be kept well away from the baby
- The baby should never be left unattended in the bed
- If the partner is sharing the bed he/she should be aware that the baby is in the bed
- Pets should never be allowed to share the bed
- If other children are sharing the bed there should be an adult between them and the baby
- Bottle feeding mothers and partners should be informed of the protective C-shaped position for co-sleeping

Adapted from the UNICEF/FSID (2001) Sharing a Bed With Your Baby

---

When a baby dies from SIDS often there are other factors involved. Ball (2001b) states that: 'the most frequent "wild card" introducing risk into bed-sharing arrangements was ... paternal alcohol consumption'. Ball found that although mothers adapted their behaviour to the presence of the baby in the bed, the fathers were less likely to do so. This occurs more commonly among certain social groups. In her findings these were groups from social class III and IV, with little post-16 education and where the men were also heavy drinkers and whose partners were breastfeeding their first infants (Ball, 2001a). Ball also highlights that as the numbers of babies being breastfed increases in this section of the population, attention needs to be paid to the wider implications of these changes in infant care practices. This is particularly relevant because of the Government's aim to increase breastfeeding initiation rates by at least 2% per year, as set out by the Department of Health (2002), and in accordance with Government initiatives to reduce inequalities such as Sure Start (Timms, 2002). Attention needs to be paid to how to reach this target population with the safety campaign message, as any attempts at behavioural change in this group are least likely to be successful (Dunkley, 2000). There are several factors that can help to minimize co-sleeping risks (*Table 9.1*).

Cultural issues

Separation of mothers and infants is seen as the norm within our society (Rapley, 2002). There is an expectation that night-time feeds will decline following the first month (Ball, 1999) and, unless parents have incorporated bed-sharing into their night-time routine they often seek alternative solutions, such as giving breastmilk substitutes at night or early weaning onto solid food. Expectations are on mothers to 'return to normal' quickly, to rate themselves according to 'how good' their baby is, and how quickly he or she sleeps through the night. They may feel tired with night-time feeding, and guilty about taking the baby into bed, although there is evidence that shows that mothers who regularly co-sleep with their baby, sleep as well as, if not better than, their counterparts whose babies sleep in a cot (Blair et al., 1999).

The Baby Friendly Initiative

Implementation of the World Health Organization/United Nations International Children's Emergency Fund (WHO/UNICEF) Ten Steps to Successful Breastfeeding (UNICEF UK Baby Friendly Initiative, 2001) has led to a change in culture within many maternity units throughout the UK. This has been from one of separation to one of togetherness of mother and baby, as described by Rapley (2002). This is significant in the implementation of Step 4 – skin-to-skin contact and the initiation of breastfeeding. Skin-to-skin contact is useful for unsettled babies, and those who are slow to initiate feeding. It also helps to reduce supplementation of breastfed babies with breastmilk substitutes, as, if a baby can be settled close to his or her mother, they are both more rested and feeding is more likely to be facilitated (World Health Organization, 1998). Step 7 – rooming in – i.e. mothers and babies remaining together 24 hours a day has been cited as one of the factors in the increased incidence, and focus on co-sleeping (FSID, 2002b).

While being a focus for breastfeeding promotion the Baby Friendly Initiative has worked to develop clear guidance for health professionals on the issue of prevention of SIDS. A sample policy and an information leaflet for parents have been developed and are available on the Baby Friendly website. It is not necessary for mothers and infants to co-sleep for a health care facility to be awarded Baby Friendly Accreditation, and, where there is a policy on co-sleeping, the aim is to promote safe practice and informed choice for parents.

Informed choice

From an ethical perspective, the issues around informed choice are vital. All health professionals have a duty to act as an advocate for their client (Frith, 1996). Respect for the parents' right to make an informed choice, as outlined in

Table 9.1.The benefits of and contraindications to co-sleeping	
Benefits	Contraindications
Facilitates breastfeeding on demand	Either parent is a smoker
Promotes early feeding in babies who are reluctant to feed	Alcohol consumption
Skin-to-skin contact helps to settle an unsettled baby	Extremely and unusually tired for any reason
Reduces chance of supplementation with formula milk	Taking of any drug which could affect level of consciousness
Breastfeeding mothers lie in protective C-shape position	Illness of parent including diabetes with unstable blood glucose or epilepsy
Promotes prolonged and exclusive breastfeeding	Illness/pyrexia of baby
Frequently occurs when mother feeding her baby at night	A baby who was born pre-term or is small

the International Code of Ethics for Midwives (International Confederation of Midwives, 1999), is also important.

Parents are responsible for the decisions they make about the care of their baby (Nursing and Midwifery Council, 2002). They require full and clear information on the benefits and any potential risks in order to make informed decisions (Seedhouse, 2001). However some of the evidence is contradictory, so parents must be allowed to weigh up the available evidence. The benefits of and contraindications to co-sleeping are outlined in *Table 9.1*.

Sensationalist media headlines do nothing to assist parents in making an informed choice. There is a constant need to gain headlines and often the comments of the coroner are 'quoted' in media reports, without enough detail to portray a balanced picture. Parents are receiving the message that bed-sharing is dangerous but not receiving the safety information around the issue.

The media do have a role to play in informing the public of relevant health issues (Crafter, 1997), but they also have a responsibility not to scaremonger. Exposure in this way is unlikely to lead to any long-term changes in behaviour (Crafter, 1997), but it is likely to cause a great deal of anxiety.

The local picture

Health care professionals in the Nottingham area had been promoting breastfeeding through co-sleeping. This had been an effective strategy, however it also became clear that the majority of the 42 babies who died in the previous 5 years had had their deaths attributed to cot death. These infants had been in bed with a parent or carer, rather than in a cot (Smith, 2002). From these findings a multidisciplinary group was formed to review the evidence.

There had been a real focus on the initiation of and support of breastfeeding in the maternity units, and an acceptance of mothers and babies co-sleeping had developed. Staff were aware of many of the benefits of skin-to-skin contact for initiating feeding where babies are reluctant to feed (World Health Organization, 1998) and encouraged this. However there are also situations where co-sleeping is contraindicated (FSID, 2002a), such as in mothers who have had opiates in labour, or who have their mobility compromised due to an operative delivery or epidural anaesthesia. Babies of these mothers are often slow to initiate feeding. There were clear guidelines in place which outlined the benefits and contraindications. However, it became clear that these were not being followed. Parents were receiving the message that co-sleeping was supportive of breastfeeding but were not becoming aware of the potential hazards (Blair et al., 1999).

The multidisciplinary group which was convened consisted of medical staff involved with parents of SIDS babies, members of the Care of the Next Infant (CONI) Scheme, representatives from child protection, community and hospital midwives, infant feeding advisors, and health visitors. This was a sub-group of a cross-trust multidisciplinary forum, which focuses on feeding issues locally.

The evidence was reviewed and staff guidelines updated. By evaluating the evidence objectively the emphasis changed from being issue-based, i.e. promotion of breastfeeding versus prevention of SIDS, to become family and evidence-based as recognized by Frith (1996). Weaknesses in current practice were identified.

A parents' information leaflet based on that accessed at the UNICEF UK Baby Friendly website was developed. This was to provide full, evidence-based, clear information about the benefits of, and the contraindications to co-sleeping, in order to facilitate informed choice for parents (Nursing and Midwifery Council, 2002). Following discussion and agreement within the group, the documents were circulated to community and hospital staff, lay groups, the coroner and the local branch of FSID for comments.

The leaflet was produced in English initially as it was seen as imperative by the group to act as quickly as possible. However there was an awareness in the group of the need to translate it into other languages and to review and update the information regularly as new research was published, due to this being an ever-changing high profile issue.

Parents' leaflet and revised guideline

The launch of the leaflet and guideline was planned with local media coverage. This included newspaper, radio and television. The coroner attended the launch, and supported the initiative. The message was presented with demonstrations of mothers lying in the protective C-shape position, and with information about the situations where co-sleeping should be avoided.

The use of the media increased public awareness of the launch. Health professionals were careful to give a balanced message, which was portrayed recognizing that the media are keen to 'make headlines', thus avoiding oversimplification of the issues as described by Crafter (1997).

Evaluation

Following the launch the effectiveness of the exercise was evaluated. Early anecdotal information was positive. Both parents and staff received it well.

While using the media increased the impact of the launch it also increased staff accountability, due to public expectations. Efforts were made to ensure that all health professionals were aware of the campaign prior to the launch. Teaching on this issue was included in breastfeeding training, thus continuing to maintain the emphasis on the important health promotion message.

One impact of the intervention was the clarification of the issues around the contraindications to co-sleeping for staff. The debate continued around the issue, however there was strength in having developed the guideline as a multi-disciplinary working group, in that the guideline was agreed by staff from varying disciplines, not just one or two.

Over a period of time other issues arose, such as the impact of the maternity units' changeover to using electric beds, which impacted on the use of 'clip-on-cots', which have been shown by Ball (2006) to improve mother and baby interaction while in hospital without the dangers of bed-sharing previously mentioned.

As other research was published (Carpenter et al., 2004) or recommendations from the Royal College of Midwives (2004) and the UNICEF UK Baby Friendly Initiative (2004) came out the guidelines needed to be reviewed in the light of them.

Latest advice

The latest recommendations for the prevention of SIDS are that the safest place for a baby to sleep is in a cot by his or her parents' bed for the first 6 months of life (FSID, 2003). This has been incorporated into Department of Health Guidance and the National Institute for Health and Clinical Excellence (NICE) guideline for postnatal care. They recommend that while it is acceptable for babies to be fed or cuddled in the parental bed, they should be returned to the cot before the parent sleeps. They warn parents never to sleep with a baby on a sofa or in an armchair, and outline that babies are at an increased risk of SIDS especially if under 11 weeks of age and if either parent is a smoker, has drunk alcohol, has taken any medication to make them sleep more heavily or is very tired. They also state that if a baby has become accustomed to using a pacifier while sleeping, it should not be stopped suddenly during the first 26 weeks of life (NICE, 2006).

NICE also recommends that all health care providers ensure that an externally evaluated breastfeeding programme such as the UNICEF UK Baby Friendly Initiative is implemented and that women are involved in planning their care to meet their needs and the needs of their babies.

UNICEF UK warns against making general statements against bed-sharing. In recent recommendations backed by the Royal College of Midwives (2004) and jointly with the National Childbirth Trust (UNICEF, 2005) it recommends that an individual risk assessment by qualified staff should be made before bed-sharing. This needs regular reviewing, good record keeping and communication with other members of staff when handing over care.

They recommend antenatal and early postnatal discussion with all mothers of the benefits and contraindications to bed-sharing, including use of the UNICEF/FSID leaflet. They also recommend that discussion should include the use of bed-sharing as a care strategy for breastfeeding mothers, and the additional risk of accidents if a baby sleeps in an adult bed, coupled with support to avoid or minimize these risks (UNICEF, 2005).

UNICEF also recommends the development of local guidelines and that staff be given adequate training to enable them to facilitate parental informed choice.

Since the launch of the local leaflet the UNICEF Baby Friendly Initiative/ FSID *Sharing a Bed with your Baby* leaflet has twice been updated, the last time being rewritten specifically for breastfeeding mothers. This is available from the UNICEF UK Baby Friendly Initiative.

Conclusions

This is a complex issue. Both breastfeeding promotion and reducing inequalities in health (Department of Health, 2002) are Government initiatives. There is evidence for the benefits of prolonged breastfeeding, and co-sleeping often occurs with breastfeeding, particularly prolonged breastfeeding.

SIDS is a devastating event when it occurs within any family. There was a dramatic reduction in the number of cases of SIDS following the Department of Health Campaign in 1991, and the figures have remained at a similar level since that time. It may be that SIDS will never be completely eradicated, however it is important that there is no complacency in ensuring parents are given information regarding the safety of their infant.

With the emphasis on mother-and-baby togetherness of the UNICEF UK Baby Friendly Initiative's *Ten Steps to Successful Breastfeeding* the issue has gained a higher profile both nationally and locally. Guidance has been provided to make co-sleeping as safe as possible, in spite of the continuing conflict in the evidence. The UNICEF UK Baby Friendly Initiative has at its heart the ethos of informed choice.

As has been discussed, the issue has to be viewed within UK culture. It is important for health professionals to give clients information on the safety aspects around co-sleeping, in the context of the promotion of breastfeeding and the prevention of SIDS, and then to support them in their chosen way of feeding and caring for their baby.

The important messages are: that parents are aware that sleeping with their baby in the same room as them for the first six months of life is protective against SIDS; that parents are aware that sharing a sofa or armchair increases the risk of SIDS more than sharing a bed; that they are aware of issues like smoking, alcohol, medications and overtiredness which increase the risk of SIDS; and that they are given the safety messages of how to make the bed as safe as possible in case co-sleeping occurs, particularly if they are breastfeeding.

The health professionals involved in the local initiative worked together to produce evidence-based guidelines. The fact that health professionals within a local area, across all disciplines, agreed and are working to the same guideline, is worth celebrating, and should lead to consistent information to parents.

Acknowledgements

I would like to acknowledge the combined work of the Nottingham Infant Feeding Forum of which the working group was a sub-group. I particularly wish to thank Lindsay Cullen, Liz Shykles, Stephanie Smith and Julie Wright for their hard work, encouragement, comments and support.

References

Alma B, Norveniusa SG, Wennergrena G, Skjærvenb R, Øyenb N, Mileradc J, Wennborgc M, Kjaerbecka J, Helweg-Larsend K, Irgensb LM on behalf of the Nordic Epidemiological SIDS Study (2001) Changes in the epidemiology of sudden infant death syndrome in Sweden 1973–1996. *Arch Dis Child* **84**: 24-30.

Ball HL (1999) *Is Bed-Sharing a Missing Element in Breastfeeding Promotion?*

UNICEF UK Baby Friendly Initiative Conference 1999.

Ball HL (2001a) *Parent-Infant Behaviour During Bed-Sharing.* UNICEF UK Baby Friendly Initiative Conference 2001.

Ball HL (2001b) *The Benefits of Bed-Sharing for Breastfeeding Babies.* Trent Regional Breastfeeding Conference, Chesterfield Royal Hospital 2001.

Ball HL (2006) *Bed-Sharing, Breastfeeding and Parental Choice.* Primary Care 2006 Conference, National Exhibition Centre, Birmingham.

Ball HL, Hooker E, Kelly PJ (1999) Where will the baby sleep? Attitudes and practices of new and experienced parents regarding co-sleeping with their new-born infants. *Amer Anthropologist* **101(1)**: 143–51.

Barker W (1993) Small Infants should not sleep in their parents' bed. *Br Med J* **315**:17–20.

Blair PS, Fleming PJ. Smith IJ, Platt MW, Young J, Nadin P, Berry PJ, Golding J (1999) Babies sleeping with parents; case-control study of factors influencing the risk of sudden infant death syndrome. *Br Med J* **319**:1457–62.

Butte NF, Lopez-Alarcon MG, Cutberto G (2002) *Nutrient Adequacy of Exclusive Breastfeeding for Term Infants During the First Six Months of Life.* Geneva: World Health Organization.

Carpenter RG, Irgens LM, Blair PS, England PD, Fleming P, Huber J, Jorch G, Schreuder P (2004) Sudden unexplained infant death in 20 regions in Europe: Case control study. *Lancet* **363**: 185–91.

Cole N (2001) Coroner's warning reinforced by health chief "Babies safer in their cots". *Scunthorpe Telegraph* 27 March.

Confidential Enquiry into Stillbirths and Deaths in Infancy (2000) *Executive Summary of the 7th Annual Report.* Maternal and Child Health Consortium, London.

Crafter H (1997) *Health Promotion in Midwifery.* Arnold, London.

Department of Health (2000a) *Reduce the Risk of Cot Death.* HMSO, London..

Department of Health (2000b) *The Sudden Unexpected Deaths in Infancy. The CESDI /SUDI Studies.* HMSO, London.

Department of Health (2002) *Improvement, Expansion and Reform: The next 3 years. Priorities and Planning Framework 2003–2006. HMSO,* London.

Dunkley J (2000) *Health Promotion in Midwifery Practice – A Resource for Health Professionals.* Bailliere-Tindall, London.

Foundation for the Study of Infant Death (2002a) *What is Cot Death? Is Cot Death on the Decline?* Foundation for the Study of Infant Deaths, London. Available from: http://www.sids.org.uk/fsid/cot.htm [Accessed 11 October 2006].

Foundation for the Study of Infant Deaths (2002b) *Bed-Sharing – A Wonderful Experience or a Danger to Babies?* Newsletter 66. Foundation for the Study of Infant Deaths, London.

Foundation for the Study of Infant Deaths (2002c) *New Cartoon Sticker Makes Cot Death Advice Stick.* Foundation for the Study of Infant Deaths, London. Available from: http://www.sids.org.uk/fsid/cartoon.htm [Accessed 11 October, 2006].

Foundation for the Study of Infant Deaths (2002d) *Nicotine and Cot Death.* Statement from the Foundation for the Study of Infant Death on the use of nicotine gum/patches during pregnancy. Foundation for the Study of Infant Deaths, London. Available from: http://www.sids.org.uk/fsid/nicotine.htm [Accessed 11 October, 2006].

Foundation for the Study of Infant Deaths (2003) *BabyZone – How to Keep your Baby Safe and Healthy.* Foundation for the Study of Infant Deaths, London.

Frith L (1996) *Ethics and Midwifery.* Butterworth-Heinemann, Oxford.

Hamlyn B, Brooker S, Oleinkova K, Wands S (2002) *Infant Feeding Survey 2000.* The Stationary Office, London.

International Confederation of Midwives (1999) *International Code of Ethics for Midwives.* Council Meeting of International Confederation of Midwives, Manila.

McKenna JJ, Mosko SS, Richard CA (1997) Bedsharing promotes breastfeeding. *Pediatrics* **100(2)**: 214–19.

Medical Devices Agency (2000) *Bed Side Rails (Cotsides) – Risk of Entrapment and Asphyxiation.* Medical Devices Agency, London.

Nursing and Midwifery Council (2002) *Code of Professional Conduct.* Nursing and Midwifery Council, London.

Rapley G (2002) Keeping mothers and babies together – breastfeeding and bonding. *Midwives* **5(10)**: 332–4.

Royal College of Midwives (2004) *Position Statement No. 8 – Bed sharing and Co-sleeping.* Royal College of Midwives, London.

Seedhouse D (2001) *Health: The Foundations for Achievement.* Wiley, Chichester: 124.

Smith S (2002) *East Midlands Today Programme BBC TV*, 2 December.

Timms M (2002) What are Osmaston and Allenton Surestart doing towards community-based breastfeeding support? A midwife's story. *MIDIRS Midwifery Digest* **12(2):** 278–9.

UNICEF UK Baby Friendly Initiative (2001) *Implementing the Baby Friendly Best Practice Standards.* UK Baby Friendly Initiative, London.

UNICEF UK Baby Friendly Initiative (2004) *Statement on Mother-Infant Bed Sharing*. UK Baby Friendly Initiative, London.

UNICEF UK Baby Friendly Initiative (2005) *UNICEF and NCT Joint Statement on mother–Infant Bed Sharing* UNICEF UK Baby Friendly Initiative. Available from: http://www.babyfriendly.org.uk/press. asp#20050928 [Accessed 11 October, 2006].

Wilson AC, Forsyth JS, Greene SA, Irvine L, Hau C, Howie PW (1998) Relation of infant diet to childhood health: Seven year follow-up of cohort of children in Dundee infant feeding study. *Br Med J* **316**: 21–5.

World Health Organization (1998) *Evidence for the Ten Steps to Successful Breastfeeding*. Family and Reproductive Health, Division of Child Development, World Health Organization, Geneva.

CHAPTER 10

Supporting infant feeding in the Bangladeshi community

Debbie Singh

Midwives are striving to help families initiate and maintain breastfeeding, in line with Department of Health and World Health Organization guidance. All families have unique issues and need individualized care, but some communities have specific needs and values of which midwives should be aware. This chapter focuses on Bangladeshi families living in England as a case study to illustrate the importance of adapting our support to meet the wide-ranging needs of our local communities.

Why focus on Bangladeshi women?

Since the 1920s, there has been a steady increase in the number of Bangladeshi families living in the UK. It is estimated that more than 280,000 Bangladeshi people now live in the UK, with the majority based in London (Office for National Statistics, 2001).

Three-quarters of Bangladeshi households have at least one child. Nationwide surveys suggest that eight out of 10 Bangladeshi people live in households with incomes below half the national average. Seven out of 10 Bangladeshi children live in households below the poverty line compared with three out of 10 other children. Bangladeshi families also have much lower levels of health compared to White families and those from Indian, African, and Chinese backgrounds (Berthoud, 1998).

A Department of Health survey found that, of mothers who started to breastfeed in England, Bangladeshi and Pakistani mothers stopped breastfeeding sooner than White or Indian mothers (Thomas, 1997). At four months, 25% of Bangladeshi mothers who had started breastfeeding were still breastfeeding compared to 39% of White mothers. There is also evidence that Bangladeshi babies in the UK are more likely than others to be underweight (Karim and Mascie-Taylor, 2001) and have low iron levels (Lawson et al., 1998).

Overall, the picture that emerges is that Bangladeshi families often live in areas of high deprivation; they may have issues with maintaining breastfeeding and introducing solid foods; and these families may have different cultural and language needs regarding the support they receive from midwives. Therefore, we wanted to find out Bangladeshi women's views about breastfeeding and introducing solid foods, to help midwives and other professionals provide the most effective support.

In 2006, in conjunction with Camden Primary Care Trust, London, we conducted a systematic review of published literature and held discussion groups and interviews with 323 Bangladeshi mothers and 99 community workers, health care professionals and social care staff. We also surveyed strategic health authorities in England to explore what issues impact on how Bangladeshi families feed their babies and what support they need with infant feeding.

We are not suggesting that Bangladeshi families have needs that are any more 'special' or serious than other groups, but rather, we are using the feedback from Bangladeshi women to illustrate how important it is for midwives to consider the individual needs of each family they work with, and to acknowledge that each family may have different needs.

What issues do Bangladeshi women face?

We systematically reviewed published literature to examine what is already known about infant feeding among Bangladeshi families. Our review found that while Bangladeshi women in the UK often initiate breastfeeding, they may not maintain exclusive breastfeeding for long. Mixed formula feeding and breastfeeding is common, but the published literature does not tell us why. There is evidence of low birth weights, low rates of exclusive breastfeeding, and problems with introducing appropriate solid foods among Bangladeshi communities in the UK (Dykes et al., 2002; Harris et al., 1983), so there is a real need for targeted and appropriate support from midwives and other health professionals.

This is similar to trends in Bangladesh, where women usually give breastmilk to their babies but often supplement breastfeeding with milk substitutes, rice, or other solid foods (Chowdhury et al., 1978; Kabir, 1986; Giashuddin and Kabir, 2004; Giashuddin et al., 2003; Roy et al., 2002). According to the literature, there is a widespread belief among women in Bangladesh that breastmilk alone is insufficient to sustain their babies (Haider et al., 1999). A variety of initiatives have been trialled in Bangladesh to improve infant feeding practices, including media and educational campaigns, baby friendly hospital initiatives, home visiting, and peer supporters in the community (Haider et al., 1997; Haque et al, 2002; Mannan and Islam, 1995; Flores and Filteau, 2002; Alam et al., 2002; Haider et al., 2002; Haider et al., 2000).

We wanted to know whether similar initiatives for Bangladeshi people had been trialled in the UK so we surveyed strategic health authority areas. The response rate was 89%. Strategic health authorities and primary care trusts in

London, the Midlands, and some parts of Northern England reported strategies to encourage Bangladeshi women to attend educational sessions as well as drop-in sessions and one-to-one support run in partnership with community groups. Drop-in sessions run by Bengali speaking peer supporters and leaflets in Bengali have been trialled in London. Other areas reported using translated versions of leaflets by the Department of Health and Food Standards Agency. These leaflets have the same content and images as English-language versions, but have been translated into Bengali.

Other research suggests that Bangladeshi women in the UK may have limited access to resources, support, and good health during pregnancy and after birth (Jayaweera et al., 2005; Parvin et al., 2004). Bangladeshi families may not be aware of the services available to assist them, may have limited contact with community nursing and social services, and may not think that the services available are appropriate for them (Merrell, 2005; Beck et al., 2005; Parvin et al., 2004; Kai and Hedges, 1999). The characteristics of professionals themselves may also be a barrier to accessing services. One study found that professionals' sex, age, ethnicity and social status affected Bangladeshi people's ability to communicate openly (Kai and Hedges, 1999).

Overall, while there are some examples of good practice, our review of published literature and current practices in different health economies identified few formal evaluations of the impacts of initiatives to improve infant feeding practices in Bangladeshi communities and even less material drawing out the key success factors or lessons that can be applied to other settings. It appears that there is a real paucity of evidence about what works well to support communities with diverse needs.

Therefore we interviewed and held 23 discussion groups with a total of 422 Bangladeshi mothers, community workers, and health and social care professionals, predominantly in the north London area.

What do Bangladeshi women think about breastfeeding?

Camden Primary Care Trust set up six discussion groups specifically to find out what Bangladeshi women think. A total of 18 other groups where mothers meet for other purposes (such as toddler groups or meetings at community centres) in London and elsewhere were also attended. One third of the discussion groups were conducted predominantly in Bengali, the rest were a mix of Bengali and English. In addition, 103 women were interviewed in community centres, at Sure Start venues, in supermarkets, and on the streets of London. The interviews were conducted mainly in English, with some translation where required. About 10% of interviews were conducted predominantly in Bengali.

The interviews and discussion groups were not recorded because we did not want to inhibit women in any way. About two-thirds of the women were mothers with toddlers or young babies, a small number were pregnant for the first time, and about one-third were grandmothers or older women. We did not attempt to gauge fathers' views.

Most of the women we spoke to thought that breastfeeding was important and healthy and could list many of its benefits. However, only about half had heard that it was important to try to breastfeed for at least six months, in line with current Department of Health guidance. Some suggested that they had received inconsistent information.

The average duration of breastfeeding among women who gave birth in the UK was about three months, although this varied from 0 to 18 months among the women we spoke to. Women who gave birth in Bangladesh said they tended to breastfeed for longer, with a range of 1–2 years. About half of the women we spoke to said that they stopped breastfeeding earlier than they would have liked, whether they gave birth in Bangladesh or in the UK. The most common reasons for this were because women thought they had insufficient breastmilk, they thought formula feeding was more convenient, and they felt they were not adequately supported to breastfeed.

'I had real trouble so I had to stop early. I didn't know how to do it. With my boy a [midwife] showed me how so I lasted for longer, but I still didn't know if I was doing it right.' (Older mother with two children)

Formula milk

Almost all of the women had used infant formula, either as a supplement for breastmilk or after they finished breastfeeding. Whether or not they breastfed, many women emphasized that giving a bottle of formula was an 'easy option'. They thought this was more convenient, less 'embarrassing' when others were around, and allowed husbands and other family members to help them feed their baby.

Twenty-one women (6%) said that they had not tried to breastfeed at all because they thought that giving their baby a bottle of formula would be easier and there were no midwives or others to help them with breastfeeding in hospital. Ten mothers mentioned that midwives in hospital automatically gave them formula milk to feed their babies.

'I had no choice about feeding because they just gave her a bottle at hospital. It was just last year.' (Young mother with one child)

Others had tried to breastfeed but had stopped after a short time (1–4 weeks) because they did not think they were producing enough milk or because they were concerned that their babies were not getting enough to eat.

'With breastfeeding you can't tell how much the baby is eating. What if it is not enough? You could be starving him and you wouldn't know. With a bottle you can see how much he eats so you know you are doing a good job of being a mum' (Young mother)

Some said they began using formula because they found breastfeeding painful. A small number of women said they stopped breastfeeding because they needed to return to work or because they wanted to use contraception.

Some women said they stopped breastfeeding because they were afraid they were being judged by other people. Babies who are formula fed might put on weight more quickly, therefore mums said they gave their babies formula so they appeared more 'healthy' to midwives, health visitors and other mums. In fact, in half of the discussion groups women said they thought that breastfeeding was 'best' but they were sometimes influenced to give their babies infant formula because of the perceptions of other people, such as health professionals, mothers-in-law, and husbands.

'I didn't want people to think I am not looking after him. I want him to put on weight and be healthy, so I use a bottle [of formula].' (Young mother)

There was a strong belief among half of the women that formula and breastmilk should be given interchangeably (mixed feeding). This was because they thought that:

- It was more convenient to use formula.
- Babies that receive only breastmilk might not grow enough.
- Babies might not get enough nutrients from breastmilk alone.
- Hospitals sometimes give formula, so it is perceived that midwives may recommend this method.
- The baby may be more difficult to wean if he or she does not receive a bottle from the start.
- Breastfeeding may give diarrhoea and tummy problems.

About half of the women felt strongly that mixing formula and breastfeeding was the best approach and they wanted hospitals and professionals to support mixed feeding, not just one option or the other. Some women felt strongly that they had to make a choice between breastfeeding or formula feeding, rather than being supported to do both.

Introducing solid foods

We also asked mothers about introducing solid foods. Almost all of the women we spoke to said that introducing solid foods and helping their children eat properly was a major problem in the Bangladeshi community. Current Department of Health guidelines suggest that most babies do not need solid foods until at least 6 months, but the age at which Bangladeshi mothers started giving their babies solid foods varied widely. Some mothers said they began feeding their babies solid food at 2–4 months, others waited until 6–9 months. Those who were exclusively breastfeeding tried to avoid solids for longer.

There was a heavy reliance on shop bought foods because they were seen as more convenient and having 'everything babies need', especially when mothers were cooking for large families and had many other chores. Many mothers thought that home-made foods would be too lumpy for young babies.

At about one year, most mothers said they were feeding babies small quantities of the foods prepared for the rest of the family. Most said they continued to give their babies milk for many years (breastmilk, formula, or a mix of both up until at least two years of age). Cows' milk was also given frequently. Solid foods included fish fingers, chicken drumsticks, and rice with spices. Sweet foods were also favoured.

Most mothers did not know when or how they should start helping their children learn to chew foods. They tended to feed their babies using a spoon, although some put mashed solids or baby rice into bottles. They thought that it was important to feed their babies with a spoon at around six months, but that as children got older they could eat with their own hands. Very few mentioned using cups or bowls.

Almost all the mothers said that they fed their children when young rather than allowing them to eat independently. This was because:

- They wanted to avoid mess.
- They did not realize the benefits of independent eating.
- They thought that feeding their children was a sign of affection.
- They felt that children do not eat enough.
- They thought it saved time to feed their baby when there is a lot of pressure to do other chores.

A large number said that feeding their baby was central to their role as a mother. Women said that they thought their main 'job' in life was to be a mother, and they put a lot of time and effort into this role. They wanted to feed their babies with spoons rather than letting babies feed themselves because they saw feeding as an integral part of the mother's role. Feeding their baby reinforced their feelings of being valuable and useful. They thought that putting food into their baby's mouth showed that mothers 'cared' for their children. Allowing independent eating was seen as somewhat neglectful.

'You feed your baby to show you care. It is your job as a mother to make sure they get enough food and to show affection for your children. That's what being a mother is all about.' (Older woman)

Issues specific to the Bangladeshi community

The mothers thought that there were differences between Bangladeshi values and behaviours and Western values about baby feeding. The most commonly mentioned differences were:

- Many Bangladeshi women in the UK do not go to work outside the home so they have more time to spend with their children and they see bringing up their baby as a very important role in life.
- Bangladeshi mums often experience a lot of problems during childbirth. This impacts on their feeding choices, for instance formula may be an easier option following a caesarean section.
- Bangladeshi women may feel uncomfortable seeing pictures of breasts in breastfeeding leaflets or in educational videos. Similarly, Bangladeshi women are private and do not like to breastfeed in public or when there are visitors. They prefer to take bottles of milk or jars of food when they are outside the home.
- Bangladeshi mothers want more support, extra help with household chores, and extra food when breastfeeding. They mentioned that living in extended families means they are always given advice and under pressure to do things a certain way.
- Bangladeshi mothers prefer to feed their babies rather than letting babies feed themselves because they do not want their children to make a mess with food. Their husbands do not like mess and mothers fed their babies to keep their husbands happy.
- Bangladeshi families may give their babies different types of food compared to White families. Bangladeshi toddlers have more spicy foods at 1–2 years. The women thought that Western babies could eat any family foods but Bangladeshi families had to be more careful because they usually ate spicy foods. The mothers thought that Bangladeshi babies might be less interested in food than Western babies. There was a perception that Bangladeshi babies and toddlers are 'fussy eaters' whereas 'White babies will eat anything'.
- Bangladeshi families often have more children and little space at home. For example, some women described families with four children, two parents, and a grandparent living in a one bedroom flat. The lack of space meant that parents got more frustrated with their children's eating habits and could not 'send them to their room' as 'punishment' for not eating well. The lack of space and finance also prohibited the use of baby chairs.

- The women thought that White mothers are more likely to follow a timetable for feeding their children (breakfast, lunch, and dinner) whereas Bangladeshi parents feed their children frequently throughout the day. Babies will be fed whenever someone comes to visit or whenever someone in the house is eating.
- Bangladeshi mothers often compare their families with others. They compare whether their baby is 'doing as well' as other babies. Mothers said they need to be told what is healthy and told that they should not compare one family to another.
- Some suggested that Bangladeshi mothers are worried about how society perceives them. They are concerned that health professionals and other parents will think they are not caring for their baby properly if the baby is not well fed (which was equated with chubby babies).

Where do mothers get information?

Mothers said that they got most of their information about feeding their babies from friends and family, health clinic staff (especially health visitors), information from products in shops and formula companies, and leaflets and books (for those who feel confident reading English). The main people 'outside the community' that women talked to about feeding were health visitors and general practitioners. Midwives were mentioned infrequently as a source of support with breastfeeding and infant feeding. But the mums thought it was important to provide education about feeding when women are pregnant. They suggested that Bangladeshi mothers do not attend antenatal courses in hospitals and health centres. Instead there was a desire for courses about birth and feeding to be held in community venues, especially if they are run by Bangladeshi workers.

> 'We don't go to those hospital courses. You have to make them in our venues and in our language.' (Young mother of two)

There were mixed feelings about the help provided by health professionals. Some said that midwives in hospital had been too busy to help them with positioning and attachment, others said that their midwife had been helpful and kind. The general perception was that health professionals were good, but often too busy to help.

Women who had had their children many years ago were most likely to feel that there was little support for breastfeeding. However, even women who had given birth within the past two years said they did not feel fully supported by professionals such as midwives and health visitors. Although they said that professionals told them it would be good to breastfeed, the mothers wanted more practical help with attachment and positioning.

'They are so busy and you do not want to press the button and disturb them. But it would be good to have help on how to do it. Not just be told it's good, but actually shown how to do it and told if you're doing it right.' (Young mother)

Almost all of the mothers said that they would like a timeline about feeding, including what foods to give at six months, nine months and so on. They thought that leaflets should be used to supplement visits to community centres and home by volunteers and health professionals. They liked the idea of group discussions to get peer support. They wanted someone to spend more than half an hour talking with them, so they could ask questions and understand more fully.

What do professionals think?

We also asked professionals to identify the key infant feeding issues facing Bangladeshi families. We gained feedback from 19 different individuals and attended 16 meetings with a mix of volunteers, community workers, and health and social care professionals in London. We spoke with 99 people in total, 27 of whom were midwives. A snowball sampling approach was used. We did not record sessions to avoid inhibiting the responses. We did not ask the professionals about their ethnicity or other demographic details, but we estimate that about one third were Bangladeshi.

Ninety out of the 99 people we spoke to believed that Bangladeshi families in the UK often have ongoing problems with infant feeding. There was a perception that Bangladeshi parents are anxious about baby feeding.

Seven out of 10 midwives working in hospital suggested that supporting Bangladeshi mothers to begin breastfeeding was increasingly becoming an issue. They said that some hospital midwives and maternity care assistants did not encourage Bangladeshi mothers to breastfeed because they automatically assumed that these mothers would not want to. They did not suggest that this was because of things that Bangladeshi mothers said or did, but rather because of inaccurate stereotyping of women into different 'types' by professionals.

'As Bengali women do not push for information, busy midwives don't always give it to them. The role of the midwife is crucial, because midwives see women earlier than health visitors. Also, maternity care assistants need training.' (Midwife)

About half of the hospital midwives we spoke to said that Bangladeshi mothers may not be assertive in asking for information or letting midwives know their preferences; instead they tend to fit in with what professionals in hospital suggest. Therefore, these midwives thought that it may be important to examine the training and development needs of professionals to help them provide culturally sensitive care in hospital after birth, where mothers should be helped to breastfeed. It was suggested that the needs of women who do not speak English well or at all need special consideration.

However, apart from hospital midwives, most other professionals and community workers did not think that encouraging Bangladeshi mothers to initiate breastfeeding was a difficulty. They believed that Bangladeshi mothers in the UK usually started breastfeeding, but did not necessarily continue for very long.

'Getting them started is not a problem, it's keeping it going that's the main thing.' (Health visitor)

Almost all the professionals we spoke to thought that Bangladeshi women needed to know more about the benefits of breastfeeding and how breastfeeding will help with their children's developmental needs. About half made the point that Bangladeshi women need further information, not just mothers. In particular, oral health workers, community midwives, health visitors, and community workers noted that older women and mothers-in-law had a central role in decision-making within their families, and that teenagers and older women could be targeted with more information, as well as women of childbearing age.

Food plays an important part in Bangladeshi culture. There are restrictions on what can be eaten and encouragement to eat certain types of foods. In common with previous studies, health professionals suggested they did not know enough about the everyday lives and eating patterns of Bangladeshi people, which may act as a barrier to providing appropriate services.

All 99 professionals who gave us feedback thought that there was a lack of knowledge among Bangladeshi mothers about what babies can and should eat at certain stages of their development. On one hand, professionals thought that Bengali mothers may give their babies solid foods very early (for example, at 1–3 months) because they are worried that their babies are hungry or because they want their babies to develop faster. On the other hand, although solid foods may be introduced early, these tend to be very smooth, pureed foods, and Bangladeshi babies often do not progress to eating firmer foods for some time.

'The child doesn't get a chance to enjoy food, so they don't like it. The mother then gets worried and tries to make the baby eat more – which makes the baby pull away even more. It's a vicious cycle and it sets up eating problems for many years to come. If they just let kids play around, eat the amount they want from their plate, and make a mess, then a lot of problems would be solved' (Health visitor)

To improve the information and support available for Bangladeshi families, midwives and other professionals suggested that they wanted more training to help them understand cultural differences and why Bangladeshi families have certain practices. An example relates to the practice of feeding babies and children by spoon or hand, rather than allowing babies to do this themselves. Some professionals think this is because mothers want to ensure that babies are eating properly or because they want to avoid mess, but Bangladeshi people often say that this is a cultural practice, and that adults may continue to feed each other on occasion as a sign of affection.

'What you might not understand is that feeding someone else is a caring gesture in our culture. One adult sister might feed another – they might be doing that still when they are 60 or 70. Mothers feeding their children is part of this caring culture.' (Community volunteer)

Other important needs identified were leaflets available in Bengali, group education sessions for professionals and mothers together; a translation service so professionals could use materials they know work well for other mothers; and assistance from peer supporters.

Almost all the professionals we spoke to thought that some Bangladeshi parents had language and communication issues that affected infant feeding. Health visitors and midwives talked about feeling frustrated about not being able to get their messages across to some Bangladeshi families, either because they did not feel that the families could understand what they were saying; or because they did not have enough supporting resources such as translated leaflets or interpreters; or because they felt that families were not receptive to the ideas of 'outsiders'. Community workers said that there were not enough Bengali-speaking professionals, and that those who were available always had more work than they could keep up with.

Some professionals said that it was difficult for them to engage Bangladeshi families because they felt their advice was 'falling on deaf ears'. There was a perception that the Bangladeshi community had its own way of doing things, and that information from non-Bangladeshi health and social care professionals may not be welcomed.

Other professionals supported this view, saying that new mothers may be undermined in their attempts to breastfeed or wean appropriately by members of their extended family. Mothers may be receiving mixed messages about appropriate practices and timeframes for weaning. About half of professionals felt that informing the whole family about feeding options may be important in changing perceptions and attitudes in the Bangladeshi community.

To help overcome these barriers, midwives, health visitors, and community workers suggested that it is important to begin providing more systematic and planned antenatal information for Bangladeshi mothers. About half of the professionals we spoke to said that midwives needed to be trained to provide culturally appropriate antenatal classes, and that experienced midwives should be asked to provide antenatal education sessions in Bangladeshi community venues. Such courses would need to be run sensitively, and perhaps not dwell on physical changes, which may be embarrassing for Bangladeshi women to talk about in public.

All of the professionals and volunteers we spoke to said that there is a need to educate professionals about the best strategies for working with the Bangladeshi community. They felt that all professionals who come into contact with Bangladeshi families should receive written materials and short training sessions to make them aware of some of the cultural differences and to remind them of the importance of being friendly, approachable, and culturally aware. In particular, there was a focus on educating midwives and health visitors.

It was suggested that midwives and health visitors should attend mandatory training with Bangladeshi women to hear their stories. Professionals wanted information about how many Bangladeshi women there are in Camden and the particular problems that face them. This would help them put the issues in context and realize how many women and families are affected.

In line with National Service Framework recommendations, it was also suggested that midwives should visit women at home once a fortnight for six weeks, extending the current visiting schedule, and that midwives could introduce peer supporters to mothers in their homes to provide a link for ongoing support. This suggestion was made by both midwifery leaders and community workers.

Practical implications for midwives

So what does this all mean for midwives? Overall, it seems that there were many correlations between published literature, mothers' views, and professionals' experience. All tend to agree that there are significant infant feeding issues facing the Bangladeshi community, and that Bangladeshi families may have some specific issues. The main considerations appear to be in terms of helping mothers maintain breastfeeding and helping them introduce solid foods appropriately.

Breastfeeding rates in the UK are one of the lowest in the developed world. One study found that decisions about infant feeding are often made prior to, or irrespective of, contact with health professionals. While health promotion campaigns in the UK have helped to inform women about the benefits of breastfeeding, this does not necessarily dissuade women from formula feeding once their decision is made (Earle, 2002). Actively promoting and raising awareness about the benefits of breastfeeding has been found to increase breastfeeding rates in ethnic minority communities and women from low income households (Ahluwalia et al., 2000). However most previous evaluations have not included Bangladeshi people. There is a real paucity of evidence about what works best to engage Bangladeshi people, especially in the field of infant feeding.

Services need to be more empowering and adapt to meet the cultural needs of the Bangladeshi community (Fazil et al., 2004). Key success factors among services that have adapted to be more accessible include making an effort to get to know Bangladeshi families, recognizing communication and cultural differences, undertaking cultural awareness training (Hawthorne et al., 2003), working with people from the Bangladeshi community to develop and provide services (Kai and Hedges, 1999), using trained interpreters and advocates (Gerrish et al., 2004), and using younger people as interpreters for family members (Free et al., 2003).

A positive finding was that women in the Bangladeshi community expressed a desire for more contact with midwives, rather than 'closing off' to the possibility of additional support. Bangladeshi women's feedback has some direct implications for the type of support midwives and others provide. For example, we may need to think about the following strategies.

Educating professionals

- Raising awareness among midwives and other professionals about the needs of Bangladeshi families.
- Providing workshops for Bangladeshi women and professionals to share views.
- Working in partnership with Bangladeshi community groups to reach more parents.

Informing women

- Providing antenatal education sessions in community venues.
- Providing targeted feeding support at the place women give birth, without women having to ask for it.
- Involving family members, such as mothers-in-law, in education sessions and informal chats.

Peer support

- Training peer supporters from the Bangladeshi community to help support women.
- Running joint drop-in sessions with peer supporters and midwives.
- Midwives taking peer supporters with them during home visits.

Printed resources

- Developing printed resources such as a timeline about different stages of feeding.
- Adapting and translating leaflets to make them more accessible to Bangladeshi women.
- Having access to a resource translation service for professionals.

Some of these are strategies that individual midwives and teams of midwives can arrange, such as running drop-in groups or considering antenatal education in community venues. Others are strategies that may need more structural and organizational support, such as arranging access to translation services. All of the strategies have one thing in common, however: they place Bangladeshi mothers and families at the centre of the care pathway, and emphasize that midwives should strive to be aware of the individual needs of the families they work with. Knowing that Bangladeshi mothers may have different views about feeding their baby and different cultural practices and expectations will help midwives adapt the availability and accessibility of information and support.

References

Ahluwalia IB, Tessaro I, Grummer-Strawn LM, MacGowan C, Benton-Davis S (2000) Georgia's breastfeeding promotion program for low-income women. *Pediatrics* **105(6)**: E85.

Alam MU, Rahman M, Rahman F (2002) Effectiveness of baby friendly hospital initiative on the promotion of exclusive breast feeding among the Dhaka city dwellers in Bangladesh. *Mymensingh Med J* **11(2)**: 94–9.

Beck A, Majumdar A, Estcourt C, Petrak J (2005) "We don't really have cause to discuss these things, they don't affect us": A collaborative model for developing culturally appropriate sexual health services with the Bangladeshi community of Tower Hamlets. *Sex Transm Infect* **81(2)**: 158–62.

Berthoud R (1998) *Incomes of Ethnic Minorities*. Institute for Social and Economic Research, Colchester.

Chowdhury M, Dutta N, Sarkar A, Dey B (1978) Breast feeding by urban mothers. *J Indian Med Assoc* 70(10): 221–4.

Dykes J, Watt RG, Nazroo J (2002) Socio-economic and ethnic influences on infant feeding practices related to oral health. *Community Dent Health* **19(3)**: 137–43.

Earle S (2002) Factors affecting the initiation of breastfeeding: Implications for breastfeeding promotion. *Health Promot Int* **17(3)**: 205–14.

Fazil Q, Wallace LM, Singh G, Ali Z, Bywaters P (2004) Empowerment and advocacy: Reflections on action research with Bangladeshi and Pakistani families who have children with severe disabilities. *Health Soc Care Community* **12(5)**: 389–97.

Flores M, Filteau S (2002) Effect of lactation counselling on subclinical mastitis among Bangladeshi women. *Ann Trop Paediatr* **22(1)**: 85–8.

Free C, Green J, Bhavnani V, Newman A (2003) Bilingual young people's experiences of interpreting in primary care: A qualitative study. *Br J Gen Pract* **53(492)**: 530–5.

Gerrish K, Chau R, Sobowale A, Birks E (2004) Bridging the language barrier: The use of interpreters in primary care nursing. *Health Soc Care Community* **12(5)**: 407–13.

Giashuddin MS, Kabir M, Rahman A, Hannan MA (2003) Exclusive breastfeeding and nutritional status in Bangladesh. *Indian J Pediatr* **70(6)**: 471–5.

Giashuddin MS, Kabir M (2004) Duration of breast-feeding in Bangladesh. *Indian J Med Res* **119(6)**: 267–72.

Haider R, Ashworth A, Kabir I, Huttly SR (2000) Effect of community-based peer counsellors on exclusive breastfeeding practices in Dhaka, Bangladesh: A randomised controlled trial. *Lancet* **356(9242)**: 1643–7.

Haider R, Kabir I, Ashworth A (1999) Are breastfeeding promotion messages influencing mothers in Bangladesh? Results from an urban survey in Dhaka, Bangladesh. *J Trop Pediatr* **45(5)**: 315–8.

Haider R, Kabir I, Hamadani JD, Habte D (1997) Reasons for failure of breast-feeding counselling: Mothers' perspectives in Bangladesh. *Bull World Health Organ* **75(3)**: 191–6.

Haider R, Kabir I, Huttly SR, Ashworth A (2002) Training peer counselors to promote and support exclusive breastfeeding in Bangladesh. *J Hum Lact* **18(1)**: 7–12.

Haque MF, Hussain M, Sarkar A, Hoque MM, Ara FA, Sultana S (2002) Breast-feeding counselling and its effect on the prevalence of exclusive breast-feeding. *J Health Popul Nutr* **20(4)**: 312–6.

Harris RJ, Armstrong D, Ali R, Loynes A (1983) Nutritional survey of Bangladeshi children aged under 5 years in the London borough of Tower Hamlets. *Arch Dis Child* **58**: 428–32.

Hawthorne K, Rahman J, Pill R (2003) Working with Bangladeshi patients in Britain: Perspectives from Primary Health Care. *Fam Pract* **20(2)**: 185–91.

Jayaweera H, D'Souza L, Garcia J (2005) A local study of childbearing

Bangladeshi women in the UK. *Midwifery* **21(1)**: 84–95.

Kabir MH (1986) Breastfeeding supplements in urban and rural areas of Bangladesh. *Rural Demogr* **13(1–2)**: 1–11.

Kai J, Hedges C (1999) Minority ethnic community participation in needs assessment and service development in primary care: Perceptions of Pakistani and Bangladeshi people about psychological distress. *Health Expect* **2(1)**: 7–20.

Karim E, Mascie-Taylor CG (2001) Longitudinal growth of Bangladeshi infants during the first year of life. *Ann Hum Biol* **28(1)**: 51–67.

Kelleher D, Islam S (1994) The problem of integration: Asian people and diabetes. *J Roy Soc Med* **87(7)**: 414–7.

Lawson MS, Thomas M, Hardiman A (1998) Iron status of Asian children aged 2 years living in England. *Arch Dis Child* **78(5)**: 420–6.

Mannan HR, Islam MN (1995) Breast-feeding in Bangladesh: Patterns and impact on fertility. *Asia Pac Popul J* **10(4)**: 23–38.

Merrell J, Kinsella F, Murphy F, Philpin S, Ali A (2005) Support needs of carers of dependent adults from a Bangladeshi community. *J Adv Nurs* **51(6)**: 549–57.

Office for National Statistics (2001) *2001 Census - Ethnic Group*. Office for National Statistics, London.

Parvin A, Jones CE, Hull SA (2004) Experiences and understandings of social and emotional distress in the postnatal period among Bangladeshi women living in Tower Hamlets. *Fam Pract* **21(3)**:254–60.

Roy SK, de Groot S, Shafique S, Afroz A (2002) Perceptions of mothers and use of breastmilk substitutes in Dhaka, Bangladesh. *J Health Popul Nutr* **20(3)**: 264–70.

Thomas M (*1997*) Infant Feeding in Asian Families: Early Practices and Growth. Stationery Office, London.

CHAPTER 11

Evaluation of bilingual peer support for breastfeeding

Shamoly Ahmed, Alison Macfarlane, Jo Naylor and Joy Hastings

Introduction

In Tower Hamlets, Bangladeshi women have a very low rate of breastfeeding and the difference between their intentions to breastfeed and actually breastfeeding is far wider than for women from other ethnic groups. In Bangladesh, breastfeeding is well rooted in its own traditional culture. A Sure Start local programme funded a Bangladeshi support worker to work with childbearing Bangladeshi women in the area; many of who are not fluent in English. A short evaluation of this work was conducted to assess the impact of bilingual breastfeeding support to women's uptake and duration of breastfeeding. The majority of women found the support worker to be the most helpful breastfeeding advisor and felt she influenced them to breastfeed. Despite this, a minority of women exclusively breastfed and most reported having problems feeding during the hospital stay. This evaluation highlighted the need for further work in this area.

In developing countries breastfeeding is a cultural norm and in Western societies women from ethnic minorities turn to their families rather than to health professionals for breastfeeding support (Baranowski et al., 1983).

The national UK Infant Feeding Survey showed that between 1995 and 2000, there was an overall increase in breastfeeding incidence in the UK (Hamlyn et al., 2000). It also showed that mothers from Asian and other ethnic minority groups were more likely to breastfeed at birth compared with White women. A survey of breastfeeding in South Asian families in 1994 found that 90% of Bangladeshi mothers at all birth orders breastfed initially compared with 82% of Indian, 76% of Pakistani and 62% of White mothers. (Thomas and Avery, 1997). This was not surprising, given that many women were likely to have recently arrived from Bangladesh where breastfeeding is the only viable option for most women. In a study of Gujarati and Bangladeshi women in Leicester there were differences in breastfeeding rates between the two groups despite their being from the same subcontinent (Katbamna, 2000).

In the 2001 census, 33.4% of the population of the London Borough of

Table 11.1. Intention to breastfeed and actual breastfeeding by ethnicity. Percentage of respondents in each group

	Intention	Actual	Difference
Bangladeshi	62	18	44
White	67	45	22
African	80	43	37
Other	73	41	32

Source: Unpublished data from Royal London Hospital, 2000

Tower Hamlets was Bangladeshi. In the three year period, 1999–2001, 58.1% of births to Tower Hamlets residents were to Bangladeshi mothers (Macfarlane et al., 2005). Many were not fluent in English.

Unpublished data from the Royal London Hospital, where the majority of these Bangladeshi women delivered showed low rates of breastfeeding which were markedly different from the national level in the mid-1990s (*Table 11.1*) Furthermore, the difference between intention to breastfeed and actually breastfeeding was far greater for Bangladeshi women than for other women. It is difficult to explain this large difference, however, one reason could be due to inadequate communication resulting in poor understanding for non-English speaking women.

The bilingual programme

As one response to this, a bilingual breastfeeding programme was developed. The first stage was a project to provide extra breastfeeding support and education to Bangladeshi women, funded by a local Sure Start programme. Two specialist midwives provided training and supervision for a Bangladeshi breastfeeding supporter. The aim was to provide help and support with breastfeeding to as many Bangladeshi women as possible within the Sure Start area. Most importantly, someone familiar with service users' language, social and cultural values and practices offered the services.

Postcodes were used to identify women who lived in the Sure Start area. The support worker made contact with the women by means of hospital ward visits and referrals made by midwives, advocates and health visitors. She then provided one-to-one support including home visits and telephone support.

This chapter reports a short evaluation of this first phase of the bilingual breastfeeding programme. The work described was used to assess the need for a second phase. The evaluation was commissioned by the local Sure Start programme.

Methods

Sample

The two midwives and the support worker had provided breastfeeding support to 194 women during the one year period, September 2001 to August 2002. Of these, 80 women received help from the support worker alone. The majority of these 80 women were Bangladeshi. For the evaluation, 15 women were randomly selected from these women.

Women who were not contactable by telephone, under 18 years of age, had not received services from the support worker, and women whose child or children were aged 4 months or over were excluded from the sample.

Approval was gained from the North East London Strategic Health Authority Research Ethics Sub-Committee, the local research ethics committee at the time.

Survey

The survey questionnaire included some open and closed questions about: women's intention to feed and their current feeding methods; breastfeeding support and information received antenatally, during the hospital stay, and postnatally; overall views on the information and support received; and some demographic details. A major part of the questionnaire was adapted from a previously piloted and validated survey (Grant et al., 2000).

Eleven interviews were conducted by SA by telephone in Sylheti, a dialect that has no written format, three in English and one in Urdu, using a female family member to translate. Interviews took 15–30 minutes to complete. Where Sylheti was used, the responses were translated directly into English for recording on the questionnaire.

Data were entered into a computer and analysed using SPSS version 10. Descriptive statistics were used for the quantitative questions and thematic analyses were used for the qualitative questions.

Results

Table 11.2 shows some of the demographic characteristics of the sample. Only three women were fluent in English with the rest being educated in Bangladesh with either GCSE equivalent or less. Seven of their partners were unemployed and 13 women were not employed outside the home. All the women that were multiparae had some previous experience of breastfeeding. The majority of women had been breastfed by their own mother.

Table 11.3 shows when breastfeeding support was received and from whom. All women received breastfeeding support at some stage of their maternity

Table 11.2. Demographic characteristics of participants (*n* = 15)		
Participant	Percentage	Base
Age		
Less than 20	7	1
20–29	53	8
30–39	33	5
40 or over	7	1
Parity		
Primipara	33	5
Multipara	67	10
Previous experience of breastfeeding		
Yes	67	10
No	33	5
Fluent in English		
Yes	20	3
No	80	12
Feeding method participant's mother adopted when feeding her		
Breast	73	11
Bottle	0	0
Mixed	20	3
Not sure	7	1
Method of feeding by participants while staying in hospital		
Breast	20	3
Bottle	33	5
Mixed	47	7

care. Women received more support postnatally, and less support during their hospital stay. More of them received support from the support worker both antenatally and postnatally than from other health professionals. The 'other' category represents women who received antenatal support but were unable to remember which health professional gave it. Those who received support during their hospital stay had received support from the hospital nurse on duty.

Most women identified the support worker to be the most helpful in terms of breastfeeding (*Figure 11.1*), and reported that she had influenced them to breastfeed. Of these women, five were multipara and all mentioned they would have liked this support while feeding their previous child or children. More

Table 11.3. When breastfeeding support received and from whom						
	Antenatally		During hospital stay		Postnatally at home	
Source of support	%	Base	%	Base	%	Base
Support worker	40	6	20	3	53	8
Midwife*	27	4	27	4	33	5
Health advocate	7	1	14	2	0	0
Health visitor	0	0	0	0	20	3
Family	0	0	7	1	53	8
Friends	14	2	0	0	20	3
Other	7	1	14	2	0	0
No help	40	6	40	6	14	2
Total	100	15	100	15	100	15

*None of these were Sure Start midwives
Some women received help from more than one source at each stage, so the totals do not add up to 100

primiparous women than multiparous women were influenced 'A lot' by the support worker.

Only two women said they needed further support with breastfeeding in addition to the help they had been receiving. Despite having contact details of the support worker and having seen and received some support from her, as well as finding her to be supportive they decided to contact other health professionals such as the health visitor or doctor for queries. This was because their social networks told them that other health professionals would be able to advise better than the support worker. This raises issues of lack of confidence in and professional recognition of the support worker as a breastfeeding specialist by women and those in their social network.

None of the women attended breastfeeding classes. Only six women reported being informed about the classes and none of those reported being informed by the support worker. It is possible that women may not have remembered being informed by the support worker at the time of questioning or may have presumed that the support worker was discussing a different workshop. Women wanted videos of breastfeeding education in their own languages, to be used in the workshops and copies for them to borrow to watch at home in privacy.

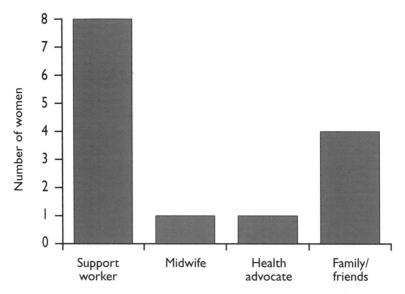

Figure 1.1. People women found most helpful in terms of support with breastfeeding.

The qualitative elements in the questionnaire showed one of the reasons most women found difficulties in exclusive breastfeeding during their hospital stay was lack of support by hospital staff. Just under half the women had caesarean sections. This was quite high compared to the overall rate of 18% in the same hospital in the same year. All except one of those who had caesareans said this had influenced the method of feeding they adopted after delivery. They said they found breastfeeding difficult due to general pain and back pain. As one woman said:

> 'Due to back pain did not breastfeed as planned, so bottle fed at hospital.' (Q2)

Two women, who had had caesarean sections, described the kind of support they would have liked during their stay at the hospital.

> 'Help in hospital after delivery, help with demonstrating how to position baby on breast, how for me to position myself ... physical demonstration rather than talking...' (Q2)
> 'To have continued support with feeding baby at hospital, especially ... who have operation [caesarean]. Then when they get home it would be easier ...' (Q15)

Good communication skills, both verbal and non-verbal, knowledge of breastfeeding, ease of access and an interest during the period while women are breastfeeding are the factors that contributed most highly to what women perceived as most helpful in terms of support during breastfeeding.

Discussion

The sample is too small to carry out statistical tests and no comparative data were collected from women who did not receive help from the support worker, but the data suggest the benefits of the additional support worker. The majority of women found the support worker to be the most helpful breastfeeding advisor with whom they had contact. This evaluation highlighted the need for further work in this area. By 2005, Tower Hamlets had similar breastfeeding projects in each of the seven Sure Start areas, employing seven part-time support workers and four part-time project co-ordinators.

The success of the scheme also suggests that other existing services are failing to offer adequate support to this group of women. A number of strategies could be adopted. Increasing time spent at ward level by a support worker and longer visiting hours may improve the support available during the hospital stay. Women's social networks provide a lot of support with feeding; the involvement of these networks in breastfeeding workshops could improve attendance.

The availability of videos in women's own languages could help to remove barriers associated with literacy and act as another tool for educating women, in particular those who feel too embarrassed and shy to be involved in an open discussion regarding breastfeeding. Since the end of the project, videos have been introduced. Careful distribution and monitoring of their impact on women's breastfeeding patterns and knowledge may enable the usefulness and practicality of such material to be assessed.

The Sure Start programmes are reaching their final stages and it is anticipated that successful projects will continue to be supported. On a larger scale, both health and economic evaluation of the second phase will need to be conducted to assess the implications of these programmes for women, their families, health care providers and whether these should or can be incorporated within the mainstream health services or children centres once Sure Start ends.

Conclusion

This evaluation was conducted to make a preliminary assessment of the impact of bilingual breastfeeding support work on Bangladeshi women and inform decisions about extending this service to other areas. The apparent success of the scheme suggested that there was a need to continue to employ local women to work as support workers.

Acknowledgements

We would like to thank Stephen Abbott from the Public Health and Primary Care Unit, City University, for his advice during the preparation of this paper.

References

Baranowski T, Bee DE, Rassin, DK, Richardson J, Brown JP, Guenther N, et al. (1983) Social support, social influence, ethnicity and the breastfeeding decision. *Soc Sci Med* **17**:1599–611.

Grant J, Fletcher M, Warwick C (2000) *The South Thames Evidence-Based Practice (STEP) Project*. Kings College, London.

Hamlyn B, Brooker S, Oleinikova K, Wands S (2000) *Infant Feeding*. The Stastical Office, London.

Katbamna S (2000) *'Race' and Childbirth*. Open University Press, Buckingham.

Macfarlane A, Grant J, Hancock J, et al. (2005) *Early Life Mortality in East London: A Feasibility Study. Summary Report. Fetal and Infant Death in East London*. City University, London

Thomas M, Avery V (1997) *Infant Feeding in Asian Families*. The Statistical Office, London.

CHAPTER 12

The impact of the high national caesarean section rate on midwives

Jacqueline Baxter

Introduction

I recently saw a woman for pregnancy booking who is expecting her first baby. At this first visit she told me that she was planning to have a caesarean section, her reason being that she is 40 years old and that this may be her only chance of having a baby. She felt that statistically her chances of having a successful birth outcome, i.e. a live healthy baby, would be greater if she has a caesarean section.

So why does this woman consider a caesarean section to be less risky than going into labour and aiming for a vaginal birth? What evidence is she basing her reasoning upon? We know that the media is a very powerful way of drawing the public's attention to specific issues and many celebrities have been reported to have had a caesarean section. She may also have friends and relatives who have given birth in this way. Also, as a medical practitioner herself, this woman will have been trained in the medical model of care where normality in childbirth is only ever confirmed in retrospect. Female obstetricians have been found to favour elective caesarean for their own birth experiences (MacDonald et al., 2002, Al-Mufti et al., 1997).

In my experience it is rare for women who have never given birth to specifically ask for an elective caesarean section and this is supported in the literature (Gamble and Creedy, 2000, 2001). However, a recent systematic review reported rates of nulliparous women requesting caesarean section in the absence of any clinical indication that ranged from 0% to 100% (Kingdon et al., 2006). As a society we appear to be losing our confidence in normal birth. The above situation illustrates the fact that we may have become blasé about giving birth by caesarean despite the procedure still being statistically more dangerous for both women and their babies than having a normal birth experience. Both elective and emergency caesarean sections are associated with complications (NICE, 2004; Clement, 1995, Francome et al., 1993). However, it needs to be recognized that this is a difficult area to study (Odent, 2004, Hall and Bewley

1999). For example, are poor outcomes due to the effects of the caesarean section itself or the long labour that went before?

As a midwife, and thus a champion of normal birth, I was able to speak with this woman and provide information indicating to her and her partner that birth can be achieved safely without surgical intervention. They had genuinely not considered this option. It would be interesting to know what the outcome in terms of decision for method of birth would have been had this woman seen another practitioner who views life through the medical model instead. Despite the recommendation in the NICE guideline (NICE, 2004) that there should be a second obstetric opinion in the event of a woman requesting caesarean section in the absence of an identifiable reason, it seems that some women are still undergoing caesarean section for choice alone. A recent study at an inner-London teaching hospital about the needs of women following caesarean section found 4% of women had had a caesarean section for maternal choice alone (Baxter and Macfarlane, 2005). This was a slightly lower rate than the 7% found nationally three years previously (Thomas and Paranjothy, 2001). It is hopeful that these findings might be indicative of a turn in this trend. However, it appears that there are still a small, yet significant, number of women undergoing caesarean sections for the reason of maternal choice alone (Hildingsson et al., 2002).

This chapter commences with a background in which caesarean section rates, both national and international, are discussed. The associated morbidity and mortality is also highlighted and the main reasons why this operation is performed given. The main body of the chapter concentrates on the important role the midwife has to play in terms of providing information and emotional support. In addition there is a description of an initiative at one London NHS trust which has improved care for women who give birth by caesarean section.

Caesarean section rates

In 1985 the World Health Organization (WHO) held a consensus conference to consider the global rising caesarean section rate. The conclusion was that there are no additional health benefits associated with a caesarean section rate above 10–15%. Since that time the National Sentinel Caesarean Section Audit has been conducted encompassing three countries of the UK leading to its publication in 2001 (Thomas and Paranjothy, 2001). The national caesarean section rate was found to be 21.3% in England, 24.2% in Wales and 23.9% in Northern Ireland. In England at that time 63% of all caesarean sections were classified as emergency and 37% elective; the primary caesarean section rate (women having a first caesarean section regardless of parity) was 17% and the repeat caesarean section rate was 67% (Thomas and Paranjothy, 2001). It is of interest that despite this very detailed audit caesarean section rates have

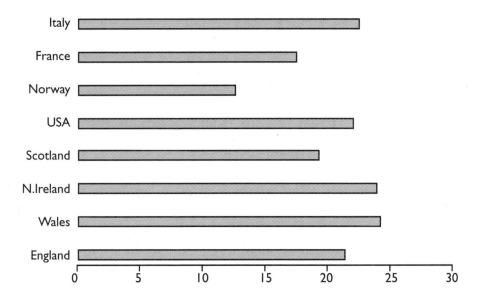

Figure 12.1. International caesarean section rates (%) 1999–2001. Source: Thomas and Parajothy (2001).

continued to rise in the past two years and the latest figure for England is 23% (Department of Health, 2005).

The authors of the National Sentinel Caesarean Section Audit commented that these rates were comparable to those in the USA (Thomas and Paranjothy 2001). Some other international rates can be seen in *Figure 12.1*. It is interesting to see a much lower rate in Norway compared to other northern countries. Even closer to home, in the UK, rates range between 19 and 24%.

Morbidity and mortality

It is not always recognized that a woman who has had a caesarean section has in fact undergone major surgery (Churchill, 1997; Clement, 1995). The decision to undertake a caesarean section should not be made lightly and each woman should be informed about the risks. Abdominal pain (relative risk 1.9), bladder injury (relative risk 36.6), hysterectomy (relative risk 44.0) and even death (relative risk 4.9) are short-term effects that occur much more commonly in women who give birth by caesarean section compared with vaginal birth (NICE, 2004). Birth by caesarean section was an identified risk factor for obstetric hysterectomy in a recent study in the south-east Thames region where 68% of all occurrences were among those who had had a caesarean section (Eniola et al., 2006). Wound infection, intrauterine infection and blood transfusion are among the long-term complications (Hillan, 1995) and more recently a reduction in fertility rates and an increase in cases of placenta praevia and uterine rupture have been reported and all these events are more likely in subsequent pregnancies of women undergoing caesarean section (NICE, 2004). In addition there is emerging evidence that suggests that having a caesarean section increases the risk of stillbirth in future pregnancies (Smith et al., 2003). Caesarean section can be riskier for the baby too. Babies are more likely to experience respiratory morbidity after planned caesarean compared with vaginal delivery (relative risk 6.8) (NICE, 2004).

It is recognized that having an elective caesarean section is safer for a woman than undergoing an emergency caesarean section but vaginal birth is still viewed as the safest way of giving birth. Case fatality for all caesarean sections was found to be six times that for a vaginal birth in 1999 and this rate rose to nearly nine times greater in the case of an emergency caesarean section (Hall and Bewley, 1999).

In two studies of women's experience of caesarean sections women were found to suffer postnatally with pain over a long recovery period (Churchill, 1997; Francome et al., 1993). This work was carried out at a time when 60% of caesareans were performed under general anaesthesia. Recovery following general anaesthesia is considered to be slower and women are more drowsy during the first few postoperative days (Bennett and Brown, 1999).

It may be that nowadays, when more than 90% of caesareans are performed under regional anaesthesia (Department of Health, 2005), this discomfort may be less. Indeed Churchill found fewer women to 'suffer' (e.g. perceived problems with bonding, not participating in the birth experience, pain following the operation, lengthy recovery period) between two different time periods, 1996 and 1991/2, during the nineties when the general anaesthetic rate was 32.5% and 58%, respectively. Rates of women reporting that they had suffered as a result of having a caesarean section were one in six in 1996, contrasting with two in five in 1991/2.

There has been concern that some women who give birth by caesarean section feel emotional loss because they miss out on a normal birth experience (Fenwick et al., 2003). In some situations women who have caesarean sections may feel a sense of failure as women and they experience a loss of confidence and self-esteem (Clement, 1995). Women have described caesarean section as traumatic (Ryding et al., 1987, 1998) and depression has been linked to the procedure (Hannah et al., 1992). In extreme situations having a caesarean section has been linked with post-traumatic stress disorder (Gamble and Creedy, 2005).

Public health

A high proportion of the maternity population gives birth by caesarean section resulting in a large number of women who, as we have seen, consequently experience morbidity. There has been concern for some time that this is

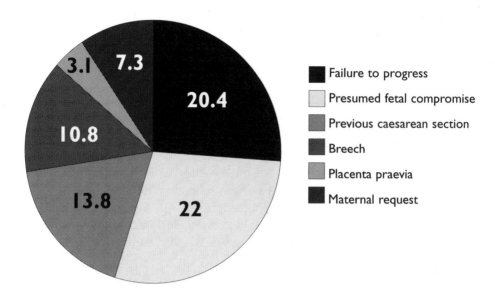

Figure 12.2. Main reasons for caesarean section (%) in England and Wales, 2000. Source: Thomas and Parajothy (2001).

therefore a public health issue (Royal College of Midwives and National Childbirth Trust, 2001; Kaufmann, 2000; Warwick, 1999). On return home women with a caesarean section scar experience far greater difficulties adjusting to life with a new baby. Those from disadvantaged groups are particularly vulnerable; they may, in addition, have to cope alone, with poor housing conditions and inadequate transport.

Reasons for women having a caesarean section

There are a significant number of women for whom caesarean section is not an option, e.g. if the baby is breech or there is evidence of human immunodeficiency virus (HIV) infection with a high viral load, or there is grade 3 and 4 placenta praevia, placental abruption, obstructed labour, or cord prolapse.

There are three main reasons why caesarean sections are performed: medical condition of the mother, untoward events during labour and factors within the fetus (e.g. fetal abnormality such as gastroschisis). The most frequent reasons cited by clinicians in the National Sentinel Audit were presumed fetal compromise, failure to progress, previous caesarean and breech presentation (Thomas and Paranjothy, 2001), see *Figure 12.2*. The adoption of and routine use of electonic fetal heart monitoring, medicolegal issues and declining numbers of vaginal breech births are all factors that have played a large contribution to the growing rates of caesarean section over the past 20 years (Dodd et al., 2004).

The role of the midwife

Providing information

Antenatally

The provision of information during childbirth is paramount to a satisfying birth experience (Beake et al., 2005) and a recent Government White Paper emphasizes the midwife's role in providing the information (Department of Health, 2006). Midwives should strive to ensure that women are fully conversant with the facts. In an Australian study women were found to be familiar with the advantages of caesarean section but far fewer knew of the risks associated with it (Gamble and Creedy, 2001). In a more recent study in north-west England women were found to base their decisions about having a repeat caesarean section on the experiences of friends and relatives rather than seeking out health professionals (York et al., 2005).

As almost one in four women will give birth in this way, it is clear that all women and their partners should be provided with information about caesarean section before birth. They should be informed about the risks of morbidity and they should also be offered information about the more practical effects of having a caesarean, such as difficulty handling the baby and mobilizing, and a prolonged healing period. This information is necessary for women to make informed choices and to reduce the risk of caesarean (e.g. medical interventions in labour such as epidural anaesthesia, augmentation with oxytocinon). In the event of a caesarean section becoming necessary, being prepared beforehand will go some way to making the experience as positive as possible (Churchill, 1997).

Information can be provided for women and couples in group settings as part of a parent education programme as well as on a one-to-one basis. Additional written information should always be given to support this. However, printed information should not replace verbal information from a health practitioner (Rosun et al., 2005). Women and their partners need to consider the disadvantages as well as the perceived advantages of having a caesarean section. They need to know the increased risks of morbidity, which can occur to women and babies. Having information also goes a long way to preparing women for the more practical effects of caesarean section: by considering some of the more difficult issues associated with caesarean section (e.g. pain, immobility) women are provided with an idea of what to expect; 'forewarned is forearmed' (Clement, 1995: 85). In a recent study some women following birth by caesarean section were found to have unrealistic expectations of care on the postnatal ward and became disenchanted when the baby was not taken away to a nursery for care (Baxter, 2006). Women need to be informed through the provision of parent education that most babies stay with their mothers as best practice suggests unless the baby is unwell.

Vaginal birth after caesarean section

Women who have had a previous caesarean section have a strong need for information from their midwife and obstetrician antenatally. As soon into the subsequent pregnancy as possible such women and their partners need to be reminded of the reason why the previous caesarean section was necessary. They can use this information together with research evidence during discussions with their midwife and obstetrician to make decisions about the forthcoming birth experience.

Successful vaginal birth following previous caesarean was achieved in more than 50% of women in published studies (Enkin et al., 2000). However, it becomes less likely among women who had their first caesarean section for failure to progress in labour. Vaginal birth following caesarean section is safe and there are no absolute contraindications. Women who achieve this do not appear to have any more complications than other women who have previously given birth vaginally (Placek and Taffel, 1988). However, recommended practice is that it takes place in a hospital and national guidance recommends that women contemplating vaginal birth after caesarean section have continuous electronic fetal heart monitoring (NICE, 2001). A small number of women weigh up the risks of scar rupture in the context of their own situation and opt to labour at home or more commonly in a birth centre. Integrated (attached to an obstetric unit) and freestanding birth centres are most commonly run by midwives and intermittant auscultation is the main form of fetal monitoring.

Supporting women who choose to act against national guidance can be challenging for midwives. It is important that the midwife is satisfied that the woman and her partner are both fully aware of the risks. If English is not the first language the support of a professional interpreter should be sought prior to any discussions taking place. In order to achieve this the couple should also be given the opportunity to speak to an obstetrician. The ideal aim is for the three parties (woman and her partner, midwife and obstetrician) to work together and create a plan of care, prior to labour commencing, that is agreeable to all (e.g. where a woman has had a previous caesarean section agrees with her midwife and obstetrician to change from her original plan for a homebirth and have care in an integrated birth centre where she will be nearer to an operating theatre in the rare event of an emergency situation arising). Best practice suggests that a woman in this situation should have care in a setting where continuous electronic fetal monitoring can be provided (NICE, 2001). Being on a hospital site within close proximity to emergency support yet in the more homely setting of a birth centre may serve as a compromise. If, following discussion, a woman still chooses to opt for a home birth or care in a centre without continuous electronic fetal monitoring a midwife should consult her named supervisor of midwives. In this event, together with the woman and her partner, the supervisor and the midwife will be able to draw up a plan of care which optimizes safety for the woman and fetus. The perception a woman has of what safety is, is sometimes different to that defined by the health professional (e.g. a homebirth request so that she can be around for her four other children when she goes into labour is a more important consideration for a single, unsupported mother than the fact that she is defined as grand multiparous and therefore does not meet the criteria for homebirth). In such situations careful discussion should take place within a caring and mutually trusting mother–professional relationship to establish a plan of care for labour that suits both mother and professional.

Postnatally

Following birth and prior to transfer home all women should have a discussion with their midwife and obstetrician. A woman who undergoes birth by caesarean section needs to know the exact reason why the caesarean section was performed so that she can make informed choices in future childbirth experiences. The jury is still out on the usefulness of routine debriefing following birth but it has been found to be effective in some situations (Lavender and Walkinshaw, 1998).

A recent study investigating the hospital care of women following caesarean section found discordance between what some women understood to be the reason why their caesarean section was performed and what was written in the case notes by the obstetrician (Baxter, in press). This same study found the indication for caesarean section by the obstetrician not always to match the reason understood by the woman herself in about one-fifth of cases. A previous study found that 20% of women were unclear or did not know why they had needed to have a caesarean section (Hillan, 1992). Despite efforts to involve women more fully in care decisions and advances in the level of information being provided since the *Changing Childbirth* report (Department of Health, 1993) some women still do not appear to know the reason why they needed to have a caesarean section. This highlights the need for the woman and her partner to have the opportunity to meet with the obstetrician who carried out the operation so that they are clear about why the caesarean section had been necessary.

Provision of emotional support

Some women have been found to fear the prospect of giving birth vaginally. For such cases counselling has been found to be beneficial to reduce the caesarean section rate (Sjogren and Thomassen, 1997). Midwives need to be aware of women's reactions to having given birth by caesarean section. Some women report the experience of having a caesarean section as being positive while others see it negatively (Clement, 1995). It is essential that women receive sufficient psychological support around the time of the caesarean section. Midwives need to ensure that a woman's partner is involved both in the

Table 12.1 Women's feelings about not having experienced a vaginal birth

Feeling	Caesarean sections		
	Planned	Emergency	All
Very disappointed	14 (9.2%)	25 (20.2%)	39 (14.1%)
Disappointed	23 (15.0%)	33 (26.6%)	56 (20.2%)
Neither disappointed nor pleased	71 (46.4%)	55 (44.4%)	126 (45.5%)
Pleased	28 (18.3%)	7 (5.6%)	35 (12.6%)
Very pleased	17 (11.1%)	4 (3.2%)	21 (7.6%)
Total	153 (100%)	124 (100%)	277(100%)

preparatory stages before the caesarean is performed and during the operation itself. Partners should be encouraged to be present as women value them being at their side during this difficult time. Partners who are present gain personally by attending the birth of their child and at the same time are able to provide support for their loved one.

Women who experience birth by caesarean section will also gain further emotional support by having continuity of carer. Pregnant women value seeing a familiar face when they give birth. The benefits for a woman of having the same carer throughout her childbirth experience are well known (e.g. reduction in the need for pain relief in labour, the baby is less likely to require resuscitation) (Hodnett, 2000). This becomes even more important for women giving birth by caesarean section. When setting up maternity services care providers should, wherever possible, aim to provide optimal support for women during a possibly frightening experience. For the large majority of women, giving birth is the first time they have been in hospital, let alone in an operating theatre. Having a midwife who is known to her and explaining procedures, will be reassuring for the woman and her partner.

From a psychological perspective, Clement (1995) stated that women's feelings about their caesarean section are influenced by three things: how necessary they perceived the caesarean section to be, the extent to which they felt informed and involved in childbearing decisions and the amount and quality of support before, during and following the procedure.

Women who gave birth by caesarean section responding to a questionnaire in 2003 were asked the question, 'How do you feel about not having had a vaginal birth?' *Table 12.1* illustrates the 277 responses where 45.5% said they were neither disappointed nor pleased with not having experienced a vaginal birth, 34% were disappointed or very disappointed and 21% were either pleased or very pleased (Baxter, in press).

The same study found differences according to whether the caesarean section was elective or emergency and a pattern emerged showing women whose caesarean sections were unplanned to have higher levels of disappointment and fewer instances of being pleased regarding not having had a vaginal birth compared with the women whose caesarean sections were planned. In contrast more women whose caesarean sections were planned said they were either pleased or very pleased about not having experienced birth vaginally and fewer in this group felt disappointed. This concurs with other studies where women were found to be less happy following emergency caesarean section (Churchill, 1997).

In the Baxter (in press) study two thirds of the women were either neutral or pleased about having had a caesarean section. This contrasts with concerns about negative feelings among women following caesarean section and confirms that some women are satisfied with this type of birth experience. The same group of women were given the opportunity to comment on their feelings about not having experienced birth vaginally. The largest theme to emerge was the feeling that the caesarean section was the right thing to do under the circumstances to achieve the outcome of a healthy baby.

'I am pleased to be able to choose the safest option for delivery for my baby. Disappointment didn't come into it.'

'There are advantages and disadvantages. I wanted my baby to be safe most of all.'

These findings concur with other work. Clements (1995) also found a positive perception of the caesarean section among women who knew that it was essential to save the baby's life or avoid serious handicap. Churchill also reiterates this phenomenon in her work in 1997. She blames the power imbalance between the obstetrician and the woman. Women believe the doctor if he or she says a caesarean section is necessary. Women are vulnerable and naturally do not want to argue with the doctor if the life of their unborn child is at risk.

Interestingly Clement also found in 1995 that women who did not consider the caesarean section to be absolutely necessary were more likely to report negative feelings about the birth.

Currently the value of postnatal debriefing is being questioned (Ayers et al., 2006; Gamble et al., 2002). The limited evidence base is conflicting with some studies showing benefits in the form of a reduction in levels of anxiety and depression at four weeks post-delivery (Lavender and Walkinshaw, 1998) while others failed to find differences in fear of future childbirth between women who received debriefing and women who received normal care (Kershaw et al., 2005). However, the process of debriefing and going through the entire birth experience with a health professional has been found to help some women and their partners to reach an understanding and draw conclusions and thus be able to think positively about future childbirth possibilities (Baxter et al., 2003). It is essential that all women who have had a caesarean section are provided with the opportunity of meeting with their care provider in order to gain a full understanding of why the procedure was performed (NICE, 2004). This will help women and their partners come to terms with the fact that they had a caesarean section and equip them with the necessary knowledge to be able to make future childbirth decisions.

An initiative to improve care for women following caesarean section

Care on postnatal wards has been found to be lacking (Baxter and Macfarlane, 2005; Beake et al., 2005). In 2002 in an inner-London NHS trust feedback from some women who experienced birth by caesarean showed them to perceive their care to be lacking following transfer to the postnatal wards. This includes requiring more help with feeding and caring for their babies, waiting for long periods before receiving pain relief and failing to receive help with personal hygiene. According to the National Childbirth Trust (NCT), following birth by caesarean section, women report a range of experience on postnatal wards from very good to very poor (NCT personal communication, 2003). An evaluation was conducted of a pilot project which aimed to improve care for women who give birth by caesarean section (Baxter and Macfarlane, 2005). Registered general nurses (RGN) and nursery nurses were recruited and added to the skill mix of the postnatal wards at night to provide further support for the midwives with the care of these women.

There is little previous work published in this area. Traditionally midwives have been the gatekeepers of the care of all women during their stay in the postnatal wards. Registered general nurses and nursery nurses do not generally feature in the skill mix of the staff in this area. However the caesarean section rate is at its highest peak for many years and the recently published NICE clinical guideline on the care of women who have caesarean sections underlines that women have more care needs following major surgery (NICE, 2004). Furthermore there is a national shortage of midwives. It was proposed that the nurses would be able to support these women with their specific nursing needs while recovering from surgery and the nursery nurses would help the women with the care of their babies.

The study set out to compare the situation before (February–April 2003) and after (September–December 2003) general and nursery nurses were introduced into the postnatal wards. Data were collected by sending postal questionnaires to women who had experienced birth by caesarean section and obtaining their views, and by reviewing their case notes. Overall some 422 questionnaires were sent out in both phases, 289 were returned – a response rate of 68%. In all 402 case notes were reviewed in both phases.

Overall satisfaction with care improved following the introduction of the nurses and nursery nurses. In phase two (after the nurses and nursery nurses were recruited) 53% of women described the care they received on the postnatal ward during the day as excellent or good compared with 35% saying the same during phase one. Differences were higher at night. In phase two 59% of respondents described their care as being either excellent or good compared to 27.5% saying the same in phase one. There were also improvements in the women's perceptions of staff appearing busy. Staff appeared less busy in phase two when 43% of women said staff were often too busy compared with 63% in phase one.

Staff availability and care of women following caesarean section were most in need of improvement according to the women. Fewer women commented about these areas in phase two. Several other themes emerged from the written general comments given by the women. These included 'a general lack of care', 'too few staff', and 'a lack of confidence in staff'.

Practical support and the provision of help and advice on the postnatal ward also improved following the introduction of the nurses and nursery nurses. In phase two 73% of women reported receiving support with feeding either always or sometimes which was significantly higher than the 48% of women reporting this in phase one. There were also statistically significant increases in the proportion of women who received help and advice with feeding the baby, caring for the baby and for their own health needs between the two phases.

Support with physical care also improved following the introduction of the nurses. When requesting pain relief, the women in phase two did not wait as long as those in phase one before pain relief was administered. Sixty five percent of women in phase one waited for more than 15 minutes compared with 34% in phase two.

More women in phase two remember a staff member inspecting their wound compared with phase one but the figures were no different than would be expected by chance and more women in phase two said they received help with personal hygiene, such as assistance to wash in bed or get to the bathroom: in phase two, 59% reported this compared with 44% in phase one.

Catheter care was also reported more frequently by the women in phase two. This was significantly higher than in phase one. More women were also found to have their fluid input and output recorded following the introduction of the nurses. In phase one 3% of notes showed that fluid balance was recorded compared with 10% in phase two.

Measurements of vital signs (e.g. blood pressure, pulse, temperature) also increased. Eighty one percent of women had their vital signs measured three or more times during the first 24 hours when they were on the postnatal ward during phase two compared with 59% in phase one.

This evaluation shows that after the introduction of the nursing staff there was a significant improvement in the overall satisfaction with postnatal care as experienced by women who have had caesarean sections. In addition differences were found in the physical aspects of care. Consequently the introduction of new roles in postnatal care at this hospital appears to have improved care for women who experienced birth by caesarean section.

Conclusion

The caesarean section rate continues to rise across the UK. While it is recognized that caesarean section is a valuable, and indeed lifesaving obstetric intervention for some women, there are others who may be experiencing this major operation unnecessarily.

As advocates for women during their experiences of childbirth midwives play a vital role in influencing rates. Together with obstetricians, midwives practise within an organizational culture. They must exercise their autonomy within the maternity team (e.g. when interpreting electronic fetal monitoring, and by establishing midwife-led birth centres). By entering into relationships with women and providing full and concise information at this time for women and their families midwives can successfully empower them to make optimal decisions about whether or not a caesarean section is necessary. When a caesarean section is undertaken midwives ensure that both practical and emotional support is provided for women and their families.

References

Al-Mufti R, McCarthy A, Fisk N (1997) Survey of obstetricians' personal preference and discretionary practice. *Eur J Obstet Gynec Repro Biol* **73**: 1–4.

Ayers S, Claypool J, Eagle A (2006) What happens after a difficult birth? Postnatal debriefing services. *Br J Midwifery* **14(3)**: 157–61.

Baxter J, (2006) Women's experience of infant feeding following birth by caesarean section. *Br J Midwifery* **14(5)**: 290–5.

Baxter (in press) Comparison of women's perceptions and clinicians' documented reasons for caesarean section. *Br J Midwifery*.

Baxter J, Macfarlane A (2005) Postnatal caesarean care: Evaluating the skill mix. *Br J Midwifery* **13(6)**: 378–84.

Baxter J, McCrae A, Dorey-Irani A (2003) Talking with women after birth *Br J Midwifery* **11(5)**: 304–9

Beake S, McCourt C, Bick D (2005) Women's views of hospital and community-based postnatal care: The good, the bad and the indifferent *Evidence Based Midwifery* **3(2)**: 80–6.

Bennett V, Brown L (eds.) (1999) *Myles Textbook for Midwives* (13th edn.) Churchill Livingstone, Edinburgh.

Churchill H (1997) *Caesarean Birth Experience, Practice and History Books for Midwives*. Hale, London.

Clement S (1995) *The Caesarean Experience*. Pandora, London.

Department of Health (1993) *Changing Childbirth*. The Stationary Office, London.

Department of Health (2005) *NHS Maternity Statistics, England: 2003-4 Bulletin 2005/10*. The Stationary Office, London.

Department of Health (2006) *Our Health Our Care Our Say*. The Stationary Office, London.

Dodd JM, Crowther CA, Huertas E, Guise JM, Horey D (2004) Planned elective repeat caesarean section versus planned vaginal birth for women with a previous caesarean birth. *Cochrane Database of Systematic Reviews* Issue 4.

Eniola O, Bewley S, Waterstone M, Hooper R, Wolfe C (2006) Obstetric hysterectomy in a population of South East England. *J Obstet Gynaec* **26(2):** 104–9.

Enkin M, Chalmers I, Keirse J (eds) (2000) *A Guide to Effective Care in Pregnancy and Childbirth* (3rd edn). Oxford University Press, Oxford.

Fenwick J, Gamble J, Mawson J (2003) Women's experiences of caesarean section: A birthrites initiative. *Int J Nurs Pract* **9**: 10–17.

Francome C, Savage W, Churchill H, Lewison H (1993) *Caesarean Birth in Britain*. Middlesex University Press, London.

Gamble JA, Creedy DK (2000) Women's request for a cesarean section: A critique of the literature. *Birth* **27(4)**: 256–63.

Gamble JA, Creedy DK (2001) Women's preference for a cesarean section: Incidence and associated factors. *Birth* **28(2)**: 101–10.

Gamble JA, Creedy DK (2005) Psychological trauma symptoms of operative birth. *Br J Midwifery* **13(4)**: 218–24.

Gamble JA, Creedy DK, Webster J, Moyle W (2002) A review of the literature in debriefing or non-directive counselling to prevent post partum emotional distress. *Midwifery* **18(1)**: 72–9.

Hall M, Bewley S (1999) Maternal mortality and mode of delivery. *Lancet* **354(9180)**: 776.

Hannah P, Adams D, Lee A, Glover V, Sandler M (1992) Links between early post-partum mood and post-natal depression. *Br J Psychiatry* **160**: 777–80.

Hildingsson I, Radestad I, Rubetsson C, Waldenstrom U (2002) Few women wish to be delivered by caesarean section. *Br J Obstet Gynaec* **109(6)**: 618–23.

Hillan EM (1995) Postoperative morbidity following caesarean delivery. *J Adv Nursing* **22**: 1035–42.

Hodnett E (2000) Continuity of caregivers for care during pregnancy and childbirth. *Cochrane Database of Systematic Reviews* Issue 1.

Kaufmann T (2000) Caesarean section: A public health issue. *RCM Midwives Journal* **3(1)**: 11–13.

Kershaw K, Jolly J, Bhabra K, Ford J (2005) Randomised controlled trial of community debriefing following operative delivery. *Br J Obstet Gynaec* **112(11)**:1504–9.

Kingdon C, Baker L, Lavender T (2006) Systematic review of nulliparous women's views of planned cesarean birth: The missing component in the debate about a term cephalic trial. *Birth* **33(3)**: 229–37.

Lavender T, Walkinshaw S (1998) Can midwives reduce postpartum psychological morbidity? A randomised trial. *Birth* **25**: 215–19.

MacDonald C, Pinion SB, MacLeod UM (2002) Scottish female obstetricians' views on elective caesarean section and personal choice for delivery. *J Obstet Gynec* **11(6)**: 586–9.

NICE (2001) *Electronic Fetal Monitoring: The Use and Interpretation of Cardiotocography in Intrapartum Fetal Surveillance*. National Institute of Clinical Excellence, London.

NICE (2004) *Caesarean Section. Clinical Guideline 13*. National Institute of Clinical Excellence, London.

Odent M (2004) *The Caesarean*. Free Association Books, London.

Placek P, Taffel S (1988) Vaginal birth after caesarean section (VBAC) in the 1980s. *Am J Public Health* **78(5)**: 512–15.

Rosun R, Curry N, Florin D (2005) *Public Views on Choices in Health and Health Care*. The Kings Fund, London.

Royal College of Midwives and National Childbirth Trust (2001) *The Rising Caesarean Section Rate: Causes and Effects for Public Health*. Royal College of Gynaecologists, London.

Ryding E, Wijma B, Wijma K (1997) Posttraumatic stress reactions after emergency cesarean section. *Acta Obstet Gynaec Scand* **76(9)**: 856–61.

Ryding E, Wijma K, Wijma B (1998) Experiences of emergency cesarean section: A phenomenological study of 53 women. *Birth* **25(4)**: 246–51.

Sjogren B, Thomassen P (1997) Obstetric outcome in 100 women with severe anxiety over childbirth section. *Acta Obstet Gynaec Scand* **76(10)**: 948–52.

Smith GC, Pell JP, Dobbie R (2003) Caesarean section and risk of unexplained stillbirth in subsequent pregnancy. *Lancet 362*: 1779–84.

Thomas J, Paranjothy S (2001) *The National Sentinel Caesarean Section Audit Report.* Royal College of Obstetricians and Gynaecologists Press, London.

Warwick C (1999) Rising caesarean section rate: A public health issue. *Br J Midwifery* **7(12)**: 731.

York S, Briscoe L, Walkinshaw S, Lavender T (2005) Why women choose to have a repeat caesarean section. *Br J Midwifery* **13(7)**: 440–5.

CHAPTER 13

Services for women with disabilities: Mothers' and midwives' experiences

Stella McKay-Moffat and Cliff Cunningham

Introduction

Although statistical data are not available, anecdotal evidence from midwives in practice for a long time and a specialist midwife who is a disability advisor (Rotheram 1989, 2006, personal communication) indicates that more women with disability appear to be meeting the challenges of parenthood. Indeed Carty et al. (1993) reported similar trends in Canada over a decade ago. The slowly burgeoning literature addressing the issues related to this area of midwifery practice and women's experiences would support this opinion. This increase in numbers is possibly due to changes in attitudes towards disability such as a decreasing societal framework of control over individual lives, and the offering of information and enabling the promotion of freedom of choice. Potentially, individuals' personal desires to express sexuality and the wish to become parents are coupled with the desire to be the 'carer' rather than the 'cared for'.

Unfortunately, the little empirical research available indicates that encounters with maternity services may well be less than optimal for these women. However, caution must be employed with interpretation of study results as the numbers of women participating in each study are often small (most researchers indicate that they had great difficulty in obtaining participants) and the length of time since they gave birth may not reflect the maternity service of today. Nevertheless, substandard care has been attributed to professionals' lack of knowledge and understanding (Smithers, 1988; Rotheram, 1989; Goodman, 1994; Thomas and Curtis, 1997; and Lipson and Rogers, 2000 from America); poor communication skills and insensitive care (Goodman, 1994; Rotheram, 1989; Lipson and Rogers, 2000). Additionally Rotheram (1989) discovered that termination of pregnancy had been offered because of the women's disability. Crucial themes in these studies parallel those found in the supporting literature that encompassed written accounts by the mothers themselves (e.g. Campion,

1990; Maternity Alliance, 1994; Crow, 2003). This was seen as creating psychological barriers to effective care, and inadequate services.

Evidence from mothers indicated their desire for normality, independence and acceptance as mothers (Campion, 1995; Maternity Alliance, 1994; Thomas, 1997; and Grue and Tafjord Lærum, 2002 from Norway) with pregnancy often undertaken after considerable thought and planning because of their disability.

Caution should be exercised in applying the evidence to maternity services in the UK today, as many of the women in the published studies gave birth some considerable number of years ago. Nevertheless, this evidence does suggest that because midwives are the main providers of maternity care, they may need more preparation to provide effectively the services that women with disabilities require. However, before specific recommendations are made, more needs to be known about the recent experiences of mothers and midwives' knowledge, experience, expertise and attitudes towards both people and mothers with disability. This was the aim of the present study.

Methodology

The study was in two parts consisting of semi-structured tape-recorded interviews with eight midwives from three different maternity units and five mothers living in the study areas. The research questions for the interviews were:

1. What are the current views and experiences of mothers and midwives?
2. What are the attitudes of midwives to pregnancy in women with a disability?

The research questions were about fact finding and describing a current phenomenon rather than testing a theory or hypothesis. This qualitative method focuses on the real world of lived experiences through thoughts and feelings that may otherwise not be identified.

Ethical considerations

Ethical committee approval was sought and given by the appropriate NHS trust committees. Oyster et al. (1987) stated that the rights and well-being of research subjects should be protected. With this in mind, participants' consent was sought and facilitated by clear information on the purpose of the project in the letter of invitation that was sent with a consent form, and again prior to interview. Participants were assured of anonymity and confidentiality which extended to destruction of the interview tapes following transcription. Immediately prior to the interview, participants were assured that the tape-recording and the interview would be halted at any time, without prejudice, if they did not want to continue. Additionally, time was offered after the interview to give participants the opportunity to discuss any issues (Robson, 1996). Thus any potential stress instigated by the interview would be acknowledged and responded to, for example provision of additional information and support or discussion about care, practice or professional issues.

Selection criteria and recruitment

Midwifery managers of three maternity units known to the researcher in the north-west of England were contacted to seek midwives with varied years in practice, with experience of providing midwifery care for mothers with disabilities who were willing to be interviewed about their experiences. This purposive sampling method ensured a cross-section of appropriate, willing participants who were likely to give insightful answers to the research questions (Robson, 2002; Rees, 2000, Cluett and Bluff, 2000). It was also a convenience sample in that the participants were within a geographical area that was easily accessible to the researcher and incurred minimal travel time and costs. Of the 12 midwives sent invitations, eight were interviewed: one was unable to attend at the last minute and three failed to reply to the invitation. A repeat invitation was not sent to avoid pressurizing the midwives to participate. *Table 13.1* gives the characteristics of the participants. Midwives 1 and 3 in unit A were known to the researcher.

A convenient purposive sample of mothers was obtained by the researcher asking the interview midwives and other midwife associates to contact mothers with a disability they knew with a child under five years old. The explicit time-scale was selected to obtain mothers who were able to reflect the current situation regarding maternity care for women with disabilities. This contact was to seek permission for the researcher to write to them inviting participation in the study. Six out of 12 mothers identified agreed to be contacted: five completed consent forms were received. *Table 13.2* gives the characteristics of the participants. Of the six mothers who did not wish to be contacted, one had achondroplasia, three were hearing impaired, one was visually impaired and one mother had an upper limb disability. This latter mother did not wish to be contacted as her new baby was unwell in the neonatal unit; no details were available why the other mothers refused. The mother who did not reply to the invitation was not contacted again as it could have been construed as applying pressure to participate.

The interview procedure

Participants were able to choose the interview time and location. All of the mothers preferred to be interviewed in their own home, while the

Table 13.1. Midwives' characteristics			
Midwife	Years of qualification	Additional qualifications	Areas of practice
Unit A			
Midwife 1	5	RGN OU Degree	Hospital and community
Midwife 2	1	Diploma in professional studies	Hospital and community
Midwife 3	22	RGN	Labour ward
Unit B			
Midwife 1	5	Diploma in higher education	Antenatal and postnatal ward
Midwife 2	6	RGN Diploma in midwifery	Antenatal and postnatal ward
Unit C			
Midwife 1	1.5		Hospital wards on rotation
Midwife 2	18	RGN	Community
Midwife 3	16	RGN, RSCN	Community

midwives chose their practice location. An active interview approach (Hoistein, 1995) was adopted. The protocol contained key questions and possible prompt questions to focus the interview on the research issues. The mothers were asked for biographical details and obstetric history. Open questions elicited details about both their disability and consequent challenges to daily living. Further questions encouraged them to talk about their experiences of maternity services. The midwives were asked about their qualifications, length of service, type and hours of practice. Open questions prompted them to share their experiences of providing care for mothers with disabilities. In each case pertinent information was explored using additional impromptu questions until no more new information was obtained.

The interviews typically lasted 1–2 hours and were conducted over a period of 8 weeks during 1999. Tape-recording the interviews enhanced the accuracy of the data collected and allowed direct eye contact during the interview. Any non-verbal clues to meaning behind the words spoken were noted immediately in writing following the interview. After completion of each interview

Table 13.2. Mothers' characteristics

Unit A

Mother 1 (age 33 years)

Type of education	Secondary school
Work	Full-time mother
Age of children	3 years + pregnant (planned)
Marital status	Married
Type of disability	Paralysed arm after road accident
Lenth of time disabled	Since early 20s

Mother 2 (age 39 years)

Type of education	Secondary school + doing literacy course
Work	Full-time mother
Age of children	19, 11, 9, 6, 2 years (last one unplanned)
Marital status	Divorced, no partner
Type of disability	Below knee amputation due to vascular disease
Lenth of time disabled	Since beginning of last pregnancy

Mother 3 (age 30 years)

Type of education	Secondary school + college
Work	Logistics for a major company
Age of children	4 weeks (unplanned)
Marital status	Single, partner not resident
Type of disability	Cerebral palsy
Lenth of time disabled	Congenital

Mother 4 (age 35 years)

Type of education	University degree
Work	Pharmacy technician
Age of children	15 months (planned)
Marital status	Married
Type of disability	Multiple sclerosis
Lenth of time disabled	3 years

Unit B

Mother 1 (age 30 years)

Type of education	Comprehensive school
Work	Civil servant
Age of children	8 months (planned)
Marital status	Married
Type of disability	Abnormal pelvis and gait
Lenth of time disabled	Congenital

participants were given an opportunity to discuss any issues (Robson, 1996) but none felt the need to do this.

Data analysis

Formal analysis began as soon as possible and was conducted manually rather than using a software package as numbers were small. All factual information, key words and phrases were highlighted. These were coded into categories and then themes. Themes from the mothers' interviews were compared; and those from the midwives were compared. General themes from each group were then compared. For personal reasons the researcher suspended the study for one year. On recommencement the transcripts were read again, to enable re-orientation to and reflection on the data. This altered the perception of the data (Riley, 1990), for example a greater similarity in some categories was noted and implicit themes were increasingly identified. Therefore the analysis was repeated resulting in greater clarity of themes and increased credibility in the results.

Credibility and reliability

To enhance the credibility and reliability of the results further and the validity of the process, an independent colleague analysed 25% of the scripts using the same process. The themes were assured as comparable results were obtained. Clear links between many of the study findings and the literature offers additional confidence in the credibility of the results.

Results

Mothers

In contrast to findings from an earlier study (Rotheram, 1989), termination of pregnancy had not been offered to any mother because of her disability. However, the mother with cerebral palsy had briefly considered termination because of her single status, and anaesthetic concerns during surgery in early pregnancy meant the mother with the leg amputation was given the option of termination.

Theme 1: The quest for normality and independence
In common with reports from mothers in the literature, three of the mothers had planned their pregnancies: indeed the mother with the abnormal pelvis had been receiving fertility treatment. The mother with multiple sclerosis (MS) had carefully considered the implications of pregnancy after advice from her specialist. One non-supportive doctor was, as she said:

'*...painting a more black picture about how it would affect me in the long term as well as in the short term.*'

The need to maintain a sense of independence and normality meant the mothers did not wish their disability to be the main focus of attention. The mother with the paralysed arm said that because she had acquired the disability 10 years earlier she felt self-conscious:

'*I don't like broadcasting it. Sometimes it's not necessary to let people know.*'

This resulted in a reluctance to seek professional help preferring to struggle to cope. However, as the mother with MS said:

'*Much as I didn't want to be labelled disabled or having MS, there was a bit of me that kept saying, "I have got needs".*'

Another mother also acknowledged that many may not want to ask for help, but she said:

'*All you can do is let people know that help is there and it's really up to them if they want to take you up on it.*'

Yet for two of the mothers, coping without asking for help was a positive aspect building self-confidence through finding their own solutions to problems.

Theme 2: The disability as paramount

Without exception all of the mothers' experiences were influenced by their disability. Mothers 2 and 3 both indicated degrees of self-consciousness and embarrassment as they felt their disabilities drew people's attention. The mother with cerebral palsy was embarrassed about her tremor and would not attend parent education classes because of it. The mother with the below knee amputation was predominantly sensitive during labour. She said:

'*[the midwife] held onto my stump if I needed to push. I was mortified, the fact that it was a stump and people thinking, "I'm not touching that" ... It does make people cringe, not that they tell you that. I was bothered about it bothering.*'

Three mothers with acquired disability blamed this for their lack of confidence and feelings of inadequacy as mothers. They not only felt less able to fulfil the role but also had concerns that others perceived them as incapable of coping.

Theme 3: Midwives' lack of knowledge

Due to what they believed was midwives' lack of knowledge and acknowledgement about their disability and its consequences, three mothers felt that their needs had largely been unrecognized. No midwife had discussed possible additional needs, therefore the opportunity to ask for help was not afforded. The mother with the paralysed arm said:

'No one has mentioned it [her disability]. The only time they notice it is when my blood pressure has to be taken, when I try to roll up my sleeve.'

Four mothers felt that midwives lacked skills to offer practical solutions for infant care to overcome the disabling aspects of their impairment. This resulted in dissatisfaction with care provision for two mothers: one even implicating her subsequent perceptions of inadequacy with her postnatal depression.

Theme 4: Disability awareness and positive attitudes

Four mothers experienced care from some midwives that was sensitive, respectful and responsive to their needs while maintaining their privacy and dignity which they valued. These factors contributed to feelings of satisfaction with their care. One mother noted the contrast to her life-long experience of other health professionals, she explained:

'...I think it was the general attitude, it was very refreshing and very relaxed ... They said, "We're here if you need us." I like that.'

Another mother stated that the midwives either failed to acknowledge her disability or watched her because of it. She said,

'It's a fine line between offering help to people and making them feel different. It must be difficult sometimes to get the balance right.'

The mother with MS felt that the midwives lacked understanding about her condition, in particular the fatigue. This she felt resulted in insensitive and intolerant care, and failure to give her prescribed medication regularly. Lipson and Rogers (2000) have noted that people with less visible disabilities often receive insensitive care. Yet for the mother with the very obvious disability of an amputated leg, the midwives appeared not to have considered her altered balance after the relatively recent loss of her limb and how that might have impacted on her during labour.

Theme 5: Effective communication

Vital to aid the mothers' satisfaction, but not always achieved, was effective communication. This was between midwife and mother and midwife and the multidisciplinary team. The mother with the leg amputation said:

> '*I was petrified of going into labour ... I kept saying to [the midwife] all through my pregnancy, "How am I going to deliver this baby if I've only got one leg?" You put both feet up don't you, to bear down?*'

But she felt less afraid and anxious when midwives gave her information and discussed issues, and went onto say:

> '*They were really, really good, the whole team [of midwives] really supportive, all the information they could possibly give me. Anything I needed or wanted. They explained everything in full. I couldn't fault them.*

However, labour and delivery conversations did not involve discussion of a 'dry run' to ascertain the best positions, leaving her bewildered and confused during labour.

Effective inter-professional communication ensured that two mothers did not have to draw attention to their disability by repeating their history. This meant less embarrassment and frustration and increased satisfaction in their care and was in contrast to their usual experience of health care. However, three other mothers felt that their care would have been enhanced if the midwives had contacted the occupational therapist or a specialist midwife to seek their expertise.

Results

Midwives

Theme 1: Midwives' lack of knowledge

All midwives had provided midwifery care for between two and six mothers with varied mobility and sensory disabilities. However, they generally felt that they lacked knowledge and experience in some aspects of care provision. This caused them some anxieties about their ability to provide effective care. Three used the word 'inadequate' to express their feelings while another said she felt 'out of my depth' and another 'anxious about missing something'. But it was clear from what one midwife said that experiential learning outside of midwifery has the potential for the development of transferable skills, she said:

> '*...[family member] is quite deaf so I am used to making sure that the person can see my face all the time. So that you don't bury your face in the cot while you are doing things and hope she will hear.*'

Another midwife offered her view:

'...*experience is a great teacher. It's what you do with that experience that is important.*'

Nevertheless, lack of educational opportunities, e.g. relevant literature and study days, had meant only limited disability education for the midwives.

Two non-nurse midwives expressed a lack of knowledge about disabling conditions generally: one specified MS in particular. Six midwives recognized that the mother was the expert in her condition and situation and therefore they would seek information from her. As one put it:

'*They probably know more about it than you'll ever do. They suffer from the condition and therefore you ask them what their boundaries are and that sort of thing, or what they need you to do.*'

Theme 2: Midwives' attitudes

In general the midwives' attitudes were positive towards mothers with disability. This was evidenced by their respect for the individual whom they felt should be treated the same as every woman, without her disability being paramount. Words like a partnership in care, the midwife as the mother's advocate, flexibility, adaptability, sensitivity, and choice were all evidence of positive attitudes towards the mothers. This was further supported by all of the midwives acknowledging a woman's right to choose to have a baby and not be offered termination because of her disability.

Three midwives emphasized the importance of seeing the mother before the disability. A comment from one midwife was:

'*I tried really hard to talk to them as they are, women who are in labour, who are pregnant...*'

Although three others found this more difficult, one in particular when the woman was a wheelchair user. This very experienced midwife with a nursing background stated:

'...*I've noticed if you ask [about the disability] you shouldn't have asked ... If you don't ask you're not acknowledging them.*'

Theme 3: Effective communication

Either overtly or implicitly, all midwives expressed the importance of effective communication to aid care planning. Although all midwives alluded to the availability of other services only two mentioned contacting other health professionals or support agencies for help.

Communication with mothers was not perceived as easy in every situation and as one midwife observed:

'If they have communication problems, that can be quite stressful [for the midwife] because you are not sure whether you are giving them the right information.'

Of particular concern was the potential to cause offence by what was said or not said, for example, appearing to undervalue people with a disability when discussing antenatal screening for fetal abnormality, or not asking about her disability thus apparently ignoring it. The challenge of communicating with a deaf mother could cause frustration for all concerned, and four midwives felt that sign language skills would be invaluable.

Limitations of the study

The main limitation of the study was the small number of participants although qualitative studies of this nature rarely contain large numbers because of time constraints (Robson, 2002). The difficulty in obtaining participants with a disability has been highlighted by other researchers (for example Goodman, 1994; Thomas, 1997; Grue and Tafjord Lærum, 2002). The mothers had a variety of congenital and acquired disabilities but there were no mothers with sensory disability which would have enriched the data by possibly identifying different issues.

The data were, like much qualitative data, vulnerable to various sources of bias. The mothers' experiences were both positive and negative. It is possible that mothers with more negative experiences did not wish to re-live those experiences by being interviewed. Therefore data from these mothers may have led to different results. Different results may have been obtained with a larger number of midwives and it could be argued that, since the midwives were self-selected, elements of bias may have been present.

Researcher bias may have been present during the interviews because of midwifery knowledge and experience. Nevertheless, careful preparation of interview protocols (Robson, 2002) helped to limit any influencing factors. On a supportive note, the researcher's credibility with the mothers and fellow midwives may have aided mutual trust and respect, and promoted acceptability to the participants aiding the honest and open sharing of experiences. Identification of themes may have been somewhat subjective because of personal values, experience and personality (Lipson and Rogers, 2000). However, the methodological checking and re-checking of transcripts and a subsequent re-analysis after some considerable time aided the thorough interpretation of data. Additionally, the validity and reliability of themes were supported by analysis from an independent colleague.

Discussion

Although the midwives were not a representative sample of the profession, they had a broad range of experience, and in their interviews discussed a wide range of issues. The practice-orientated approach to the gathering of evidence was grounded in the real-world experiences and perceptions of both mothers and midwives. The mothers had a variety of congenital and acquired disabilities offering a wide perspective on 'managing life with an impairment' and perceptions of maternity services.

Despite the small numbers, the results appear to reflect some of the findings from previous studies and accounts from mothers, while refuting others. None of the mothers was offered termination of pregnancy because of their disability. The experiences of the mothers in the study and the reflections of the midwives indicated a lack of disability knowledge and, in some cases, a lack of helping skills similar to the findings of Smithers (1988), Rotheram (1989), Goodman (1994), Thomas and Curtis (1997) and Lipson and Rogers (2000), and the mothers' accounts in the literature. This caused the midwives concern about their ability to offer effective care. Midwifery care seemed, in the main, to be provided with sensitivity unlike reports from Goodman (1994), Rotheram (1989) and Lipson and Rogers (2000).

There were two striking findings. Firstly, the conflict between the mothers' need for independence and desire to be treated as normal, which paralleled the findings of Thomas (1997) and Grue and Tafjord Lærum (2002), and the need to have acknowledgement of the disabling aspect of their impairments. This caused them dilemmas about drawing attention to their disability and seeking midwives' help, possibly aggravated by a lack of confidence in the midwives' ability to offer assistance.

Secondly, specific elements of communication were identified as opposed to communication in general, as highlighted in the literature (Rotheram 1989, Goodman 1994, Lipson and Rogers 2000). These specific areas related to the difficulty that some midwives identified in knowing what to say to the mothers and how to ask questions without being perceived as insulting, particularly related to antenatal screening for fetal abnormality and about the disability. This then had implications for discussing needs and appropriate help, and had the potential to inhibit preparation for parenthood. As a consequence of the midwives' unwillingness to engage with the mother they relied on the mother to ask for help. In a sense this reluctance of both mothers and midwives to address the issue of the disability can be seen as a form of collusion to avoid potential painful or embarrassing topics.

When mothers and midwives described instances of effective communication there were many signs and statements that mothers felt less anxious and more satisfied with their care. A further specific communication issue appeared to relate to the lack of liaison with other health professionals to seek their support and expertise, for example, the occupational therapist and specialist midwife. None of the mothers had been afforded the opportunity by the midwives for referral to others. Only two midwives seemed clear about the referral process or had actually made contact with experts for assistance. The others appeared not to consider the potential value of expert help to either the mothers or themselves.

Evident from the midwives, and highlighted in more recent UK (Rotheram, 2002) and Canadian (Carty, 2002) literature was their need for further general education about disabilities and specific education related to meeting mother's additional needs. From what the mothers said it is apparent that those needs may be different for the mother with acquired disability, especially if relatively recent, compared to a congenital or long-term disability where adaptability and acceptability are more likely. Therefore, different supportive techniques and abilities are essential.

Conclusion

Although there appears to be some improvement in services for mothers with disability, there is still much to be achieved. Midwives need to develop a proactive, confident service within a partnership of care. The knowledge and demands of service users should be utilized, and the expertise of specialist professionals and organizations brought together. This sharing of skills through collaborative working will enhance women's childbirth experiences by improving standards of care, resulting in service satisfaction for both mother and midwife.

References

Campion MJ (1995) *The Baby Challenge: A Handbook on Pregnancy for Women with Physical Disability.* Routledge, London.

Carty E (2002) Health care for women with disabilities in British Columbia. *Disability Pregnancy and Parenthood International* **40**: 11.

Carty E, Conine T, Holdbrook A, Riddell L (1993) Guidelines for serving disabled women. *Midwifery Today* **27**: 2–37.

Cluett E R, Bluff R (eds.) (2000) *Principles and Practice of Research in Midwifery.* Bailliere Tindall, Edinburgh.

Crow L (2003) Invisible and centre stage: A disabled woman's perspective on maternity care. *Midwives* **6**: 158–61.

Goodman M (1994) *Mothers' Pride and Others' Prejudice: A Survey of Disabled Mothers' Experiences of Maternity.* In: Maternity Alliance

Disability Working Group Pack. Maternity Alliance, London.

Grue L, Tafjord Lærum K (2002) 'Doing motherhood': Some experiences of mothers with physical disabilities. *Disabil Soc* **17**: 671–83.

Hoistein JA (1995) *The Active Interview*. Sage Publications, London.

Lipson JG, Rogers JG (2000) Pregnancy, birth and disability: Women's health care experience. *Health Care Women Int* **21**: 11–26.

Maternity Alliance (1994) *Listen to Us for a Change: A Charter for Disabled Parents and Parents to Be*. In: Maternity Alliance Disability Working Group Pack. Maternity Alliance, London.

Oyster TC, Hanten WP, Llorens LA (1987) *Introduction to Research. A Guide for Health Services Professionals*. Lippincott Co, Philadelphia.

Rees C (2000) *An Introduction to Research for Midwives*. Books for Midwives Press, Oxford.

Riley J (1990) *Getting the Most From Your Data. A Handbook for Practical Ideas on How to Analyse Qualitative Data*. Billing and Sons Ltd, Worcester.

Robson C (1996) *Real World Research: A Resource for Social Scientists and Practitioner Researchers*. Blackwell Publishers, Oxford.

Robson C (2002) *Real World Research* (2nd edn.) Blackwell Publishers, Oxford.

Rotheram J (1989) Care of the disabled woman during pregnancy. *Nurs Stand* **4(10)**: 36–9.

Rotheram J (2002) The maternity needs of disabled women. *Disability Pregnancy and Parenthood International* **40**: 10–11.

Smithers K (1988) Practical problems of mothers who have multiple sclerosis. *Midwife Health Visit Community Nurse* **24(5)**: 165, 167–8.

Thomas C (1997) The baby and the bath water: Disabled women and motherhood in social context. *Sociol Health Illn* **19(5)**: 622–43.

Thomas C, Curtis P (1997) Having a baby: Some women's reproductive experiences. *Midwifery* **13**: 202–9.

CHAPTER 14

Midwives and travellers

Kath Jones

Introduction

The provision of maternity services to women from diverse and ethnic backgrounds can often prove challenging to midwives. Understanding the complex issues surrounding culture, ethnicity and race is paramount to meaningful engagement with these groups. It is acknowledged that access to health care is poor and that health inequalities are greater among ethnic minority groups.

This chapter will describe the health care given to gypsy travellers and how the use of multidisciplinary, multi-agency forums can break down barriers and provide greater access to health and social care.

Who are gypsy travellers?

Gypsy travellers are defined by the Caravan Act (1968) as 'people of a nomadic habit or lifestyle whatever their race or origin'. In the UK the term is used to include Romany gypsies, and Irish, Welsh and Scottish travellers. They are recognized as a racial group in case law applicable to England and Wales, and Irish travellers have been given statutory recognition that they are part of a racial group in Northern Ireland.

The 1976 Race Relations Act identified that Romanies are an ethnic minority. However in the document *New Deal for Communities: Race Equality Guidance* (1999) there is no category of traveller included in the definition of black and ethnic minorities.

Because of the wide spectrum of travellers and lifestyles, it is often difficult to describe precisely who is a gypsy traveller. For the purposes of this chapter, the group described will be gypsy travellers whose membership is dictated by birth and consists of subgroups of English, Welsh and Irish travellers.

Not included are: gypsies who have originated from Europe and obtained refugee status; show and fairground travellers; bargees and other families living in boats; and new age travellers who are a diverse group with varying beliefs and backgrounds who live a nomadic existence.

Gypsy travellers have various patterns of residence. Some live an entirely nomadic lifestyle, while others reside in permanent, private or unauthorized campsites. Many live a settled lifestyle in housing but retain their gypsy traveller identity.

Okley (1983) suggests that the definition of travellers should be based on descent. She argues that a traveller's status is ascribed at birth and reinforced by upbringing and commitment to travellers' values and lifestyle.

The health status of travellers is significantly poorer than the settled population (Linthwaite, 1983). While it is acknowledged that travellers have poor health there is scant reliable research on travellers' health status. Studies by Feder (1998) and Hajoff and McKee (2000) have focused on child and maternal health, infant mortality, perinatal death rates, low birth rate and childhood accidents. The major problems relating to health appear to be coronary heart disease and mental health problems. Much of this evidence is anecdotal. A salient factor appears to be the poor access to health services that this group encounters, thereby exacerbating any underlying health inequality (Feder, 1998). A small local study by McDonald and Roberts (2001) identified increased mental health problems such as depression and psychosis, linked to alcohol abuse, and schizo-affective disorders. They also identified alcoholism as a local problem along with an increasing use of cannabis.

The problem of substandard living accommodation is a factor that impacts on health. Pahl and Vaile (1988) reported that traveller mothers identified problems in caring for their children due to the dirt, traffic, overcrowding, poor washing facilities and lack of education provision.

The policy document *Saving Lives: Our Healthier Nation* (Department of Health, 1998) identifies social, economic and environmental factors as the primary causes of ill health. A report by Morris and Clements (1999) found that 'travellers experience levels of deprivation in these areas which is possibly without parallel'.

Access to health care for travellers is a significant factor. The positioning of sites, often long distances from health centres, coupled with poor literacy, means that appointment compliance is poor. This in turn leads to removal from general practitioner and dentist lists as they are perceived as a difficult group. This often leads to the inappropriate use of accident and emergency departments where gypsy travellers often suffer discrimination due to lack of cultural understanding.

Government legislation towards addressing inequalities in health is in place. *Saving Lives: Our Healthier Nation* (Department of Health, 1998), aims to improve the health of everyone, but the health of the worst in particular. It does not however emphasize ethnic minorities or travellers.

Acheson (1998) recommended that 'policies considering inequalities of health should include consideration of the application of those policies to ethnic groups as a matter of course'.

In Ireland a specific strategy to address the inequalities in health of travellers called the *National Strategy for Travellers' Health 2002–2005* was produced by the Traveller Health Advisory Committee (Department of Health and Children, 2002). This strategy was developed with traveller involvement and identified factors that adversely affect traveller health.

Challenges for midwives

The challenges that face midwives providing care to traveller women encompass both cultural and health-related issues. For care to be effective, women need to access the service early. It is important that they are aware of their named midwife and how to contact midwifery services.

In areas where this is well established the service works effectively. This trusting relationship, built on advocacy and respect, enables both the woman and the midwife to develop and sustain a working partnership. Midwives who provide this care need to have knowledge of the culture of gypsy travellers in order to maximize their understanding. Reid (2005) stresses that

'Negative stereotyping may prevent midwives from communicating effectively with traveller women leading to care that is ineffective and inappropriate – care that frustrates and creates and maintains inequalities.' (p.24)

The antenatal booking interview is best carried out by a midwife known to the women. Many women are often embarrassed at their lack of literacy. Traditionally gypsy traveller women will not take up screening for Down's syndrome as their cultural and religious beliefs, mostly Roman Catholicism, will not allow termination of pregnancy. Increasingly, women are having antenatal screening but will not act on negative results.

Pregnancy and birth are traditionally seen as women's work and there is very little involvement of men. When care takes place it is usually women family members who are present and the men are out at work or congregating in groups around the site. There is a slight cultural shift developing and some men will accompany the women for scan appointments or to the labour ward. The older women discourage men from attending the birth so they are often outside the room. Celebrations often start with the onset of labour so men will often arrive at the maternity unit having consumed alcohol. Because large numbers of women accompany the labouring woman to the hospital it can have an impact on the labour ward staff as they can perceive this as threatening. There is often conflict between family members when there is an emotional occasion such as birth or death. This is dealt with in a very open and public way with very little thought for other women or staff.

Home birth is not the norm, trailers are seen to reflect women's personal cleanliness and they would not want them contaminated by the 'mess' of birth. This contrasts with the often untidy and dirty conditions outside the trailers.

In the author's experience, gypsy traveller women do not tend to want early discharge postnatally. Celebrations of the birth are often loud with large numbers of visitors attending the wards. They often suffer discrimination from other women and their relatives and members of staff. Liaison with a midwife assigned to the travellers can often diffuse these situations.

The cultural stereotype of young gypsy traveller women is that of loud, garish and scantily dressed women. This is in direct opposition to the modesty that is displayed in exposing their bodies for examination. Abdominal palpations can be difficult when there is a reluctance to remove or move clothing. While most of the women agree and understand the benefits of breastfeeding, very few actually use this method of feeding. The exposure of the breasts is seen as 'shameful' and even those who do breastfeed would not do so in front of men or in public.

The health promotion aspect of midwifery care to travellers is particularly challenging. This author's experience has been that this group has poor diet, usually very high in fat, and the young women constantly 'yo yo' diet with the tendency to stop eating meals and take slimming tablets or drinks.

Smoking and alcohol consumption has always been a health hazard in this group. While many will agree to commence smoking cessation programmes, their lifestyle makes it difficult to sustain. Most of the women will reduce their alcohol consumption while pregnant but events such as weddings or funerals increase the consumption often to the level of binge drinking. The use of illegal drugs is not a major problem but there is an increase in cannabis smoking among the men.

Sexually transmitted diseases such as chlamydia are increasing as with the general population. This may be diagnosed following childbirth when a baby develops an eye infection. It is extremely problematic as the men are reluctant to attend specialist clinics. Most of the women have only had one sexual partner and when they are given the information that the infection is sexually transmitted, it often exacerbates domestic abuse as the men have been exposed for committing adultery.

Accessing family planning and well woman clinics is difficult. Again, the literacy problem and often chaotic lifestyle can inhibit the uptake of these services. Gypsy traveller men are reluctant to take responsibility for contraception. They perceive large families as a sign of their virility. Many women do not inform their partner that they are using contraception and so the preferred method is the intra-uterine contraceptive device or, increasingly, contraceptive implants. The author's experience differs to that of Rigal (1997) who identified that the oral contraceptive is preferred. Uptake of cervical screening is poor, and, along with the large number of pregnancies experienced by women, there is a high incidence of gynaecological problems. Dealing with problems such as incontinence is made more difficult in the confined space of a trailer with inadequate sanitation or washing facilities.

In the author's experience domestic abuse is often a way of life for these women. Families will not interfere, and while the consequences may lead to hospital admission, the women rarely press charges. If they do enter a women's refuge, they will often give information about their whereabouts to a family member. This information will then be passed on to the partner who will contact the woman and beg forgiveness. She then returns into the cycle of abuse. This is problematic for agencies such as the Women's Aid movement. Enquiries about domestic abuse can be made by midwives because partners are rarely present at consultations. Disclosure is not usual unless there are obvious signs of injury. It is acknowledged that screening is more effective when carried out by a professional who the woman knows and trusts.

This is confirmed by Bacchus et al. (2001) who suggest that routine enquiry needs to be conducted in a safe, confidential environment by a trained, non-judgemental, empathic health professional without time constraints and limited resources. The difficulty often faced by this group and other ethnic minorities is that the presence of family members can block disclosure.

There is little evidence of child abuse among gypsy travellers. However, due to the nature of sites the accident rate is high. Children are often observed wandering around outside the trailers inappropriately dressed for the weather conditions. Gypsy traveller children tend to have a higher hospital admission rate than the settled population.

Understanding the gypsy traveller culture is important in order to access the women and provide a service that is relevant to their needs. The culture observed surrounding death is particularly relevant in relation to caring for women after the loss of a baby. It is their practice to burn any possessions of a dead person. Many women will be unable to accept the mementos that are now encouraged, such as a keepsake box, although more women are now keeping photographs. Grief is displayed very publicly with large numbers attending the funeral. This has implications for policing and local councils when large numbers of caravans descend on an area. The support from other women is tremendous with the grieving person being 'nursed' back to health.

The increase in multi-agency travellers' forums has highlighted the health deficits and socioeconomic problems faced by gypsy travellers. One of the primary aims is to develop a more inclusive service for this vulnerable group. The involvement of gypsy travellers in the forums leads to more effective development of local policies and service provision.

The forums usually comprise representatives from health, education, police, local council, social services and the church. Members can be co-opted where specific expertise is required.

Forums give voice to the travellers, enabling them to address issues specific to them in a formal arena which is non-threatening. Forums enable a specialized body of knowledge to be built up and shared with other professionals.

While many travellers do not wish to be included in mainstream society, the marginalization which occurs in terms of access to health, housing and education is prevalent. Forums are an effective way of developing and evaluating local policy initiatives. Travellers are encouraged to take responsibility and to be accountable within the forum. This is often the first time older travellers have had this type of responsibility afforded to them.

Working in partnership has a definite positive effect on health promotion. Events can be staged with all agencies involved raising awareness. Using such arenas, subjects such as domestic abuse can be explored and groups set up to encourage women to be assertive and raise their self-esteem.

Children are encouraged to take part in events such as healthy eating and are involved in shopping for and preparing food.

When there are named professionals involved with a traveller community, the sharing of knowledge becomes easier. They can identify potential problems and work together to support the families. Traditionally there have been poor relationships with authorities such as local councils and the police. By involving these agencies, a greater understanding by all parties can be achieved and this leads to improved relationships. The opportunities for improving both the health and social needs of travellers is greater when there is collaborative working within multi-agency groups.

The work of a midwife with gypsy travellers is not purely the provision of midwifery care. It means becoming integrated into their culture and providing a holistic approach to health. Listening to the women and hearing their stories is a valuable means of greater understanding. Midwives are in a privileged position to be able to impact, not only on the immediate health of this vulnerable group, but also on the future health of the families.

References

Acheson D (1998). *Independent Inquiry into Inequalities in Health*. HMSO, London.

Bacchus L, Bewley S, Mezey G (2001) Domestic violence in pregnancy. *Fetal Matern Med Revi* **12**: 249–71.

Department of the Environment, Transport and the Regions (1999) *New Deal for Communities: Race Equality Guidance*. HMSO, London.

Department of Health (1998) *Saving Lives: Our Healthier Nation*. HMSO, London.

Department of Health and Children (2002) *Traveller Health: A National Stategy 2002–2005*. Stationary Office, Dublin.

Feder G (1998) Traveller gypsies and primary care. *J Royal Coll Gen Pract* **39**: 425–9.

Hajoff S, McKee M (2000) The health of the Roma people: A review of the published literature. *J Epidemiol Community Health* **54**: 864–9.

Linthwaite P (1983) *The Health of Traveller Mothers and Children*. East Anglia Save the Children, London.

Morris R, Clements L (1999) *Disabilty, Social Care, Health and Travellers*. Traveller Law Support Unit. Unpublished.

Okley J (1977) Gypsy women: Models in conflict. In: S Ardener (ed.) *Perceiving Women*. Dent, London.

Okley J (1983) *The Traveller-Gypsy*. Cambridge University Press, Cambridge.

Pahl J, Vaile M (1988) *Health and Health Care Among Travellers*. University of Kent Health Research Unit, Canterbury.

Rigal J (1997) Family planning for Irish traveller women: Gender, ethnicity and professionalism at work. In A Byrne, M Leonard (eds.) *Women and Irish Society: A Sociological Reader*. Colour Books, Dublin.

Reid B (2005) Re-visioning the provision of maternity care for traveller women. *Royal College of Midwives: Evidence Based Midwifery* **3(10)**: 21–5.

Roberts A, McDonald K (2001) *An Assessment of the Health Needs of the Travelling Population of Wrexham and Deeside*. Unpublished manuscript.

CHAPTER 15

Exploring midwives' attitudes to teenage pregnancy

Debrah Shakespeare

Introduction

Midwives have been told for a number of years that Britain has a problem with teenage pregnancies (Department of Health, 1992, 2004a, b). This is usually followed up with statements providing evidence that Britain has the highest teenage pregnancy rates in Europe (Social Exclusion Unit, 1999). With evidence and statements such as these, a commitment was made by the (then) Government to reassess issues surrounding this subject. It sought to explore reasons why this 'problem' was occurring, and how best it could manage it. However, it is fair to say that parts of British society appear to have adopted a belief that teenage pregnancy occurs as the result of reckless behaviour (Health Education Authority, 1998).

This prompted the author to question whether such views were evident within the midwifery profession. Hence, do midwives hold the same feelings and attitudes towards teenage pregnancy as those present in society? And, more importantly, does this affect the care that they deliver? With this, a study was conducted to explore the attitudes of six community midwives working in the north of England. It adopted a phenomenological approach, as it sought to examine the lived experiences of these midwives and the experiences they had in relation to teenage pregnancy. There were some common themes and sub-themes that emerged from the data. Elements of these data in the form of actual text are presented in this chapter. There are also elements of discussion and analysis presented relating to the findings. They show that the midwives had indeed encountered some real dilemmas through their experiences with pregnant teenagers and with the care that they had provided to this group of clients. In conclusion, there are some implications for future midwifery practice identified from the text, including the need for support for those midwives experiencing some tough dilemmas throughout their daily practice. The midwives' own words and phrases have been used where direct quotations are given, no alterations have been made by the author.

Britain has a problem with teenage pregnancy (Department of Health 1992, 2004a, b,). There are well-documented health risks involved with early sexual intercourse. These include increased risks of cervical cancer and sexually transmitted diseases (University of York, 1997). It is also recognized that teenage pregnancy and early motherhood are associated with poor educational achievement, poor physical and mental health, social isolation and poverty (Health Education Authority, 1998). Poverty and social disadvantage are risk factors that increase a woman's likelihood of dying throughout pregnancy and early motherhood (CEMACH, 2004). This is an issue that midwives need to consider, given that many teenage mothers are said to experience both social disadvantage and social exclusion.

The issue of teenage pregnancy is also compounded by evidence suggesting that teenagers are becoming sexually active at a younger age and that contraceptive uptake is generally dependant on the climate surrounding the sexual health of young people (Wellings and Kane, 1999).

The teenage years deal with much risk-taking behaviour (Flinn et al., 1998), yet they involve a transition from being a child to emerging an adult. During this time the individual undertaking the transition has to deal with new feelings and emotions, some of which could carry life-long consequences. For health care professionals to minimize such risks, a greater understanding into the subject of teenage sexuality and pregnancy is needed.

However, problems can arise when the general view of certain phenomena is different to the view of the individuals encountering it. The media and some Government reports depict teenage pregnancy as being morally wrong and linked with poverty and low social status (Social Exclusion Unit, 1999).

A greater understanding may be achieved by examining the experiences of those dealing with teenage pregnancy on a daily basis. The close examination of these experiences, reflections and attitudes could serve to identify whether the beliefs of these individuals hold with the wider beliefs of society in general. It could also serve to identify areas of conflict if the beliefs differ.

Study design

This study was written in 1999 and examines six community midwives' lived experiences of teenage pregnancy. Some of the references have been updated to reflect recent publication and guidance. However, the bones of the research have not been altered in any way and the findings have been presented in their original form. The study explored the midwives' existing knowledge into this subject and identified the sources of this knowledge. It also described how certain issues influence the attitudes of the midwives, which may affect the care they aim to provide to this group of clients. The study adopted a phenomenological approach.

Databases including CINAHL and MIDIRS were searched in a selective literature review.

The most common problem encountered while undertaking the literature review was that the articles on the whole appeared to consist of collections of quotations and references from previous articles. Careful examination of the many articles enabled some consistencies and contradictions to be identified, and some common themes emerged. These were:

- Lack of professional knowledge and education concerning sexuality.
- Poverty and social deprivation.
- Contraceptive issues.
- Sexual health.

There appeared to be a common theme that Britain appears ill-equipped to deal with issues relating to sexuality and sex education (Minns, 1994), and this related to health care professionals, teachers and parents alike (Wellings et al., 1994).

There have been strong links between teenage pregnancy and negative social and health outcomes for those involved (Minns, 1994; Mander, 1999; Woods and Sellars, 1999). There is a general undertone in some articles that there was a financial implication associated with teenage pregnancy (Woods and Sellars, 1999). This fails to differentiate between any intended or unintended pregnancy, which is an important issue within the subject of teenage pregnancy. In contrast, other articles stated that poor social outcomes are not inevitable (Wellings et al., 1994; Health Education Authority, 1998). It is clear that cultural and political influences can affect the way individuals perceive teenage pregnancy.

In England almost 90,000 conceptions per year occur to teenagers, and of these 56,000 result in live births (Social Exclusion Unit, 1999). Within the urban area of south Yorkshire where the study was conducted, the overall birth rate for 1999 was 3176. Of these, 346 occurred to women aged 12–19 years, representing 10.8% of the total births. A second search revealed that of these, 34 births occurred to women aged 12–16 years, representing 1.07% of the total.

Methodology

This study centred on a phenomenological approach, which predominantly deals with the 'lived experience' (Beauchamp and Childress, 1989). To explore the attitudes and feelings that community midwives hold towards teenage pregnancy, in-depth interviews of six community midwives were conducted and tape-recorded. No interview schedule was used.

Each interview lasted 30–40 minutes. The information obtained from these interviews, once transcribed verbatim, underwent rigorous and careful analysis using Colaizzi's seven-stage process of data analysis (Colaizzi, 1978). The findings are presented as such, and implications for future practice identified.

Ethical considerations

The decision whether to approach the local ethics committee was given much consideration, yet it was decided that, as there was no direct patient contact within the study, ethical approval would not be sought. However, this study was conducted in 1999/2000 and it is recognized that recent changes to guidance around research and ethical approval would now require this to be taken to the local ethics committee before undertaking this type of study. A consent form was signed by all participants who were told that they could withdraw from the study at any stage if they wished to.

Findings and themes

What is 'the problem'?

The first theme that appeared to emerge from discussions with the midwives was how they tried to rationalize what 'the problem' with teenage pregnancy was. For example, the midwives were asked to estimate the teenage pregnancy rates for the area. All of them overestimated the rates, yet it was noted that they appeared uncomfortable at being asked to make an estimation. The highest over-estimation was 25% of all deliveries.

A sub-theme emerged when the midwives attempted to make links with the socioeconomic profile of the area and went on at lengths to offer descriptions of the communities in which they practised. They described a very socially deprived area, built up, with high levels of unemployment, poor housing and a community that consisted of many underprivileged people:

> *'...a working class, it's a lower social class area, an ex-pit village ... quite socially deprived really...' (M3)*

The midwives made clear links between teenage pregnancy rates and social deprivation, but on the whole were unable to offer references for such knowledge:

> *'... I don't know exact figures but I would imagine rates are higher than what they would be in better social class areas.' (M4)*

There was also reference to high levels of single-parent families, with the midwives suggesting a link between this and a cultural link to teenage pregnancy.

A sub-theme that emerged from these discussions appeared to present many of the midwives with a clear and identifiable discourse – the sub-theme being what was the view of a teenager?

The midwives were asked to consider the term 'teenager'. All thought that it best described an age group rather than the individuals within the group. There was a strong sense of respect for individuality among the midwives and a feeling that respect should be afforded to all women regardless of age. It was thought that the term teenager could be used in the wrong context and was thus open to abuse and misrepresentation. They thought that the term did not represent the maturity of the individual and that there are huge diversities between the physical and mental maturity of women of the same age:

'I think you use the term teenager to express 13–19-year-olds don't you? That doesn't mean that every 13-year-old is exactly the same in maturity. Similarly, you could have a 19-year-old who is exactly as young as a 13-year-old ... er, I don't know what we term young people.' (M1)

The common belief was that the stereotypical label of 'teenager' was not wholly appropriate, yet before being asked, the midwives had not really thought about it.

General perceptions of teenage pregnancy, and the midwives' perception of this emerged as another sub-theme. The midwives expressed some conflict between what society thinks about teenage pregnancy, established through media coverage, and what they had actually seen in daily practice:

'Everybody knows what you mean by teenage pregnancy ... the word teenager conjures up the picture of an uncaring, probably troublesome person, which isn't necessarily the case.' (M3)
'...Well if you say a teenage pregnancy you think it's a bad thing don't you? ... It's got bad connotations ... you are labelled aren't you!' (M2)

However, through daily practice a different picture emerges. The midwives described the teenagers that they encountered as being quiet, shy people, nervous at accessing health care, yet needy and willing to learn. The uptake of maternity care by these people was said to be good. There were of course exceptions to this, yet there were the same exceptions for women in all age groups. This picture describes an individual who may be accessing health care for the first time in a predominantly adult service. A young person who may be facing responsibilities greater than ever before. On one hand they are being told they are children, yet on the other hand they are expected to behave as adults:

'We treat them like adults but accept that they have got extra needs.' (M5)
'It's all foreign to them and they don't know what they are letting themselves in for ... once they feel secure with us they start to come on their own.' (M3)

The midwives all commented on the fact that their experience of teenagers who were pregnant differed from the view held by society in general. This led to further discussions around how they thought that the Government and media are suggesting that teenage pregnancy is inherently wrong and as such needs controlling in some way. The message was being sent to the public that in some way poverty breeds poverty, and ultimately society will pay the price for these young people becoming pregnant at a young age. Hence, the general thought of this group of midwives was that society was led to believe that the real problem that teenage pregnancy brought to this country was one of 'financial burden':

'I mean there's a big thing about them getting benefits and seeing it as a way to get houses quicker, and I think they do!' (M2).

However, on closer examination of this belief, and by her own admission, this midwife had been brought up in a professional household and thus these were the beliefs that had been suggested to her by family members throughout her upbringing. In contrast, another midwife (M1) had a traditional 'working class' upbringing and appeared to be much more accepting of the phenomenon. Another (M2) vigorously argued the fact that she did not allow her personal beliefs to affect her work, however, she went on to say that she did feel that teenagers who became pregnant, were in effect 'ruining their lives'. Midwife 4 presented a similar view stating:

'They are going to miss out on so much – but that's my perception because they [the teenagers] might see that they are getting everything they wanted. If they do just want to be a mother that's what they are going to do anyway.' (M4)

One midwife remained totally neutral in expressing her feelings of teenage pregnancy, but did suggest that in accepting it, society could be seen to be encouraging it. She also spoke of her family's beliefs about teenage pregnancy which differed to her professional experience. However, she did not feel the need to challenge the assumptions that other family members were making about teenage parents.

Education

The second large theme that emerged from the data related to issues around education and health promotion. Education was a common theme that ran throughout all the interviews. Once again it led to much discussion, particularly around when and what to offer. This was thus separated into sub-themes, the first relating to education before teenage pregnancy had occurred.

The timing of sex education was discussed at length. It was generally thought that some forms of sex education should be offered to children at a younger age than at present:

'Well obviously if they are getting pregnant at 13 then we need to get there before then don't we?' (M5)

It was also thought that the responsibility of offering some form of sex education should be placed with the parents, hence encouraging a more open approach to sex and sexuality in general, rather than 'sweeping it under the carpet'. Interestingly, however, one midwife stated that she believed that young people need educating in such matters at an earlier age, yet she would not want that for her own daughters.

The content of such educational programmes was also criticized, although the majority of the midwives thought that the media assisted in educating young people. However, the media were also criticized by one participant who vehemently argued that:

'It's fine to talk about sex, you know, it's all in the media and these programmes on channel 5, then there's nothing happening, nothing about contraception ... it's just like saying sex is absolutely fine ... kind of glorifying sex without any kind of responsibility. I don't think they know enough about the facts of life.' (M6)

It was agreed by all that an authoritarian approach to delivering sex education would render the sessions ineffective. It was suggested that sessions would be best delivered by knowledgeable, supportive and non-judgemental professionals, not necessarily by teachers or other professionals in uniform, including midwives. Indeed, one participant thought that teenagers would view midwives as being too authoritarian in their approach. It was interesting also that the midwife thought that teenagers themselves should be canvassed on the content of such sessions:

'I don't think they expect teachers to be talking about that type of thing ... it needs to come from a person they can relate to.' (M2)

Surprisingly, none of the midwives interviewed mentioned the school nurse as being appropriate at delivering such education.

All midwives interviewed placed much emphasis upon offering pregnant teenagers some form of specific parent education. It was identified that there was local provision for this, yet numbers were limited and quite precious.

The midwives felt that, on the whole, teenagers did not access parentcraft education classes for a variety of reasons. Communication was a problem in the respect that it was felt that teenagers were not good at communicating their needs to health care professionals. This in itself led to them being misunderstood and labelled as not being bothered:

> 'They can't speak their needs very well. She may be classed as, "Oh! she won't be able to cope with her baby very well." ... They don't like to say anything, the midwives attitude may be, "Oh! not another one she's on income support, we're supporting her basically!"' (M6)

Half of the midwives explicitly suggested the specific needs of teenage parents in relation to smoking and diet, yet again they went on to suggest that midwives may be seen as being too authoritarian in their approach to education.

Peer support was an idea initiated by those questioned and all thought it to be a good approach to consider. However, one midwife went on to contradict her suggestion that peer support would work for younger clients by saying:

> 'I think if you have got a few youngsters in together then it'll give them some peer support amongst themselves.' (M4)
>
> 'You need the right sort of teenagers don't you ... they've got to be motivated really haven't they?' (M2)

This, in some respects, is true, but as to who decides what the right 'type' of teenager is could generate some conflict.

Support

The final theme that emerged from the data related to support. This, again, could be divided into two sub-themes, those of support from family and friends and support offered by health care professionals.

Looking at the first of these sub-themes, the issue of support from family and friends, the midwives felt that in the communities where they practised, the stigma of being a teenage parent was not as evident as in the past. They had found that the communities were much more accepting of this phenomenon than previously expected:

> '... I think the community as a whole takes on board these women as mothers, it's not seen as something outrageous I don't think, as much, any more. They accept it and get on with it.' (M4)
>
> 'There's no surprise, there's no shock and it's normal to see them. It's the inevitability that their daughter is going to reproduce at a young age.' (M3)

The mothers of the teenagers were repeatedly mentioned. It was generally felt that the mothers offered much support and frequently attended antenatal clinics with their daughters. It was also noted that they were more than often the main source of support in the early postnatal period, and often assisted in long-term childcare for those teenagers returning to education. However, it was also explicitly mentioned that the mothers did not appear to be taking over the role of parent for the newborn infants, rather they were there as support for the teenage mothers.

When asked whether the mothers took over, one midwife claimed:

'No, no way, when I say support, they're helping them, supporting them financially as well as psychologically!' (M5).

However, in contrast another midwife stated:

'I think sometimes the mothers do take over don't they, because they still see their teenager as a child and that they are still looking after them – I think they probably see it as a natural thing to do.' (M2)

There was mixed feelings about the role partners had to play. Initial reactions suggested that the partners were often absent following delivery:

'The lads still really want to go out like young lads do ... to have a good time before they settle down.' (M6)

However, given time to reflect on these feelings, many of the midwives went on to state how they had experienced very supportive partners who were willing to take on the demands of a new father.

The ability of teenage mothers to parent was a source for much discussion, and it was concluded that they were perfectly capable of coping with the demands of motherhood. However, it was also accepted that midwifery care covers only 28 days following the delivery, when the mothers are in a state of euphoria. Hence, any real problems with parenting may not be seen by midwives if they occur past this initial postnatal period, and that health visitors would probably be able to offer more insight into this:

'They are still in that, "Oh the baby's lovely" stage ... I think it's more the health visitors that see them getting [if they are getting] postnatal depression or if they aren't coping very well.' (M6)

It was felt that the ability of the teenager to cope and prosper is directly affected by the amount of support available to them. In this community the teenagers appear to adjust very well to parenthood, socially there is much support and acceptance towards them.

The midwives also provided discussions on the second sub-theme – that of support from health care professionals dealing with teenage pregnancy. This issue was presented in differing ways, some more obvious than others.

There was the feeling among the midwives that many of those teenagers who had fallen pregnant had done so intentionally. The reasons behind these actions were suggestive of the fact that pregnancy would increase the 'status' of the young women among their peers, particularly in relation to the individuals becoming eligible for benefits and housing. They also felt that teenage women became pregnant to provide them with something to love:

'I think that they want this thing to love them unconditionally and they want something to focus on, so I think some of it is planned to a degree and obviously they see their role in life as being a mother, and the status that brings'. (M6)

Finally the midwives were asked to comment on reasons why they thought other midwives held certain attitudes to teenage pregnancy. Lack of knowledge and prejudicial attitudes that stigmatize minority groups were common reasons offered:

'I think a lot of it is to do with personality, if you are tunnel-visioned then it doesn't matter how much you read or try to develop yourself, you just have to be non-judgemental. But I think that goes across the board anyway. I think we should be non-judgemental in our role full stop.' (M5)

On reflection this is a quality that would not solely benefit the midwifery profession, it could also serve to benefit society.

Conclusion

There were numerous conflicting discourses that emerged from the experiences of the community midwives interviewed in this small qualititive study. The community midwives presented a very different picture of the pregnant teenager from that presented by the media. These personal observations and opinions were formulated through their own practice and observation.

Teenage pregnancy appeared to be much more accepted within the local communities. It was also noted that there were also significant numbers of teenage pregnancies that were planned as it was seen as culturally normal to do so.

There was a strong commitment by the midwives in preserving the qualities of individuality and the provision of non-judgemental care despite pressures from other sources encouraging them to act towards pregnant teenagers in a given way.

All the midwives expressed the desire to contribute to the specific needs of pregnant teenagers yet wondered whether this was achievable within an already stretched service. However, they were acutely aware of the benefit that support and encouragement through education would bring to teenagers, thus encouraging these teenagers to make real choices for themselves.

Six years on from when this research was first commenced, teenage pregnancy is still an ongoing problem for a variety of reasons (Department of Health 2004a, b, CEMACH 2004), and while it is the opinion of this author that huge achievements have been made, we are a long way from achieving our goals, and those that were defined in the Social Exclusion Unit report (1999), namely to:

- Halve the under-18 conception rate by 2010.
- Provide support to teenage parents to reduce the long-term risk of social exclusion.

The subject of teenage pregnancy has obtained a higher profile among senior policy makers and this in turn has resulted in some rapid and effective action (Teenage Pregnancy Unit, 2005). However, the same evaluation suggests that while conception rates and birth rates have fallen among teenagers in the first four years of the strategy, there is still work to do. The 2010 target is considered, by most, to be 'challenging' and thus continued and sustained effort of all those working and caring for young people and parents is as important as ever.

The following recommendations were made when this study was first completed:

- Midwives need a forum within which they can identify safely, and without fear of repercussions, any personal or professional dilemmas resulting from conflicting discourses.
- Midwives are in an ideal position to offer their wealth of knowledge of health and social issues into mainstream education. However, resources are needed to support this.
- Development of peer group support and parenting groups specifically for pregnant teenagers should be encouraged.

It appears that these recommendations continue to be of relevance.

References

Beauchamp TL, Childress JF (1989) *Principles of Biomedical Ethics* (3rd edn.) Oxford University Press, Oxford.

CEMACH (2004) *Why Mothers Die 2000–2002*. Royal College of Gynaecologists Press, London.

Colaizzi P (1978) Psychological research as a phenomenologist views it. In R Valle, M King (eds.) *Existential Phenomenological Alternatives for Psychology*. Oxford University Press, Oxford.

Department of Health (1992) *The Health of the Nation: A Strategy for Health in England*. HMSO, London.

Department of Health (2004a) *Maternity Standard, National Service Framework for Children, Young People and Maternity Services* Department of Health, London.

Department of Health (2004b), *Choosing Health: Making Healthy Choices Easier*. HMSO, Norwich.

Depoy E, Gitlin L (1994) *Introduction to Research: Multiple Strategies for Health and Human Services*. Mosby, St Louis.

Flinn SK, Davis L, Pasarell S, Shah J, Zare R (1998) Adolescent pregnancy and too early childbearing. In A Henderson, S Champlin S (eds.) *Promoting Teen Health*. Sage, California.

Health Education Authority (1998) *The Implications of Research into Young People, Sex, Sexuality and Relationships*. Health Education Authority, London.

Mander R (1999) Teenage pregnancy: A challenge or a problem and for whom? *Midwives J* **2(9)**: 280–1.

Minns H (1994) Teenage pregnancy, *Modern Midwife* **July**: 12–14.

Social Exclusion Unit (1999) *Teenage Pregnancy*. HMSO, London.

Teenage Pregnancy Unit (2005) *Teenage Pregnancy Strategy Evaluation: Final Report*. Available from: http://www.dfes.gov.uk/teenagepregnancy/dsp_Content.cfm?PageID=85 [Accessed 11 October 2006].

University of York (1997) Preventing and reducing adverse effects of unintended teenage pregnancy. *Effect Health Care Bull* **3**: 1–12.

Wellings K, Field J, Johnson A, Wadsworth J (1994) *Sexual Behaviour in Britain*. Penguin, Harmondsworth, UK.

Wellings K, Kane R (1999) Trends in teenage pregnancy in England and Wales: Can we explain them? *J R Soc Med* **92**: 277–82.

Woods R, Sellars K (1999) Too much too young. *Sunday Times*. **5 Sept**: 13.

CHAPTER 16

Is perinatal depression a 'White woman' thing'?

Dawn Edge

Introduction

In light of research suggesting strong and consistent links between ethnicity and mental illness (Baker et al., 2002; Bhopal, 2001; Lloyd, 1998; Modood et al., 1997; Nazroo, 1997), it is reasonable to hypothesize that Black Caribbean women would be over-represented among those receiving treatment for depression during pregnancy and in the early postnatal period or 'perinatal depression'. However, despite the presence of putative risk factors such as poor partner support, high levels of lone parenthood, limited social support, and significant levels of deprivation and disadvantage (Baker et al., 2002; Baker and North, 1999; Smith et al., 2000) this does not appear to be the case. Anecdotal evidence from primary care practitioners (midwives, general practitioners, and health visitors) suggests that Black Caribbean women are less likely than the general population to consult with depression during pregnancy or in early motherhood.

In addition to their absence from clinical data, Black Caribbean women are also largely absent from the research into perinatal depression. This contrasts sharply with the picture for White and South Asian women in the UK among whom much research has been undertaken (see for example, Bostock et al., 1996; Fenton and Sadiq-Sangster, 1996; Appleby et al., 1994; Bolton et al., 1998; Evans et al., 2001; Taylor, 1999).

In this context, it occurred to me that, despite media reports about the prevalence and potentially serious consequences of depression; Black Caribbean women in my family and social networks were not engaged in the discourse on mental illness – including 'women only' mental illnesses such as postnatal depression, which have become sufficiently mainstream as to appear in television soap operas and other sections of the popular media (see for example, Reeder, 1999). In contrast to White British women within my social networks who spoke openly about their personal experiences of perinatal depression, Black Caribbean women neither related personal stories nor spoke of knowing other Black women who had been diagnosed with and/or treated for perinatal mental illness.

A number of explanations may be advanced for Black Caribbean women's absence from both clinical and research data. For example, it has been reported that Black Caribbean people not only have poorer access to services but are also more likely to report negative experiences and outcomes of contact with mental health services (Takei et al., 1998; Lloyd, 1993; Keating et al., 2002). Additionally, indirect racism and the use of negative racial stereotypes have also been shown to influence clinical encounters with associated consequences for outcomes of the diagnostic process (Littlewood, 2001; Ahmad, 1993; Hickling and Hutchinson, 1999; Spector, 2001). It is suggested that these factors might decrease the likelihood of Black Caribbeans receiving diagnoses with common mental illness such as depression and anxiety while increasing their risk of being diagnosed with serious and enduring mental illnesses such as schizophrenia and psychosis (Littlewood, 2001).

Although this may partly account for low levels of diagnosed perinatal depression among Black Caribbean women, the absence of this ethnic group from published research means that these hypotheses have not yet been formally tested. For example, to date, there has been little research into perinatal psychopathology or the role of ethnic/cultural factors in the aetiology, prevalence, models of care, and help-seeking among Black Caribbean women in the UK.

Outlining the research

Against this background, I undertook a mixed-method, longitudinal cohort study among women of Black Caribbean origin living in Manchester, UK (Edge, 2002; Edge et al., 2004). The aim of the quantitative component of the study was to investigate whether Black Caribbean women experienced depression in pregnancy and early motherhood and to estimate the prevalence of perinatal depressive symptoms among them compared with White British women living in the same geographical area and under similar socioeconomic circumstances. The purpose of the qualitative aspect of the research was to explore Black Caribbean women's beliefs about mental illness in general and perinatal depression in particular and to examine whether and how such beliefs influenced their attitudes to help-seeking.

During 12 months of data collection, I approached 429 women at antenatal clinics in central Manchester, UK of whom 297 self-labelled as being 'White British' and 132 of 'Black Caribbean origin'[1] – all of whom were in the final trimester of pregnancy. A self-selected sample of 301 women (101 Black Caribbean and 200 White British) consented into the study – a response rate of 70.1%. Participants self-completed an antenatal questionnaire (see Edge, 2002 for detailed methodology), which included demographic items and others related to generally agreed risk factors

---

[1] *The sample included all women who described themselves as being of 'Black Caribbean origin' including those who described themselves as being of 'mixed ethnic origin' or 'Black-British' but had at least one parent who originated from the Caribbean.*

for perinatal depression such as the number, nature, and sources of close personal supports and life events and difficulties. The questionnaire also incorporated the Edinburgh Postnatal Depression Scale (EPDS), a 10-item self-report psychometric measure used by health care professionals to assist in the detection of depression during and after pregnancy (Cox et al., 1987; Murray and Cox, 1990).

Of the original sample, 200 women (130 White British and 70 Black Caribbean) also completed postnatal questionnaires around six weeks after giving birth. In addition to the EPDS, the postnatal questionnaire included items relating to women's experience of labour and delivery, their health and well-being in the postnatal period, and the health and temperament of their babies – all of which have been linked with the onset of postnatal depression (Lyons, 1998; O'Hara and Swain, 1996; Cooper et al., 1996).

A sample of Black Caribbean women was subsequently selected for the qualitative phase of the study from women who completed both antenatal and postnatal questionnaires (details appear in the 'Qualitative study' section). The research received ethical approval from the Central Manchester Local Research Ethics Committee.

Quantitative findings

Data analysis

Data were analysed using the Statistical Package for Social Scientists (SPSS) (Bryman and Cramer, 2001; SPSS Inc., 2003). Although validated with a recommended cut-off of 12/13 postnatally (Cox et al., 1987) and 14/15 during pregnancy (Murray and Cox, 1990), the threshold for probable caseness was set at EPDS ≥ 12 because this was the threshold used by health visitors in routine clinical practice in the area in which the research was undertaken. Using this cut-off therefore facilitated comparisons between findings from this study and data derived from clinical practice.

Univariate relationships between ethnicity, psychosocial risk factors, and socio-demographic characteristics were examined using chi-square (χ^2), Fisher's Exact, and Mann-Whitney U tests as appropriate. Mean EPDS scores for Black Caribbean and White British women were compared using the independent samples t-test. Within group scores over time were examined using the paired samples t-test.

Results

Two-thirds of the sample ($n = 200$) were White British and one-third ($n = 101$) Black Caribbean. The oldest woman was 43 and the youngest 18. The mean age was 28.82 (*SD* 6.59). *Table 16.1* indicates that, compared with their

White British counterparts, there were significantly greater levels of social and socioeconomic risk for onset of perinatal depression among Black Caribbean women. For example, they were significantly more likely than White women to have lived in the most deprived areas of the city[2] (χ^2 = 12.08, df = 2, p < 0.01). They were also almost twice as likely to be bringing up their babies alone. Virtually half (48.5%) the Black Caribbean women (compared with (26.5% of White British women) were lone parents (χ^2 = 15.50, df = 2, p < 0.001). Additionally, those Black women who were married or cohabiting were significantly more likely than White women to report receiving little or no support from their partners (χ^2 = 8.64, df = 2, p < 0.05) or having confiding relationships with their partners (χ^2 = 4.14, df = 1, p < 0.05).

However, despite these risk factors, Black Caribbean women appeared to be less depressed than their White counterparts. Not only did they record lower mean EPDS scores than White British women but (at a cut-off of EPDS ≥12) 26% of Black Caribbeans compared with 38% of White British women (χ^2 = 4.16; df = 1; p < 0.05) scored above threshold suggesting that they had symptoms severe enough to equate to moderate clinical depression *(Table 16.1)*. Perhaps unsurprisingly in light of these findings, Black Caribbeans were significantly less likely to report having received treatment for depression (χ^2 = 7.77. df = 1, p < 0.01) or postnatal depression (χ^2 = 3.83, df = 1, p < 0.05).

Table 16.1 also shows that women who completed both surveys were less socioeconomically deprived than the antenatal sample. However, even among this more affluent group, Black Caribbean women were more likely to live in the areas of highest deprivation (χ^2 = 13.34, df = 2, p < 0.001) and be lone parents (χ^2 = 7.00, df = 2, p < 0.05). They continued to report dissatisfaction with partner support but were also less likely than White British women to receive support outside their spousal/cohabiting relationships (Fisher's Exact Test, 2-sided, p = 0.05). They also reported being more socially isolated – 64% (n = 45) compared with 45% (n = 58) of White British women reported being unable to get out as much as they wanted to (χ^2 = 7.05, df = 1, p < 0.01) and encountered multiple barriers to getting out (χ^2 = 15.02, df = 4, p < 0.01).

Taken together, these findings disprove the earlier hypothesis that suggested that Black Caribbean women were more likely to be more depressed than their White British counterparts. Despite experiencing higher levels of material deprivation and other social risks for onset of perinatal depression, Black Caribbean women were no more likely than their White British counterparts to experience depressive symptoms in the early postnatal period and were

---

[2]*Wards of the city in which participants lived were analysed using Department of Environment, Transport and the Regions deprivation indices (Department of Environment, Transport and the Regions, 2000) and sub-divided into three categories: the 'least deprived', 'most deprived', or 'middle' third of wards.*

Table 16.1. Characteristics of the sample

Variables	Antenatal sample (n = 301)			Postnatal sample (n = 200)			Non-respondents (n = 101)		
	White (n = 200) n (%)	Black (n = 101) n (%)	p-value	White (n = 130) n (%)	Black (n = 70) n (%)	p-value	White (n = 70) n (%)	Black (n = 31) n (%)	p-value
Mean age (±SD)	29.0 (6.4)	28.4 (6.8)	0.453	30.0 (6.2)	30.1 (7.0)	0.882	27.2 (6.3)	24.6 (5.3)	0.053
Unemployed	109 (55)	63 (63)	0.192	59 (45)	39 (56)	0.184	50 (71)	24 (77)	0.630
Living on benefits	69 (35)	39 (39)	0.525	35 (27)	25 (36)	0.201	34 (49)	14 (45)	0.830
Single	53 (27)	49 (49)	0.000	28 (22)	27 (39)	0.030	25 (36)	22 (71)	0.005
Most deprived	59 (30)	46 (46)	0.002	28 (22)	30 (43)	0.001	31 (44)	16 (52)	0.429
First baby	100 (50)	40 (40)	0.088	72 (55)	23 (33)	0.002	28 (40)	17 (55)	0.196
Poor partner support	12 (6)	17 (17)	0.013	20 (15)	16 (23)	0.287	13 (19)	9 (29)	0.385
History of depression	54 (27)	13 (13)	0.005	31 (24)	10 (14)	0.142	23 (33)	3 (10)	0.014
History of PND	15 (8)	2 (2)	0.050	6 (5)	2 (3)	0.716	9 (13)	0 (0)	0.036
EPDS mean (±SD)	9.9 (5.9)	8.8 (6.6)	0.309	9.1 (5.7)	9.1 (6.9)	0.998	11.6 (5.8)	7.9 (6.0)	0.005
Antenatal EPDS ≥12	75 (38)	26 (26)	0.042	39 (30)	19 (27)	0.671	36 (51)	7 (23)	0.007
Postnatal EPDS ≥12	–	–	–	27 (21)	19 (27)	0.307	–	–	–

significantly less likely to have done so during pregnancy (*Table 16.1*). A number of factors might account for these findings.

One possible explanation could be that generally agreed risk factors carry different salience for Black Caribbean women and might not therefore impact their mental health in ways that have been previously reported. For example, lone parenthood has been repeatedly implicated as carrying a high risk for onset of perinatal depression (Greene et al., 1991; Baker and North, 1999). Yet, despite significantly higher levels of lone parenthood among Black Caribbean women in this study, they were no more depressed than their White British peers. Similar findings have previously been reported by Lloyd (1998) who found that, while lone parenthood increased the risk of depression for Asian and White women, this was not the case for Black Caribbeans. Additionally, findings from the Fourth National Survey of Ethnic Minorities (Berthoud and Nazroo, 1997) indicate that, whereas marriage reduces the risk of depression for the general population, it appears to increase the risk of onset for Black Caribbeans – results which have been endorsed by findings among African Americans (Jackson, 2002).

This suggests that, compared with previous reports on White and South Asian women, there might be important aetiological differences in terms of the relationship between social risk and the onset of perinatal depression for Black Caribbean women. It may be, for example, that there are factors which ameliorate the impact of negative life events and adverse social circumstances in the lives of Black Caribbean women thereby affording them a measure of protection from onset of perinatal depression.

The qualitative study

In order to explore these issues further, a sample of Black Caribbean women was purposefully selected and interviewed in depth about their experiences of pregnancy, childbirth, and early motherhood as well as their beliefs about mental illness and perinatal depression in particular. The aim of this aspect of the research was to gain insight into the meaning that Black Caribbean women attribute to generally agreed social risk factors, to explore their coping strategies for managing adversity, and to explore their attitudes to accessing help and support.

Women were interviewed when their babies were between 6 and 12 months old since, according to the psychological literature, women at this stage were likely to have recovered from perinatal depression and are therefore able to describe and discuss their experiences and feelings without aggravating their condition or causing undue distress (Cooper and Murray, 1998). All the women chose to be interviewed in their own homes – although all were offered alternatives. With their consent, women's interviews (lasting between 45 minutes and 2 hours) were audiotaped and field notes recorded.

In order to facilitate the interview process, I used qualitative 'freetext', (collected during the quantitative study and from feedback obtained during development and piloting of the survey questionnaires) to develop an interview guide (Lofland, 1971). The interview guide (see Edge, 2002 for details) established a framework in which to undertake 'guided conversations' while enabling each interview to evolve – following its own path while allowing interviewees to recount their stories in their own way, thereby eliciting 'rich, detailed materials' for analysis (Lofland, 1971: 76).

Interviews were subsequently transcribed verbatim by the author and analysed thematically. Glaser's (1978) constant comparative approach was used to group themes into categories and sub-categories. These were then examined for 'goodness of fit', and re-organized into key themes. The interviews generated a total of 18 key themes comprising 235 sub-categories. QSR NUD*IST4 (Qualitative Solutions and Research, 1997) was used to facilitate data management. Women's responses were made anonymous and are reported here using interviewee-assigned numbers.

Qualitative findings

Black Caribbean women's construction of perinatal depression

Black Caribbean women's responses suggested that, on balance, they considered depression during and after pregnancy to be existent conditions. However, a recurring theme in their narratives was their unfamiliarity with the symptoms and nature of depression in general and perinatal depression in particular. The following woman's response typifies the difficulty women in the study experienced when trying to define perinatal depression. Her response epitomizes other women's views that it is difficult to recognize a condition such as postnatal depression when one is unfamiliar with its salient features.

> *'I don't know, I don't know what postnatal depression is ... I don't know what postnatal depression is supposed to be, how you're supposed to feel, look or whatever, I don't know. I have no idea ... you hear about people killing their babies 'cos they've been having postnatal depression. What exactly is postnatal depression? What are you supposed to be doing, saying or whatever? I don't know.' (Participant 9)*

Despite their relative unfamiliarity with perinatal depression, Black Caribbean women nevertheless theorized about its nature and causes. In common with other lay groups and health professionals, they subscribed to biopsychosocial theories for the genesis of depressive illness. However, like other lay groups, they did not grant equal credence to all components of this model but ranked social and psychological triggers over biological triggers. According to one woman, if biological factors trigger perinatal depression,

> *'Why hasn't everybody had it? What sort of hormones have they got different to me or you? [Laughs]' (Participant 9)*

Typically, women suggested that psychological and social triggers might coalesce into 'overload'. Although particular events may appear to trigger depression, they are likely to be merely the 'tip of the iceberg'. Depression represented a final common pathway – the result of trying to manage multiple layers of adversity and psychosocial stressors such as financial problems and difficulties in close personal relationships.

> *'...he [GP] actually sat down to me and said,"Look, you're putting a lot of stress on yourself." He says, "You're trying to do too much." ... He said, "Your husband's from abroad, he can't work ... you've just had a baby ... you're older, you've just had a baby and ... he's not helping you ... you can't do it. You will get ill. It will wear you out. It's simple".' (Participant 1)*

Women also advanced a variety of theories about the relationship between perinatal depression and other forms of mental illness. For example, some women believed that perinatal depression exists on a continuum with happiness at one end and more serious mental illnesses such as schizophrenia at the other. However, the absence of a clear line of demarcation between normality and mental disorder made it difficult for women to determine where normal feelings such as unhappiness, loneliness, or boredom ended and something more serious began, as suggested by this woman who had been diagnosed with postnatal depression.

> *'What's the difference between madness and sane? What is going mad? What is mad? I don't know what the answer is. What is mad? I don't know ... I don't feel mad.' (Participant 1)*

Despite suggestions from the literature that women from Black and ethnic minority groups are more likely to somatize psychological distress, none of the women in this study mentioned somatic symptoms. Instead, they echoed other lay views (Rogers et al., 2001) that inability to cope with the activities of daily living or to manage associated psychological and emotional distress were the most significant indicators of depressive illness. In this context, uncharacteristic behaviours such as tearfulness, anxiety, irritability, sleep disturbance, and thoughts of deliberate self-harm were deemed to be the most salient indicators of depression.

'I just kept crying. I was thinking, "I'd rather not have had children because if I die what will they do without me?" I was feeling like I didn't want to be here any more. But I didn't have the ... the guts to take pills or anything like that. I just stuck it out.' (Participant 5)

However, from women's narratives there emerged a sense that depression was not the inevitable outcome of coping with even the most extreme adverse circumstances. According to these women, 'depressive symptoms' did not equal 'depressive illness'. As observed elsewhere (Cornwell, 1984; Schnittker et al., 2000), some Black communities attribute mental illness to moral failings or character flaws. In this context, it becomes a moral imperative to take responsibility for one's feelings and related actions – remaining stoical in the face of great and enduring adversity. Individuals who fail to subscribe to this model might receive blame rather than support. This sense of depression being indicative of moral weakness or lack of moral fibre is hinted at in this woman's response:

*'I keep asking, "What are **they** doing to be depressed? How do **they** get themselves in that state?"' [Emphasis added] (Participant 9)*

Perceptions of differences between Black and White women

The belief that it is possible to exercise control over the onset of depressive illness led to exploration of Black Caribbean women's perceptions of differences between their attitudes to mental illness and those of their White British counterparts. While there was a consensus that depressive symptoms are universal, women suggested that resistance to onset of depressive illness per se is a major distinguishing feature between their attitude to and strategies for managing psychological distress and those of White British women.

'... you get depressed, everybody does but ... I think Black women don't allow themselves to get depressed. They keep themselves on top of it ... I don't think we allow ourselves to get bogged down with anything ... but some English ladies sit down and ... let things get on top of them ... I don't think Black women allow it to get that far.' (Participant 4)

The Black women in this study spoke of histo-political and socioeconomic forces that have shaped their lives suggesting that the ability to withstand adversity and disadvantage was not only self-enhancing but is also a cultural signifier; something unique to Black women; which serves to reinforce their self-concept and sense of social cohesion. While sharing a common lay perspective in which agency is privileged over structure in the struggle to preserve mental health (see for example, Rogers et al., 2001), it appears that, against a background often steeped in adversity and disadvantage, Black Caribbean women in the UK have drawn on their cultural heritage to evolve a unique ideology of self-reliance and autonomy which is mirrored in their strategies for help-seeking.

> *'I think it all relates back down to slavery – when we had to be strong for our kids because of what was going on at home. We had to protect them, had to be strong for them. We couldn't show ... what we were actually feeling inside ... just basically had to ... hold the family together. And it's just been instilled into the daughters the idea that you need to be strong, to hold your family together. You can't depend on no man. At the end of the day, if the man goes out and gets killed now, what's gonna happen? ... You need to be a strong.' (Participant 5)*

However, as suggested by the quote above, while sociocultural factors were potentially powerful protectors from perinatal depression, they could also be something of a double-edged sword; acting as strong cultural and social imperatives to minimize or deny psychological distress which militate against either acknowledging symptoms or seeking help.

> *'I do think that Black people get depression, but I don't think we're allowed to have depression. I think it's quite a matriarchal society and therefore you've got to cope. You've got to sort your family out, and so therefore you are not allowed to be depressed.' (Participant 7)*

In this context, women suggested that the apparent 'under-diagnosis' of perinatal depression and other common mental illnesses among Black Caribbean women was not necessarily evidence of the absence of symptomatology or even of resistance to psychiatric labelling. Under-diagnosis might be partly due to Black Caribbean women's failure to recognize the nature and potential seriousness of depressive illness, rendering them unable to access formal diagnosis, care, and treatment.

> *'I don't think they [Black Caribbean women] see the seriousness of depression. I think they think they're just feeling down and can just pick themselves back up – so, basically, they're dealing with it by themselves.' (Participant 5)*

Black Caribbean women's attitudes to help-seeking

Not all women agreed that Black Caribbean women's failure to recognize depressive symptoms was the reason why so few apparently consulted practitioners in primary care. Others suggested that deeply-ingrained unwillingness to discuss either diagnosable mental illness or psychological/ emotional distress among Black Caribbeans was a more plausible explanation – one that provides further evidence of culturally mediated responses to dealing with adversity and stressful situations.

> *'Black people don't really talk about things. I think its more pride than anything. I find a lot more White people, they speak about anything and everything, anywhere, whereas Black people don't. We tend to hold back ... I know that I keep a lot to myself ... and I think that's what a lot of Black people do, they don't speak about their experiences or problems, [they] hold it in.' (Participant 2)*
>
> *'I'm not saying it's totally a White person's thing. I think it is amongst Black people but it's just that it's unheard of ... if they haven't recognized that there is a problem, [they're] not going to seek help, are they?' (Participant 9)*

While unwillingness to disclose symptoms of emotional or psychological distress was inextricably linked to women's ability both to hold and project positive self-images, there was evidence of other sociocultural factors that constrained women to internalize distress, to 'keep it to themselves' in order to be seen to cope, thereby fulfilling expectations of being 'Strong-Black-Women' (Edge and Rogers, 2005). For example, women repeatedly stated that, even though they might be willing to access 'talking therapies', this was problematic because of the cultural imperative not to 'talk your business' outside the family, especially if doing so involved talking about other people.

> *'I don't mind talking about things that affect me but I don't want to be disloyal to my family. So I know that I wouldn't want to talk through certain things.' (Participant 7)*

There was evidence that Black Caribbean women were willing to seek help for depressive symptoms.

> *'I'm going to counselling at the moment ... I didn't get a referral, I walked in off the street ... I thought ... "No, I don't have to cry, there's a place I can go. Someone will help me." So I went there [Voluntary Sector Agency].' (Participant 6)*

However, these women adopted a lay hierarchy in help-seeking, which meant that they approached statutory health care providers as a last resort (Rogers and Pilgrim, 1997). Firstly, they attempted to problem-solve by personal agency and ingenuity. When those strategies failed, they turned to their social networks and voluntary sector agencies. Only when self-reliance and other strategies failed did they turn to health professionals.

Interestingly, women reported that when they approached health care professionals they were unlikely to receive the support they wanted. Instead, their encounters with practitioners (examples cited include general practitioners, health visitors, midwives, and hospital consultants) reinforced their social construction of perinatal depression.

> 'He [GP] said, "You're not depressed." He said, "Will you stop thinking you're depressed?" He said, "I will send you for counselling – if you want to go to counselling so you can talk, but you are not depressed." He [said] I wasn't depressed, I was doing too much and running myself down.' (Participant 1)
>
> 'I mean when I went to see the consultant about my hypertension a couple of week's ago ... and when I told him [about diagnosis with postnatal depression] he said, "You haven't got postnatal depression. You're too cheerful and bright and laughing."' (Participant 7)

It has previously been suggested that Black people are more likely than their White counterparts to turn to prayer and consult religious leaders for help with personal and psychological problems (Schnittker et al., 2000). This was certainly the case in this study. A significant finding from the quantitative aspect of the study was that when asked to whom they would turn 'if you had a problem' only Black Caribbean women said that they would turn to God, prayer, or to other religious sources. None of the 200 White British women did so. Although few of the women went to church, they cited the practical and emotional support that they derived from their faith communities as well as from private prayer and reading their Bible.

> "... the support brought me through it [domestic violence, still birth, life-threatening illness, and marital breakdown], believe – the support pulled me through it! There's no doubt! And also like I was reading my Bible and I do follow the Rastafarian faith.' (Participant 1)
>
> 'There are people in church who are very, very good. A lady from church, she came. She said, "I've come with my gloves and bathroom cleaning stuff and I'm doing your bathroom." She cleaned my bathroom, which was lovely.' (Participant 7)

According to Schnittker and colleagues (2000), although both Black and White people were equally likely to accept environmental aetiologies for onset of mental illness, Black people were more likely to attribute mental illness to 'bad character' and 'God's will' and therefore to reject psychological treatments. Black religious leaders were also more likely to emphasize the importance both of prayer and willpower in overcoming psychiatric problems (Schnittker et al., 2000). If this stance was adopted by the religious leaders to whom Black Caribbean women turn, this could serve to reinforce their concept of mental illness as a sign of moral weakness and the need to draw on personal agency in order to counter onset of depression thereby reducing the likelihood of women from this ethnic group seeking help from health care professionals.

Discussion

Despite the presence of social risk factors, Black Caribbean women in this study were no more likely to record high depression scores than their White British peers postnatally and were significantly less likely to have done so during pregnancy. However, around one-quarter of the Black Caribbean sample experienced perinatal depressive symptoms of sufficient severity as to equate with diagnosable mental illness. Nevertheless, few sought help from health care professionals and when they did so, they were unlikely to receive treatment. Instead, health care professionals were likely recursively to reinforce Black Caribbean women's social construction of depression (Edge and Rogers, 2005).

A number of factors may account for these findings. Firstly, and somewhat surprisingly given that women were recruited at antenatal clinics, Black Caribbean women appeared to be unfamiliar with the symptoms of perinatal depression. According to these women, this was at least partly because of the absence of a lay discourse about mental illness within their communities. This made it difficult for them to conceptualize depressive feelings and low mood as 'symptoms'. It also raises questions about the efficacy and/or cultural sensitivity of current antenatal education and health promotion initiatives such as the Defeat Depression Campaign (Paykel et al., 1998).

There was evidence of a strong relationship between Black Caribbean women's sense of identity, their need to exercise control over their lives, and their response to managing depressive symptoms. Black Caribbean women appeared to believe that they are less susceptible to psychological distress than their White British counterparts. It may be that disproportionate exposure to disadvantage and adversity has fostered greater sensitivity to the social origins of depression among Black Caribbean women causing them to regard perinatal depression not as illness, but as the obvious, 'natural', sequelae of dealing with childbirth in the context of adversity and disadvantage (Edge and Rogers, 2005). According to Hall and Tucker (1985), these women's self-concept as 'Strong-Black-Women' may serve a self-enhancing function affording protection against mental illness. Alternatively, it might lead women to believe that conditions such as perinatal depression are 'life problems' and therefore not amenable to treatment thus forcing them to draw on depleted inner resources.

Despite their ambiguity about the nature of perinatal depression and the presence of cultural imperatives to minimize distress, women were willing to seek help from health professionals but only when they were unable to manage symptoms themselves or failed to receive adequate support and/or treatment from their own social care networks or voluntary agencies. However, when Black Caribbean women approached health professionals, they did not have their distress validated or receive diagnosis and treatment. Instead, health professionals reinforced their social construction of perinatal depression. It also appears that health professionals were unable to see beyond the efforts women made to mask their feelings – which led Dalton (1980) to call postnatal depression 'the smiling depression'. If women presented as being (too) cheerful, professionals appeared to believe that they could not possibly be depressed.

Counter-intuitively, Black Caribbean women appeared to regard the failure of health professionals to recognize their depressive symptoms or offer them treatment in a somewhat positive light. It would appear that health professionals' response forced them to continue to deal with their feelings (Edge and Rogers, 2005; Edge et al., 2004). Not receiving a diagnostic label appeared to act both as a counter to depressive feelings and, perhaps more importantly, to construct their feelings as 'symptoms'. While this may be positive for women's self-concept, it raises important questions about the long-term consequences of minimizing or denying psychological distress. It has been suggested that failure to acknowledge and actively manage psychological distress might have serious consequences for physical health and well-being resulting in high levels of stress-related illnesses such as diabetes and stroke that have been reported among Black populations (Jackson, 2002).

It has been previously reported that spirituality and religious beliefs are potentially powerful counters to the onset of mental illness (Gabe and Thorogood, 1986; Graham, 1993; Fisch et al., 1997; Cinnirella and Loewenthal, 1999). In this study, women also reported the importance of their spirituality and a sense of being supported as protectors from the onset of depression. Not only did some women resort to private prayer and seeking support directly from God, they also cited the practical and emotional support that they derived from within their faith communities. However, according to Schnittker et al. (2000), the messages women receive from faith communities might reinforce their view of mental illness as moral weakness thereby reducing the likelihood of women seeking help and/or accepting treatment from health professionals.

Conclusions

Despite initiatives to increase detection, all forms of depression remain under-diagnosed in primary care (Littlejohns et al., 1999. The absence of a discourse on mental illness among Black Caribbean women may make them even less likely than the general population to receive treatment as they may lack the frames of reference that would enable them to reconstruct their feelings as 'symptoms'.

In this context, health care professionals might need further education about the ways in which different ethnic groups conceptualize depression and other forms of mental illness and how this might influence the diagnostic process. Health professionals might also need increased awareness of the need to guard against stereotyping and to look beyond the façade which women often present in order to recognize the true nature and level of their psychological distress.

However, it may be that further studies into the coping strategies that Black Caribbean women adopt could provide health professionals with additional approaches for dealing with perinatal depression among other ethnic groups.

Finally, women's accounts of the support they received from spirituality and religious institutions and their willingness to access care and support via the voluntary sector suggests that there might be scope for developing partnerships between these groups. In this context, the religious institutions which women spoke of might come to be regarded as community mental health resources both for offering care and support and for delivering health promotion and health education about the nature, cause, and potential treatability of mental illness.

References

Ahmad WIU (1993) Making Black people sick: 'Race', ideology and health research. In: WIU Ahmad (ed.) *'Race' and Health in Contemporary Britain*. Open University Press, Buckingham: 11-33.

Appleby L, Gregoire A, Platz C, Prince M, Kumar R (1994) Screening women for high risk of postnatal depression. *J Psychosom Res* **38(6)**: 539–45.

Baker D, Mead N, Campbell S (2002) Inequalities in morbidity and consulting behaviour for socially vulnerable groups. *Br J Gen Pract* **52**: 124–30.

Baker D, North K (1999) Does employment improve the health of lone mothers? *Soc Sci Med* **49**: 121–31.

Berthoud R, Nazroo J (1997) The mental health of ethnic minorities. *New Community* **23(3)**: 309–24.

Bhopal R (2001) Ethnicity and race as epidemiological variables: Centrality of purpose and context. In: H Macbeth, P Shetty (eds.) *Health and Ethnicity*. Taylor and Francis, London: 21–40.

Bolton HL, Hughes PM, Turton P, Sedgwick P (1998) Incidence and demographic correlates of depressive symptoms during pregnancy in an inner London population. *J Psychosomat Obstet Gynec* **19**: 202–9.

Bostock J, Marsen M, Sarwar Z, Stoltz S (1996) Postnatal depression in Asian women. *Community Nurse* **Nov/Dec**: 34–6.

Bryman AA, Cramer D (2001) *Quantitative Data Analysis with SPSS Release*

10 for Windows: A Guide for Social Scientists. Routledge, Hove, UK.

Cinnirella M, Loewenthal KM (1999) Religious and ethnic group influences in beliefs about mental illness: A qualitative interview study. *Br J Med Psychol* **72**: 505–24.

Cooper PJ, Murray L (1998) Clinical review: Postnatal depression. *Br Med J* **316(20)**: 1884–6.

Cooper PJ, Murray L, Hooper R, West A (1996) The development and validation of a predictive index for postpartum depression. *Psychol Med* **26**: 627–34.

Cornwell J (1984) Hard-Earned Lives: *Accounts of Health and Illness From East London*. Tavistock Publications, London.

Cox JL, Holden JM, Sagovsky R (1987) Detection of postnatal depression – development of the Edinburgh Postnatal Depression Scale. *Br J Psychiatry* **150**: 782–6.

Dalton K (1980) *Depression After Childbirth*. Open University Press, Oxford.

Department of Environment Transport and the Regions (2000) *Indices of Deprivation 2000: Regeneration Research Summary. Report Number 31*. Department of Environment Transport and the Regions, London.

Edge DE (2002) *Perinatal Depression Among Women of Black Caribbean Origin: A Longitudinal Cohort Study of Prevalence, Beliefs, and Attitudes to Help-seeking*. Unpublished PhD Thesis. University of Manchester: Manchester, UK.

Edge D, Baker D, Rogers A (2004) Perinatal depression among Black Caribbean women. *Health and Social Care in the Community* **12(5)**: 430–8.

Edge D, Rogers A (2005) 'Dealing with it': Black Caribbean women's response to adversity and psychological distress associated with pregnancy, childbirth, and early motherhood. *Soc Sci Med* **61**: 15–25.

Evans J, Heron J, Francomb H, Oke S, Golding J (2001) Cohort study of depressed mood during pregnancy and after childbirth. *Br Med J* **323(4)**: 257–60.

Fenton S, Sadiq-Sangster A (1996) Culture, relativism and the expression of mental distress: South Asian women in Britain. *Sociology of Health and Illness* **18**: 66–85.

Fisch RZ, Tadmor OP, Dankner R, Diamant YZ (1997) Postnatal depression: A prospective study of its prevalence, incidence and psychosocial determinants in an Israeli sample. *J Obstet Gynaec Research* **23(6)**: 547–54.

Gabe J, Thorogood N (1986) Prescribed drug use and the management of everyday life: The experiences of Black and White working-class women. *Sociological Review* **34**: 737–72.

Glaser BG (1978) *Theoretical Sensitivity: Advances in the Methodology of Grounded Theory.* Sociology Press, Mill Valley, CA.

Graham H (1993) *Hardship and Health in Women's Lives.* Harvester Wheatsheaf, New York.

Greene SM, Nugent JK, Wieczorek-Deering D, O'Mahony P, Graham R (1991) The patterning of depressive symptoms in a sample of first-time mothers. *Irish Journal of Psychology* **12(2)**: 263–75.

Hall LE, Tucker CM (1985) Relationships between ethnicity, conceptions of mental illness, and attitudes associated with seeking psychological help. *Psychological Reports* **57**: 907–16.

Hickling FW, Hutchinson G (1999) Roast breadfruit psychosis: Disturbed racial identification in African-Caribbeans. *Psychiatric Bull* **23**: 132–4.

Jackson J (2002) *Health and Mental Health Disparities Among Black Americans.* Visibility/Invisibility Conference, Andrew Sims Centre for Professional Development, Leeds, UK.

Keating F, Robertson D, McCulloch A, Francis E (2002) *Breaking the Circles of Fear: A Review of the Relationship Between Mental Health Services and African and Caribbean Communities.* The Sainsbury Centre for Mental Health, London.

Littlejohns P, Cluzeaut F, Bale R, Grimshaw, J, Feder G, Moran S (1999) The gravity and quality of clinical practice guidelines for the management of depression in primary care in the UK. *Br J Gen Pract* **49(440)**: 205–10.

Littlewood R (2001) 'Culture' in the field of race and mental health. In: H Macbeth and P Shetty (eds.) *Health and Ethnicity.* Taylor and Francis, London: 209–222.

Lloyd K (1993) Depression and anxiety among Afro-Caribbean general practice attenders in Britain. *Int J Soc Psychiatry* **39(1)**: 1–9.

Lloyd K (1998) Ethnicity, social inequality, and mental illness. *Br Med J* **316**: 1763–70.

Lofland J (1971) *Analyzing Social Settings: A Guide to Qualitative Observation and Analysis.* Wadsworth, Belmont, California.

Lyons S (1998) A prospective study of post traumatic stress symptoms one month following childbirth in a group of forty-two first time mothers. *J Repro Infant Psychol* **16(1)**: 5.

Modood T, Berthoud R, Lakey J, Nazroo JY, et al. (eds.) (1997) *Ethnic Minorities in Britain: Diversity and Disadvantage.* Policy Studies Institute, London: 339–59.

Murray D, Cox JL (1990) Screening for depression during pregnancy with the

Edinburgh Postnatal Depression Scale (EPDS). *J Reprod Infant Psychol* **8**: 99–107.

Nazroo JY (1997) *The Health of Britain's Ethnic Minorities: Findings From a National Survey.* Policy Studies Institute (PSI), London.

O'Hara MW, Swain AM (1996) Rates and risk of postpartum depression - A meta-analysis. *Int Rev Psychiatry* **8**: 37–54.

Paykel ES, Hart D, Priest RG (1998) Changes in public attitudes to depression during the Defeat Depression Campaign. *Br J Psychiatry* **173**: 519–22.

Qualitative Solutions and Research (1997) *QSR NUD*IST. (4 - Users' Guide).* Richards, Melbourne.

Reeder J (1999) Killer in the mind: Depths of depression can be deadly. *Manchester Evening News* 17–18

Rogers A, May C, Oliver D (2001) Experiencing depression, experiencing the depressed: The separate worlds of patients and doctors. *J Ment Health* **10(3)**: 317–33.

Rogers A, Pilgrim D (1997) The contribution of lay knowledge to the understanding and promotion of mental health. *J Ment Health* **6(1)**: 23–35.

Schnittker J, Freese J, Powell B (2000) Nature, nurture, neither, nor: Black–White differences in beliefs about the cause and appropriate treatment of mental illness. *Social Forces* **78(3)**: 1101–130.

Smith GD, Chaturverdi N, Harding S, Nazroo J, Williams R (2000) Ethnic inequalities in health: A review of UK epidemiological evidence. *Critical Public Health* **10(4)**: 375–408.

Spector R (2001) Is there racial bias in clinicians' perceptions of the dangerousness of psychiatric patients? A review of the literature. *J Ment Health* **10(1)**: 5–15.

SPSS Inc (2003) *SPSS for Windows Statistical Software.* SPSS Inc, Chicago.

Takei N, Persaud R, Woodruff P, et al. (1998) First episode of psychosis in Afro-Caribbean and White people. *Br J Psychiatry* **172**: 147-153.

Taylor A (1999) Postnatal mental disturbance. http://www.net.uk/home/marce. uk/pmd.htm

CHAPTER 17

Pregnancy, parenting and substance misuse

Faye McCrory

Introduction

The *National Service Framework for Children, Young People and Maternity Services* (Department of Health, 2004) establishes clear standards for promoting the health and well-being of children, young people and mothers; and for providing high quality services that meet their needs. There are 11 standards (see *Box 17.1*), and the last one addresses the requirements of women and their babies during pregnancy, birth and after birth. It includes women's partners and their families; and it addresses and links to pre- and post-conception health promotion and the Child Health Promotion Programme. It should be read in conjunction with Standards 1–5.

Hidden Harm: Responding to the Needs of Children of Problem Drug Users (Home Office, 2003) states that parental drug use can, and often does compromise children's health and development at every stage from conception onwards. The complexity of the situation means it is not possible to determine the precise effects on any individual child. However, a large proportion of the children of problem drug users are clearly being disadvantaged and damaged in many ways, and few will escape entirely unharmed. *Why Mothers Die* (CEMACH, 2004) also underpins the need for changes in drug and alcohol treatment services.

The above documents are crucial in terms of drivers for change in health care delivery and are seminal to this chapter.

The true extent of drug taking in women is largely unknown as reliable figures are hard to obtain. It is clear however, that smoking, alcohol and illicit drug use in women of reproductive age is increasing and the continued use of drugs during pregnancy is common (DrugScope, 2005). Although nicotine and alcohol are legally available it is important not to confuse legality with safety. Maternal use of tobacco is well researched and known to have significant harmful effects on pregnancy. Alcohol has the clearest association with fetal teratogenesis and has well-documented adverse effects associated with high maternal intake. The increased national profile of the risks of alcohol, particularly associated with female fertility and pregnancy, is to be welcomed.

Box 17.1. National Service Framework (Department of Health, 2004)

Standard 1: Promoting Health and Well-being, Identifying Needs and Intervening Early

Standard 2: Supporting Parenting

Standard 3: Child, Young Person and Family-Centred Services

Standard 4: Growing Up into Adulthood

Standard 5: Safeguarding and Promoting the Welfare of Children and Young People

Standard 6: Children and Young People Who Are Ill

Standard 7: Children and Young People in Hospital

Standard 8: Disabled Children and Young People and Those With Complex Health Needs

Standard 9: The Mental Health and Psychological Well-being of Children and Young People

Standard 10: Medicines for Children and Young People

Standard 11: Maternity Services

Risk assessment in itself presents an enormous challenge because of the highly variable course of drug misuse, and becomes more problematic when other variables such as mental illness and domestic abuse are introduced. Interventions should therefore not just take account of the medical treatment, but also include the broader social issues that affect the lives of families.

The inherent tensions and potential conflicts will be explored within the political and personal context. While pregnancy and substance misuse is the focus, the often associated complexities will necessarily form part of the discussion. The aim is not to provide definitive answers, but to generate discussion about a difficult and sometimes painful part of the responsibilities that professionals must carry when working in this minefield of multiple need.

The needs of women are central to the Government's programme of reform and investment in public services and to our commitment to addressing discrimination and inequality. Modernizing mental health services is one of our core national priorities. *Women's Mental Health: Into the Mainstream* (Department of Health, 2002a) highlights that women make up over half of the general population, play a significant role in the workforce and assume the major responsibility for home-making and for the caring of children and other family members. At the same time, many women experience low social status and value. Social isolation and poverty are much more common in women, as is the experience of childhood sexual abuse, domestic violence and sexual violence. Both mental health care and drug treatment services must therefore be responsive to these differences (Department of Health, 2002b).

Drug and alcohol misuse can be chaotic and unpredictable, and serious health and social consequences are common. The National Treatment Agency's models of care (2002) set out a national framework for the commissioning of adult treatment for drug misuse expected to be available in every part of England to meet the needs of diverse local populations. It advocates a systems approach to meeting the multiple needs of drug and alcohol users by having explicit links to the other generic health, social care and criminal justice services, including through-care and aftercare.

Pregnancy brings a unique set of challenges to adults living with drug and/or alcohol problems, and to those involved in their care. When there are also mental health and other issues present, the situation becomes more complex. Many factors affect the outcome of pregnancy and the health and well-being of mother and baby. Many conditions carry with them an element of risk or uncertainty, greater during pregnancy. Drug use is just one factor. Other factors include lifestyle and social circumstances, physical and psychological health, nutrition, breastfeeding, sexually transmitted and communicable diseases, and antenatal and postnatal care (DrugScope, 2005).

The Confidential Enquiry into Maternal Deaths (CEMACH, 2004) is the longest running example of national professional self-audit in the world. For the first time, the report *Why Mothers Die 1997–1999* (Confidential Enquiry into Maternal Deaths, 2001) was able to fully evaluate other factors that may have played a part in the women's death. These findings are of great concern, showing that maternal mortality rates among the socially excluded, including women from lower socioeconomic classes, very young girls and specific ethnic groups, are higher than among the population as a whole. There has always been a large degree of under-ascertainment of deaths from mental illness or substance abuse by this Enquiry. However, a pilot Office for National Statistics linkage study showed that the Confidential Enquiry into Maternal Deaths (CEMD) was unaware of over 40 extra deaths from suicide or deaths from violent causes, and another eight where the Coroner recorded an open verdict. In addition, 11 unreported women died from an accidental drug overdose. This is of particular relevance to this chapter.

Eleven deaths in women who were drug or alcohol dependent were also discussed in the Enquiry. In contrast to the other women who died from suicide, these women are characterized by their high levels of social adversity, homelessness, poor uptake of services (particularly substance misuse services), poor attendance for either psychiatric or antenatal appointments, and by their youth and single status (Confidential Enquiry into Maternal Deaths, 2001).

Within this context it is additionally important to note that there are a number of health problems and needs that are specific to women in prison, particularly with regard to both substance misuse and mental health.

Pregnancy, substance misuse and care of the newborn

The care of women and their newborns with antenatal drug and alcohol exposure is increasingly recognized as a significant health problem. Effective care for women and their families must therefore involve an effective and well-co-ordinated teamwork approach. Key to reducing risk is working in partnership with the woman, thus enhancing her capacity to control her drug or alcohol use, and to access the support she needs.

Various guidelines published have no legal standing. However, they can and should play an important role in improving services and clinical governance (Baldacchino et al., 2003). They provide a framework within which maternity services for drug users and their children can be evaluated

A goal of any programme should be to promote positive health practices that contribute to the health of mothers and their newborns. Specific objectives are to:

- Improve nutrition.
- Decrease smoking.
- Decrease alcohol and drug use.
- Raise self-esteem.
- Encourage breastfeeding.
- Promote dental health.
- Encourage physical activity.
- Encourage early and continuing antenatal care.
- Promote social and community support.
  (British Columbia Reproductive Care Program, 1999)

The main aims of any guidelines should be twofold. Firstly, to achieve the co-operation and involvement of women and their families in a negotiated package of care, and secondly, to develop robust strategies that enable parents and professionals to provide supportive care for both women and their babies (Thajam and Carroll, 2006). The importance of a multidisciplinary approach to care cannot be overemphasized. A negotiated individual care pathway, and use of a multidisciplinary team approach will facilitate the identification of the multiple and complex needs of drug using families, and provide opportunities to reduce any negative impact on parenting abilities.

Illicit drug use is a chronic relapsing condition, and clients presenting for treatment will invariably have been using drugs on a dependent basis, for several years (Macrory, 1997). The treatment of both drug and alcohol misuse is therefore a planned exercise, and must involve those best qualified to plan treatment and care.

Fear of being judged by professionals, previous social services involvement, or the presence of secondary amenorrhoea may mean that some women access services late, or intermittently in pregnancy (Thajam and Carrroll, 2006). However, pregnancy can be a catalyst for change and midwives are ideally placed to support the woman with appropriate information and interventions, as outlined in the National Treatment Agency's models of care (2002) and the Standing Conference on Drug Abuse guidelines (1989). Sharing information is essential not only to meet the outcomes and work to best practice, but also to meet the recommendations in *Hidden Harm* (Home Office, 2003) and *Why Mothers Die* (CEMACH, 2004).

Aims and outcomes include:

- Pregnant women who misuse drugs and/or alcohol will seek and engage with maternity services.
- Maternity services recognize and act upon the complex needs of women and their families.
- Families receive accurate and honest information regarding the risks associated with drug and alcohol use in pregnancy.
- Women feel their voice is heard and their opinions respected.
- Individual care pathways reflect realistic risk reduction and harm minimization strategies, that are negotiated with the woman.
- Babies receive supportive care and remain with their mother, unless medical or legal reasons indicate otherwise.
- Strategies that support effective communication are in place.
- Any concerns about the mother or baby are identified and acted upon.
- Normal psychological and physiological aspects of pregnancy, rather than drug use, remain the primary focus of care.

Care in labour, including pain relief, should follow the women's preferences, hospital policies, and the agreed care plan. Methadone, if prescribed, should continue through labour. It will not produce a significant analgesic effect and should not replace other forms of pain relief. To ensure that there is no gap in the provision of prescribed medication, and that community prescriptions are not collected while the woman is in hospital, it is essential that the key drug worker is informed of any admission.

The mother and baby should be transferred to the postnatal ward together, unless legal or medical reasons indicate otherwise. Ensure that normal psychological and physiological aspects of parenthood, rather than drug use, remain the focus of care.

While the value of score charts is questionable in the assessment of withdrawal symptoms (Hulatt, 2000), the baby should be closely observed on a regular basis and the mother should be involved in the process. If a score chart is used, it should not be seen as a prescriptive tool, but as a guide to overall observation. The aim is that babies are able to feed and settle between feeds, and that medically worrying signs of withdrawal are acted upon. Babies are often fractious even if they do not require treatment and parents should be encouraged to cuddle/gently rock their baby. Kangaroo care can also be soothing. A calm atmosphere, with dim lighting and keeping noise to a minimum is also recommended (Thajam and Carroll, 2006).

It is essential that all parents, particularly those with drug or alcohol problems, are advised that they should *not* sleep with their baby either in bed, on a chair, or on the sofa.

The named specialist midwife and others identified in the care plan should be informed that the mother is on the ward. If considered appropriate, or if it has been identified in the care plan, a pre-discharge planning meeting should be organized. The key drug worker and other involved agencies should also be informed of discharge.

Breastfeeding

Most drugs of misuse do not pass into the breast milk in quantities which are sufficient to have a major effect on the newborn baby. Apart from all the well-documented benefits, breastfeeding will certainly support the mother in feeling that she is positively comforting her baby, should it be hard to settle. There may be some effect on the baby, such as drowsiness with opiates or tranquillizers. However, the important point is, that women should be given all the information they need to make an informed choice about breastfeeding, and having made that decision, they should be fully supported by all professionals involved (DrugScope, 2005).

Research also suggests that breastfeeding should not be discouraged in those who are either hepatitis B (Carey, 1995), or hepatitis C (Lin et al., 1995) positive.

There is no scientific evidence on which to base an expert opinion regarding substance misuse and breastfeeding. Therefore, in dealing with what is essentially a theoretical situation, many professionals promote it on that basis. In theory, it could be considered inadvisable because the baby will get small doses in the milk. However, in theory and practice the risk is relative since the fetus was exposed to larger doses before birth. And because these are generally low birth-weight and vulnerable babies and at increased risk of sudden infant death syndrome (SIDS) through maternal smoking, drug use and poor nutrition, breastfeeding should be promoted and supported. As there is no scientific evidence that it is detrimental – although there is plenty of personal opinion – those of us experienced in the field go with the view that it is more good than bad. However, it is extremely important to ensure that the mother does not receive 'mixed messages' from health professionals. While the baby will be helped to settle, and any withdrawal effects will be reduced by breastfeeding, giving the baby any amount of their his or her own methadone, however small, is extremely dangerous and can lead to a fatal outcome. It should also be reiterated that parents using both licit and illicit drugs, including alcohol must not sleep with their baby.

Parenting assessments

The impact of problematic parental substance misuse on family life and children's well-being cannot be overstated. It can affect whole families, and there are often powerful tensions between the rights of children to be cared for and protected, and the needs of parents who themselves are under stress due to their drug or alcohol using lifestyle. There is no doubt that this may represent a risk for their children.

The central question is the extent to which, in the longer term, a parent's drug or alcohol problem so reduces their ability to parent that their children's lives become damaged beyond effective repair? When is this point reached? How can this be effectively assessed and managed? These are the issues that all professionals working in the community need to bear in mind whether they are involved with parents or their children or both (Weir, 1999).

Beck-Sander (1999) in discussing ways to reduce conflict between services, suggests that a fundamental caveat of all risk management work is that all risks posed by parents to their children cannot be prevented. At best risks can only be reduced. It is not even feasible to aim to identify all risks – and any service adopting this aim would be doomed to failure. Furthermore its workers would be over-cautious in a vain attempt to avoid any possible harm occurring. Such a service would also be unable to work effectively with other services because of its unrealistic expectations. The task of risk management is therefore to carefully weigh up the harms and benefits in a risk calculation – nevertheless this can be another source of potential conflict between services. What may appear a 'reasonable risk' (i.e benefits outweigh harm) to one service may appear unreasonable (i.e. harm outweighs benefits) to another (Beck-Sander, 1999).

Under UK law, the Children Act 1989 (Department of Health, 1989) leaves us in no doubt that the needs of the child are paramount in all Children Act court proceedings where a conflict of interest arises between parent and child. Adult and child services must therefore act in accordance with the child-centred philosophy behind this Act. However, it is acknowledged that difficulties and conflicts can arise when it is felt that what professional judgement suggests is the patient's best interests, conflicts with the interests, or needs of the children for whom they are caring.

When making an assessment of parenting capability, the following questions should be considered by all involved key workers. The impact of domestic violence, mental health, sexual abuse and prostitution must also be included in the assessment.

- When does an adult's substance misuse pose a conflict of interest within a family?
- When does a parent's substance misuse pose risks for the safety and well-being of his or her child?
- How does the ability to parent become impaired in these circumstances?
- What is a child's capacity to tolerate the changed and often detrimental care that he or she may receive?
- How can these risks be assessed and how can they be managed?
- Who decides when those risks become acceptable?
- What services need to be available to meet the needs of both adults and children in these circumstances?
- How do professionals working in these circumstances need to be trained and supported?
- What can be done to bridge the gulf between the professionals who are trying to meet the respective needs of children and parents?
- How can the different agencies involved ensure consistent practice and good communication between each other?
(adapted from Weir and Douglas, 1999)

The concept of resilience

Over the past 25 years researchers studying risk factors have identified certain individuals – termed resilient individuals – who are better able to resist destructive behaviours, even in the presence of identified risk factors. While protective factors typically are defined as influences external to a person that contribute to his or her well-being, resilience has been conceptualized as a set of strengths internal to the individual (Wolin and Wolin, 1993). Many protective factors contribute to a resilient personality. Just as multiple risk factors predict more severe outcomes, multiple protective factors improve one's chances for positive outcomes (Davis, 1999). It must be noted that risk and protective factors change as a product of an individual's age and developmental stage – therefore, prevention programmes must be matched to the appropriate developmental stage of the individuals for which they are designed.

However, as Field (1993) reminds us, that there is another group of children who seem to cope in the midst of striking adversity. These are the ones who seem to be 'managing' in a situation where the quality and quantity of care they receive is very far from what most children would need. The importance of mental illness and/or substance misuse in one parent is that it may pose a risk to a child. However, the contribution of the other parent must be considered, and this may be positive or negative. While the factor of resilience is the one quoted most often in relation to children, Field finds reliance on children's resilience to be worrying, and liable to lead to false optimism. Additionally, emotional abuse can be difficult to identify, but may produce lasting difficulties. Let us now address the real and potential impact of both mental health and substance misuse on the child.

The impact on the child

Over the past 50-plus years there has been a growing awareness of the importance of attachment in infant/carer relationships. Attachment is generally understood to indicate the relationship that develops between an infant and its primary caregiver (usually the mother) during its first few months of life. Our modern understanding began with the pioneering work of John Bowlby (1944, 1951) in which he emphasized that children's experiences of interpersonal relationships were crucial to their psychological development. He argued that the formation of an ongoing relationship between child and primary caregiver was as important to the child's development as other factors, such as the provision of experiences, discipline and child care (in Cole and Fearnley, 1998). Bowlby went on to postulate that each infant develops 'an internal working model' about attachment figures, in which the infant's sense of self and others unfolds through interactions with the primary caregiver. It has also been suggested that any interruption in the development of a reciprocal relationship between an infant and his/her primary caregiver may be experienced as stressful, and may have a detrimental effect on the child's attachment process (Cole and Fearnley, 1998).

Certain experiences, particularly if met before the age of two, act as risk factors in the development of an attachment disorder (Fearnley and Howe, 1999). These include pre-birth and birth traumas, sudden separations from the primary caregiver, frequent moves between different carers and/or placements, chronic maternal depression/mental illness/substance misuse, and where the primary caregiver has experienced serious childhood trauma that remains unresolved. Severe neglect and physical, emotional, and sexual abuse are also significant risk factors.

Lau (1999) in discussing the needs of children and families from different cultures is clear that of particular concern is the finding of parental violence, or potential threats against the children, severe behavioural disturbances (e.g. drugs/alcohol), self-destructive acts and repeated suicide attempts. She reminds us that it is important to find out what has happened to the exercise of authority in the traditional extended family, which would normally serve the function of providing a source for mediating family conflict, as well as containing and restraining extreme behavioural disturbance in any one family member. One could argue that in some circumstances, the very exercise of authority denies women the opportunity of the care and support so desperately needed – instead they are hidden from society, ostracized from their family and have their rights denied.

Conclusions and recommendations

Because outcomes for these families are multiply determined, there are many opportunities and potentially effective strategies for interventions. These must focus on ensuring a safe and stable home environment, reducing parent–child discord and improving communication, developing parenting skills, reducing environmental stressors and supporting children's resilience in order to improve outcomes for parents and children. Henry and Kumar (1999) remind us that assessing what constitutes 'good enough' parenting is very difficult, and many authors have commented on the fact that parenting remains a very difficult construct to measure because of its complex multidimensional quality (Mrazek et al., 1995).

People with co-occurring disorders have lives and families, hopes and dreams, responsibilities and needs. They can be mothers, fathers, grandparents, students, teachers, plumbers or pianists. Too often these individuals pay a high price for having co-occurring disorders: lost dreams, lost families, and in some cases, lost lives (Substance Abuse and Mental Health Services Administration, 2002). While the experiences of adults with substance misuse and/or mental illness are similar to those of all parents in many ways, the literature emphasizes their unique circumstances, but most commonly, their deficits and failures.

For many women, unresolved issues from their past debilitate presenting behaviours and understanding, especially around relationships. If these needs are not addressed and met, parents may never achieve family unity and the goal of good parenting may remain beyond their reach. If it is only within warm, consistent, accepting, and reciprocal relationships that children can learn to be empathetic and socially competent (Fearnley and Howe, 1999), the future looks bleak for families where drug use and mental illness is present.

Of course it will not always be safe to keep children at home. Maya Angelou, the poet, has put very poignantly the dilemma for those of us who have to intervene in family life:

> *'How is it possible to convince a child of its own worth after removing him from a family which is said to be unworthy, but with whom he identifies.'*
> *(in Weir and Douglas, 1999: 9)*

Into the Mainstream (Department of Health, 2002a) emphasizes the importance of listening to women and that we must take heed of what they are saying. They want to be listened to, their experiences validated, and most of all to be kept safe while they recover from mental health problems. They also want importance placed on the underlying causes of their distress in addition to their symptoms; support in their mothering role; and their potential for recovery recognized.

Perhaps the most compelling justification for a distinct response to women's health in particular is the fact that it carries a higher individual and social cost than men's. The aim is to promote a co-ordinated approach so women with a range of problems and needs can feel assured that the departments and agencies responsible for providing help and support respond to their needs as a whole, rather than in isolation (Department of Health, 2002b). Improvements in services are an investment in the health of the future, as well as present generations. Meaningful and effective interventions have the potential to impact positively on physical and mental health, impact on parenting in the long-term, and reduce the need for children to be placed in care. They are essential if we are to break the present cyclical nature of drug use, mental illness, poverty and despair.

References

Baldacchino A, Riglietta M, Corkery J (2003) *Maternal Health and Drug Abuse: Perspectives Across Europe.* European Collaborating Centres in Addiction Studies (ECCAS), Denmark.

Beck-Sander A (1999) Working with parents with mental health problems: Management of the many risks. In: A Douglas A Weir (eds.) *Child Protection and Adult Mental Health: Conflict of Interest?* Butterworth Heinemann Press, Edinburgh.

Bowlby J (1944) Forty-four juvenile thieves: Their characters and home life. *Int J Psycho-Anal* **25**: 19-52.

Bowlby J (1951) *Maternal Care and Mental Health.* WHO Monograph Series, no.2. World health Organization, Geneva.

British Columbia Reproductive Care Program (1999) *Guidelines for Perinatal Care of Substance Using Women and Their Infants.* British Columbia Reproductive Care Program, Vancouver BC.

Carey P. (1995) Hepatitis B, pregnancy and the drug user. In: C Siney (ed.) *The Pregnant Drug Addict.* Books for Midwives Press, Cheshire.

Cole J, Fearnley S (1998) *Attachment Therapy: A Preliminary Report of an Attachment Therapy Model Being Pioneered at the Keys Attachment Centre as a Treatment for Children Assessed as Having an Attachment Disorder.* Available from Keys Attachment Centre, Rawtenstall, Lancashire, UK.

Confidential Enquiry into Maternal Death (2001) *Why Mothers Die 1997– 1999. The Fifth Confidential Enquiry into Maternal Deaths.* Royal College of Gynaecologists Press, London.

Confidential Enquiry into Maternal and Child Health (2004) *Why Mothers Die'2000–2002. The Sixth Report of Confidential Enquiries into Maternal Deaths in the United Kingdom.* Confidential Enquiry into Maternal Deaths, London.

Davis KL (1999) Risk and Protective Factors for Alcohol Abuse and Dependence. *Journal of Neuropsychopharmacology: 5th Generation of Progress.* National Institute of Mental Health. Rockville, MD.

Department of Health (1989) *The Children Act 1989.* HMSO, London

Department of Health (2002a). *Women's Mental Health: Into the Mainstream. Strategic Development of Mental Health Care for Women.* Department of Health Publications, London.

Department of Health (2002b). *Mental Health Policy Implementation Guide: Dual Diagnosis Good Practice Guide.* HMSO, London.

Department of Health (2004) *National Service Framework for Young People, Children and Maternity Services* (Standard 11). Department of Health Publications, London.

Douglas A, Weir A (eds.) (1999) *Child Protection and Adult Mental Health: Conflict of Interest?* Butterworth Heinemann, Edinburgh.

DrugScope (2005) *Substance Misuse in Pregnancy: A Resource Book for Professionals.* DrugScope, London.

Fearnley S, Howe D (1999) Disorders of attachment and attachment therapy. *Adoption and Fostering* **23(2)**: 19–30.

Field IM (1993). Enhancing parent sensitivity. In: NJ Anastonion, S Harel (eds.) *At Risk Infants: Interventions, Families and Research.* Paul Brooks Publishing, Baltimore: 81–9.

Henry LA, Kumar RC (1999) Risk assessments of infants born to parents with a mental health problem or a learning disability. In: A Douglas, A Weir (eds.) *Child Protection and Adult Mental Health: Conflict of Interest?* Butterworth Heinemann Press, Edinburgh.

Home Office (2003) *Hidden Harm: Responding to the Needs of Children of Problem Drug Users.* Report of an Inquiry by the Advisory Council on the Misuse of Drugs. Available from: www.drugs.gov.uk [Accessed 17 October 2006].

Hulatt J (2000) Neonatal abstinence syndrome: How and where should babies with this condition be cared for? *J Neonatal Nursing* **6(5)**: 159–64.

Lau AY-H (1999) Understanding the needs of children and families from different cultures. In: A Douglas, A Weir (eds.) *Child Protection and Adult Mental Health: Conflict of Interest?* Butterworth Heinemann Press, Edinburgh.

Lin H-H, Kao J-H, Hsu H-Y, Ni Y-H, et al. (1995) Absence of infection in breast-fed infants born to hepatitis C virus-infected mothers. *J Pediatrics* **126(4)**: 589–91.

Macrory F (1997) *Drug Use, Pregnancy and Care of the Newborn. Guide to Good Practice.* Unpublished manuscript. Available from author.

Mrazek DA, Mrazek P, Kimnert M (1995) Clinical assessment of parenting. *J Am Acad Child Adolescent Psychiatry* **34**: 272–82.

National Treatment Agency (2002) *Models of Care for the Treatment of Adult Drug Misusers, Framework for Developing Local Systems of Effective Drug Misuse Treatment in England.* National Treatment Agency, London

Standing Conference on Drug Abuse (SCODA) (1989) *Drug Using Parents and Their Children: The Second Report of the National Local Authority Forum on Drug Abuse in Conjunction with SCODA.* Association of Metropolitan Authorities, London.

Substance Abuse and Mental Health Services Administration (1999) *Report to Congress on the Prevention and Treatment of Co-Occuring Substance Abuse Disorders and Mental Disorders.* Substance Abuse and Mental Health Services Administration (SAMHSA), National Institute of Mental Health, Rockville, MD.

Thajam D, Carroll H (2006) *Guidelines for Working with Pregnant Drug and/or Alcohol Using Women.* Manchester Specialist Midwifery Service (MSMS). In preparation.

Weir A (1999) An introduction to the issues: A new holistic approach outlined. In: A Douglas, A Weir (eds.) *Child Protection and Adult Mental Health: Conflict of Interest?* Butterworth Heinemann Press, Edinburgh

Wolin SJ, Wolin S (1993) *The Resilient Self: How Survivors of Troubled Families Rise Above Adversity.* Villard Books, New York.

Index